THE RESEARCH PROCESS

BOOKS AND BEYOND

Myrtle S. Bolner
Gayle A. Poirier

Louisiana State University

KENDALL/HUNT PUBLISHING COMPANY
4050 Westmark Drive   Dubuque, Iowa 52002

Formerly entitled *Library Research Skills Handbook*

Copyright © 1997 by Kendall/Hunt Publishing Company

ISBN 0-7872-1915-0

Printed in the United States of America

10 9 8 7 6 5 4 3 2 1

Contents

Preface

The evolution of civilization is really the story of learning. Beginning with the infancy of the universe, the first inhabitants gathered and used information just as they gathered food and other essentials of life. With this knowledge base they were able to create new knowledge and to make advancements that changed the way they lived. As the knowledge base has grown, so has the complexity of the research process—the process by which information is stored, retrieved, and used in the creation of new knowledge. Information can enlighten us as to the physical environment, the political and social order, the scientific and technical accomplishments, and, indeed, all aspects of life. Viewed in that light, it is clear that learning research skills is an essential part of the education process.

We live in an information age in which we are constantly being bombarded by various information media ranging from books and journals to the Internet. It has become increasingly important that individuals develop the ability to conduct research in a variety of media. Research today can be both amazingly simple and amazingly complex. Technology has played an important part in simplifying the way we locate information. At the same time it is quite easy for the researcher to be overwhelmed not only by the sheer volume of information but also by all the tools of research—especially those in less traditional formats such as the Internet.

In order to exploit today's knowledge base to its fullest the researcher must have access to information—both within libraries and beyond, learn how information is organized, and have some ability to use that knowledge. In other words, the user must become *information literate*. It is our aim to provide a book that will serve a threefold purpose: (1) make researchers aware of the different kinds of information that is available in libraries and beyond, (2) provide them with a guide to the means of accessing information, and (3) help them to evaluate and use information productively. The authors recognize that along with basic retrieval skills the user must acquire what is the most important ingredient for the effective research tool—the ability to analyze and use information critically. Critical thinking in the context of research involves a certain attitude and disposition on the part of the information user, a willingness to challenge the propositions and assertions encountered as one taps the information sources. Most importantly, critical thinking calls for the testing of values and beliefs in the light of knowledge and evidence discovered in the course of an information search.

The book discusses the ways information is organized and the principal tools for accessing information—library catalogs, reference books, indexes, government publications, CD ROMs, online databases, and the Internet. The authors have suggested many titles of reference books, indexes, and electronic databases on a variety of subjects. The more frequently used sources are described in some detail, while others are simply listed.

Earlier versions of this book were published under the titles *Library Research Skills Handbook* and *Books, Libraries, and Research*. This new version and new title reflect a change in authorship as well as a change to reflect new technologies in information storage and retrieval. We wish to thank the reference staff of the Louisiana State University Libraries, and in particular the Library Instruction staff for suggestions. Special thanks are due Denise Sokolowski, Librarian, University of Maryland, European Division, and her staff for their many excellent suggestions and continuing interest in the book.

Introduction

The student will find that research skills are essential to achieving success in the courses of the college curriculum and that research is, in effect, an extension of classroom instruction. Yet, many students lack the skills necessary to use the information resources which their college or university provides. One of the best ways to acquire research skills is through specific instruction, and many institutions provide formal courses designed to familiarize students with library resources and research techniques. In other instances, librarians and instructors cooperate to design research strategies that support classroom instruction.

This book is designed so that it may be used either in a formal course or as a guide to research. While the chapters are arranged in a step-by-step progression that the authors have found useful, they may also be used out of sequence to suit individual styles of instruction.

Chapter 1 provides an overview of the changing role in the way that information has been processed throughout history. Chapter 2 provides an insight into the academic library by describing the resources and services. Chapter 3 describes the various information media. Basic techniques for searching materials in electronic format are previewed in Chapter 4. Chapter 5 contains an overview of the classification of information into systems of knowledge. Chapter 6 explains how to use library catalogs effectively to retrieve information. Chapter 7 defines and explains the Internet and lists some popular Web sites. Chapter 8 explains how to select, use, and evaluate reference sources. Chapter 9 introduces periodical literature, explaining the distinction between popular and scholarly material and providing a list of sources used to locate periodical literature. Chapter 10 continues a discussion of citations and articles by providing selection tools for book reviews and literary criticism. Chapter 11 introduces biographical dictionaries, indexes, and other sources used to find information on the lives of individuals. Chapter 12 treats government publications in all formats. Chapter 13 provides a guide to statistical sources.

With this foundation, the reader is led to a discussion of the research paper in Chapter 14, which includes hints on selecting a topic and a guide to writing and documenting the final formal research paper. It also provides guidelines for selection and critical evaluation of materials. There is a discussion of plagiarism followed by examples showing how to document research. The forms recommended are based on the *MLA Handbook for Writers of Research Papers* (4th ed. New York: MLA, 1995).

The questions and exercises at the ends of the chapters are designed to provide a review of the material covered in the chapter and to reinforce learning by giving students hands-on experience with the library resources essential to successful research. Some chapters contain several exercises. It is expected that the instructor will choose those exercises which they think are most appropriate for their students. The authors have chosen to use the topic, "women and employment," to illustrate the many facets of information retrieval. Where that topic was not appropriate to the sources under discussion, other subject headings were used.

The concept of using a research project to provide students with an opportunity to collect, organize, evaluate, and use information is the methodology which the authors have found to be effective in teaching research skills. Once students have mastered this technique they should be able to vary their research activity according to subsequent demands, regardless of the topic involved. The student selects, or is assigned, a topic which serves as the framework for the project. Other steps are the formulation of a thesis statement, preparation of a working outline, gathering information, evaluating the relevance and worth of the information, and compiling and documenting the information. The final product varies: it may be a brief research paper or an annotated bibliography. In lieu of a formal paper assignment, shorter projects may serve to provide the student with similar experiences in research. Several of these sample projects are included in the book.

College and university libraries vary from simple collections of mostly paper materials located in a single room to very large and complex collections located in multiple buildings and in information networks beyond the library. Similarly, the format of library materials ranges from the familiar paper format of books and magazines to highly technical information sources in a variety of formats. Elementary library research for information in paper format is often baffling; when one adds retrieval of information stored in electronic format and on the Internet, the task seems almost overwhelming. In this book students are introduced to information in a variety of formats, for example both the card catalog and the online catalog are discussed in great detail; both print and electronic indexes are included. Students will recognize that advances in electronics and communications will continue to change the way that information is stored and retrieved. It is expected that the foundations acquired in using this book will enable students to progress to more complex information systems as these evolve.

INFORMATION PROCESSING PAST AND PRESENT

"The present is the living sum-total of the past"
—*Thomas Carlyle*

A PREVIEW

Humankind's progress through the ages has been dependent on the creation, storage, and transmittal of information. This process, which had its beginning in the need for human beings to communicate with one another, has progressed from crude drawings on cave walls to highly technical electronic systems such as CD-ROMs and the Internet. The purpose of this chapter is to show the development of writing, books, libraries, and computer technology as part of the large picture of the evolution of information creation, storage, and retrieval.

KEY TERMS AND CONCEPTS

Information Processing
Transmission of Information
Development of Language
Development of Writing
Recording Information
Books
Non-Book Information Sources
Information in Electronic Format
Libraries
Trends in Information Storage and Retrieval

INTRODUCTION

Information may be defined as knowledge in the form of ideas, facts, or data created by the human mind. *Information processing* is all of the ways that humans transmit, record, store, retrieve, and use information. In the process, information goes from the creator to a receiver; it is stored, accessed, and used to generate new information.

1

Transmitting Information: Oral and Written

Language

The transmission of information began with the oral tradition. Long before human beings could write, they communicated by means of grunts and cries accompanied by gestures. Speech sounds probably developed into language as human beings became more social and began to engage in community activities. Culture, traditions, and historical accounts were passed from generation to generation in stories, folklore, songs, and poetry. The limitations of an oral means of communication unassisted by technology are self-evident. Speech can only be preserved by repetition. Not only is the possibility for distortion great, but only those in close proximity can receive the information.

Writing

Writing, considered by many to be the greatest human accomplishment, developed because of the need to record and preserve information uninhibited by limitations of memory and distance. There were three distinct stages in the evolution of writing: (1) *pictographic,* (2) *ideographic*, and (3) *phonetic*. It is difficult to identify, with certainty, the dates of each stage which led to the development of writing, especially since some cultures such as the Chinese still use an ideographic form of writing. The Indian tribes of North America used pictographic and ideographic forms of writing until recent times.

In the *pictographic* stage simple pictures of objects were drawn mostly on natural surfaces such as cave walls and small pieces of wood, ivory, and bone. These early records of humankind's attempt to communicate, discovered in a region extending from Europe to Siberia, date from about 40,000 BC to about 10,000 BC.

Ideographs were drawings of an object representing an idea. For example, a drawing of an eye with tears dropping from it represented sorrow. Ideographic writings have been discovered in many ancient civilizations in North and South America, Africa, and China. The Sumerians developed a system of writing idea-pictures on clay tablets using a stylus which produced wedge-shaped impressions. This style of writing, *cuneiform*, began about 5000 BC From the Sumerians, writing spread to neighboring cultures with each culture borrowing symbols from the other.

In the *phonetic* stage, symbols came to represent sounds and are the precursor of the alphabet. Phonetic writing passed through three distinct stages: (1) *word symbol*, with a single symbol representing a word; (2) *syllabic*, with a symbol representing each syllable; and (3) *alphabetic*, with a single symbol representing a single sound. There is no clear timeline for the emergence of each step, but a progression can be discerned as trade spread among peoples of the ancient world.

Around 3000 BC the Egyptians developed a form of word symbol which was refined by the Phoenicians and from there transported to Greece, where the first alphabet was created. The Roman alphabet, the parent of the English alphabet, came to us from Greece. The Romans simplified the alphabet by reducing it to a manageable 23 letters, and using a single sound as the name of a letter, instead of words as with the Greek alphabet (for example, A instead of alpha). The Roman alphabet spread over Europe, and, except for the addition of three letters and changes in the form of script, it has remained unchanged.

Recording Information: From Stone Age to Electronic Age

Information processing includes not only the means to transmit information, but also the recording and storing of information. The material on which information is recorded plays an important part in the evolution of information processing.

Cave Walls and Clay Tablets

As we have seen, information was first recorded on natural forms—cave walls, bones, pieces of bark. Later small clay tablets and larger pieces of stone were used for recording information.

Papyrus

While the people of Mesopotamia, the Sumerians, the Babylonians, and the Assyrians were writing on clay, the ancient Egyptians were writing on papyrus, a paper like product made from a plant which grew along the Nile River. Papyrus was used in the countries bordering the Mediterranean Sea, most notably Egypt, Greece, and Rome, from about 500 BC to 300 AD.

Parchment and Vellum

Parchment, a refined form of animal skin, is thought to have been invented at Pergamum (which is now Turkey) around 200 BC. Parchment was made from specially prepared and untanned skins of animals, usually sheep, calves, or goats. Vellum is a finer quality parchment made from the skins of kids, lambs, and young calves. Parchment, which gradually replaced papyrus, was used extensively as a writing material until it was replaced by paper.

Paper

Paper was invented by the Chinese about 105 AD, but it was a thousand years before this great invention reached Europe. The introduction of paper in Europe coincided with the beginning of the Renaissance in the late 1400s. There was at this time an interest in classical learning accompanied by an increased demand for books. This demand for reading material resulted in two events which changed civilization—the use of paper as a writing material and the invention of the printing press.

Books

The first form of the book as we know it today, the *codex,* was developed around the first century AD by the Romans. The codex was made of folded sheets of parchment or vellum which were laced together with leather thongs and covered with wood. In later forms, the pages were stitched together and leather was stretched over the wood covers. Many of the early codex were beautifully decorated with carvings and gold and jewel inlay. The contents were written slowly and laboriously by hand. It took months, and even years, to hand-copy a book. Consequently, books were available only to a few privileged scholars. A form of handprinting had been developed in China about 1,000 years before, but it is doubtful that people in the West were aware of it. The first printed books in the West were handprinted from letters carved into wooden blocks. This was a difficult and time-consuming process and was no improvement over the hand-copying method of producing books.

Printing Press

The invention of a movable type printing press about 1450 made a monumental contribution to the intellectual development of humankind. Johann Gutenberg, a German printer, is generally credited with the invention. The *Gutenberg Bible* was the first book to be mass produced on movable type. Within a few years printing spread throughout Europe, and the number of books being produced increased tremendously. By the end of the fifteenth century printing techniques were perfected, and books became widely available. During the 17th century the first newspapers were printed in Europe, followed later by the publication of journals. The availability of books as a result of the invention of the printing press brought about extraordinary changes in the lives of people. It opened up the possibility for education and learning and for participating in the advancement of science, culture, politics, and economics.

Book Publishing

During the Industrial Revolution, several events caused an increase in the availability of books: manufacturers developed ways to produce paper more efficiently and cheaper; printers acquired new types of presses and typesetting devices which increased the speed of printing, and the use of cloth and paper covers became commonplace. This was followed by the introduction of photo typesetting and the use of photography to reproduce images. As books became more and more affordable, the demand grew, resulting in a tremendous increase in the numbers and types of publications. The trend in mass printing of books and other types of printed matter continues today.

Non-Book Information Sources

Although the written word printed on paper is the predominant way that information is stored, the advent of technology beginning in the nineteenth century made possible the transmission of sounds and images rapidly and over long distances. The telegraph was invented in 1837; the telephone, in the 1870s; radio, between 1901 and 1928; and television, in the 1920s. During this same time period new materials were developed on which to record and store information. Non-book information storage materials include: microform (microfilm and microfiche), phonograph records, tape recordings, and video tapes.

Information in Electronic Format

The invention of the computer in the 1940s heralded the beginning of a new age in information processing. Information in electronic format includes any information that is created in machine readable form by a computer, stored on magnetic tape or on computer disk, and retrieved by using a computer. In today's libraries we find online catalogs, online databases, CD-ROMs, local area networks (LANs), and Wide Area Networks (WANs). Information of every type is available in electronic format.

Information Storage: The Development of Libraries

Throughout history information has been accumulated, organized, and transmitted in libraries. The word library comes from the word *liber*, meaning book, or collection of books. The libraries of today are not merely collections of books; rather they are collections of information stored in a variety of formats: books, microforms, phonograph records, video tapes, and computer tapes and disks. Libraries exist not only to preserve information but to provide access to information. The development of libraries from the stone age to the electronic age is part of a continuum in the process of storing and retrieving information.

The Stone Age

Information storage began with the writing that was preserved on cave walls. A more systematic way of collecting and preserving information was developed when clay tablets were put into organized collections. These collections of clay tablets were actually the first "libraries."

Ancient Libraries

The great libraries of ancient Egypt, Greece, and Rome consisted of papyrus rolls. The greatest collection of scrolls in the ancient world was in Alexandria, Egypt. The collection numbered about 700,000 scrolls and was reputed to have included a copy of every scroll in existence. No one knows the fate of the library, but speculation is that it was destroyed by Christians around 391 AD in their campaign against pagan literature.

The Greeks are credited with establishing the first public libraries in Athens about 500 BC. The period was marked by a great interest in education and learning. Libraries were established to provide the public with literature. After the Roman invasion of Greece, what remained of the collection was taken to Rome in 88 BC. Roman soldiers brought back scrolls taken from Greek libraries, but most of these ended up in the homes of the wealthy. Rome's first public library was built about 33 BC. There were 26 public libraries in Rome in 476 AD when the Vandals destroyed all signs of Roman learning and culture and plunged Rome into the Dark Ages. Little remains of all the great papyrus libraries of ancient Greece, Egypt, and Rome.

The Middle Ages

The fall of the Roman Empire was followed by a decline in educational and artistic activity which lasted until the late 1400s. However, classical culture and literature were preserved mainly in the monastic libraries throughout Europe. Most of the monasteries contained a *scriptorium*, a room where the monks laboriously copied by hand whatever ancient manuscripts they could collect—religious tracts, the Bible, Latin grammars, and a few secular books.

Modern Libraries

The first modern European universities appeared about 1100 AD as the Dark Ages were ending. By the end of the 15th century books were readily available. They were placed on open shelves in libraries where they were easily accessible. Libraries began to resemble modern libraries. The 1600s and 1700s are known as the "Golden Age of Libraries." Many of the great libraries of Europe were founded during this period. The British Museum (1759) which is now part of the British Library and the Bibliotheque Nationale of France (1789) are among the world's greatest libraries.

Libraries in the United States date back to the founding of the Harvard University Library in 1638. Subscription libraries were established beginning in 1731, making books available to the public. The first subscription library, the Library Company of Philadelphia, was established by Benjamin Franklin. Subscribers paid dues which entitled them to borrow the books free of charge. Other subscription libraries spread throughout the colonies. Congress established the Library of Congress in 1800 for the purpose of providing reference service to the United States Congress. Today it is the largest library in the world and serves as the national library. The collection contains over 100 million books, periodicals, films, tapes, manuscripts, recordings, microforms, optical disks, and computer-stored records. Approximately a half million items are added to the collection annually.

Libraries in the United States have been closely associated with the ideal of free schooling for everyone. The first tax-supported library in the United States was established in Peterborough, New Hampshire, in 1833. The idea of public libraries spread rapidly and received its greatest impetus in the late 1800s when Andrew Carnegie donated millions of dollars for the construction of free public libraries. His generous gift helped build more than 2,500 libraries in the United States and other English-speaking countries, but more than that, it helped to foster the notion that libraries are a necessary public service.

Today libraries of every type exist to serve the information needs of various constituent communities. The types of libraries are: *public libraries*, supported by taxpayers and serving a wide variety of citizens in the community; *school libraries*, supporting the curriculum of elementary and secondary schools; *academic libraries*, connected to colleges and universities and supporting the teaching and research mission of the parent institution; *research libraries*, dedicated to specific scholarly needs; *special libraries*, usually affiliated with private corporations and businesses or government agencies; and *national and state libraries*, dedicated to preserving the literature of the country or state and serving the information needs of the government.

Trends in the Development of Information Storage and Retrieval

During the last half of the twentieth century a new concept of the role of libraries emerged. We no longer think of libraries as storehouses for information sources. Rather, the emphasis is on libraries as purveyors of information. Libraries have played a leading role in the scientific advancement that has brought about so much change and progress in the world today. They serve as information centers, disseminating information for immediate use and application. In turn, the application of scientific and technological advancements to the library has enhanced its performance as an information center.

Just as the printing press changed the course of history, so also has the computer revolutionized information processing. Almost every library function has been affected by advances in computer technology—circulation, record keeping, online catalogs, inter-library lending, and reference services. The use of computers to automate library services began in the early 1960s with the automation of circulation and routine record keeping. The Library of Congress began to produce machine readable catalog records in the mid-1960s, and by the end of the 1980s online catalogs had replaced the card catalog in many libraries. Today, online databases, CD-ROMs, and the Internet have begun to replace books in libraries.

If the changes in information processing of the last half of the twentieth century continue at the same rate over the next decade, we are likely to see drastic changes in libraries. Some are predicting a totally electronic library in which all materials and services will be in electronic format. They envision a "paperless society"' in which printed books and magazines will be replaced by CD-ROMs and online databases. Others are predicting that library buildings as we know them will no longer exist, and information will be transmitted to individuals electronically. Probably neither of these scenarios will be entirely realized. It is unlikely that libraries will get rid of the books in their collections, nor is it likely in the near future that publishers will cease to publish books in paper format. It *is* likely that advances in automation will continue to occur, that we will see more and more publications in electronic format, and that more services will be automated.

Regardless of how automated a library becomes, it will continue to serve the basic human need for information. The materials of the past, both distant and recent, will still be present, augmented by the services which are continually being developed to facilitate their use. Library users will be expected to become more information literate in order to take full advantage of the services made possible by technological progress.

WORKS CONSULTED

Chiera, Edward. *They Wrote on Clay*. Chicago: University of Chicago, c.1938.

Diringer, David. *The Alphabet: A Key to the History of Mankind*. 3rd ed. Rev. New York: Funk & Wagnalls, 1968.

"Inventions and Discoveries." *World Almanac and Book of Facts 1994*, 159-161.

Johnson, Elmer D. *Communication: A Concise Introduction to the History of the Alphabet, Writing, Printing, Books, and Libraries*. New Brunswick: Scarecrow, 1955.

"Libraries." *Microsoft Encarta*. c.1994. CD-ROM.

McMurtrtrie, Douglas. *The Book: The Story of Printing and Book Making*. New York: Oxford, c.1943.

"Library of Congress: General Information and Publications." Online. Library of Congress. Available HTTP: http://www.loc.gov/

Ogg, Oscar. *The 26 Letters*. Rev. ed. New York: Crowell, 1971.

Rider, Alice D. *A Story of Books and Libraries*. Metuchen: Scarecrow, 1976.

Instructor: _____   Name: _____

Course/Section: _____   Date: _____

Review Questions for Chapter One

1. What is information processing?

2. Why was writing developed?

3. What were the three stages in the evolution of writing?

4. What are the stages in the development of the English alphabet?

5. Name other forms of writing material used before the development of paper.

6. What effect did Johann Gutenberg's invention of movable type have on civilization?

7. Name four non-book sources which one might find in libraries today.

8. What are the types of libraries in existence today?

9. How has the perception of the role of libraries changed in the last half of the twentieth century?

10. Describe three developments in library services as a result of electronic technology.

11. What services are automated in your library? Name any publications in your library in electronic format.

ACADEMIC LIBRARIES

A PREVIEW

College and university libraries offer a variety of materials and services that are designed to support the teaching and research missions of the institution. Those who use the library in the research process will find it helpful to know how materials are organized and arranged in libraries, what materials are available, and how to retrieve those materials. Although library arrangements and services vary from library to library, there are many elements which are common to all of them. This chapter gives an overview of the arrangement of library materials and the various functions and services commonly found in college and university libraries.

KEY TERMS AND CONCEPTS

Research
Arrangement of Library Materials
Library Services

INTRODUCTION

We have probably all heard the adage "there is nothing new under the sun." This saying can be applied to research. The purpose of research is to understand and interpret the achievements, knowledge, and ideas of others whether recorded on cave walls, clay tablets, papyrus, parchment, paper, film, computer disk or magnetic tape. Many of the assignments students receive in higher education require them to use the library for research. To do this they must become familiar with its collections and services. Many students are introduced to libraries in elementary or high school, or perhaps they are familiar with their public library. They will find, however, that the college or university library is more complex; it is often larger than the library with which they may be familiar; it probably provides a greater variety of services; and it may use a different scheme for classifying its materials.

The mission of the college and university library is to provide books, periodicals, and other information-related materials and services to meet the research and instructional needs of the students and faculty. The rising costs of materials and new technologies make this difficult in all but the wealthiest institutions. The library is frequently hampered in this effort by financial constraints and by the destructive acts of those it seeks to serve. Mutilation and theft of library materials by patrons are major problems in college and university libraries. All such acts ultimately result in a decrease in the materials available and a lessening of services. It is incumbent on library users to share the responsibility of preserving library materials by seeing to it that such destructive acts do not occur.

Arrangement of Library Materials

While there is some uniformity of arrangement of the materials among college and university libraries, there are also many variations. Differences in arrangement among libraries is governed by a number of factors: size of the institution, educational mission, and availability of resources. Some schools have separate libraries for undergraduates; other schools have only one central library; many universities have a central library as well as branch libraries which serve various colleges or departments within the university.

In addition to locating library facilities on campus for maximum use, librarians are also concerned with arranging materials within the library. Most libraries arrange materials by function or by service provided. Typically, all the books are shelved together on shelves in what is called a stack area; non-book materials such as microforms and audio materials, are housed in other areas; and access services such as reference assistance, circulation, and inter-library borrowing are provided at specially designated service desks. Many libraries provide guides to their collections and services; others have self-guided tours; and still others offer a computer-assisted tour of the library. These will provide a good starting point in learning where materials are located and how they are arranged. The functions and services discussed below are common to many college and university libraries. The student will need to know about these functions in order to use the library effectively.

Stacks

The library's main collection of books is arranged by call number on rows of shelves called *stacks*. Some libraries have "closed" stacks to which only library staff and those with special permission have access. Patrons present a "call slip" to a library attendant who gets the material. Having closed stacks reduces the loss of library material by theft and mutilation. It also reduces the number of books which are out of order in the stacks. In most libraries, however, books are shelved in "open" stacks where patrons are free to browse and select materials for themselves. Browsing is helpful in locating materials which the user might not have discovered in the library catalog. Some libraries have a combination of the two systems—the general stack areas are "open" while special collections are "closed." In some college and university libraries, stacks are open to faculty and graduate students, but closed to undergraduates.

The Library Catalog

The key to locating materials in the library is the *catalog*. When a library acquires a book or other information source, it is assigned a call number which determines where it will be located in the library. A catalog record is created that includes call number, author's name, title, publication information, and a note giving the size of the book and other descriptive information such as availability of maps, illustrations, and/or bibliographies. Subject headings are assigned in order to help the library user locate the book by its subject. The catalog record is placed in the library's catalog where it is available to library users.

There are several different types of library catalogs. The *card catalog* is one in which the cards for each book are inserted alphabetically in file drawers. Some libraries have their catalog records in books, called *book catalogs*; others have *COM catalogs* (Computer Output Microform), which are lists on microfiche that have been generated from computer tapes; others have their catalog records on *CD-ROM* (Compact Disk-Read Only Memory). Still others have *online catalogs* where the catalog records are stored on computer tapes and made available via computer terminals.

Reference Collection

Perhaps the single most useful collection in any library is the reference collection. This collection consists of encyclopedias, dictionaries, almanacs, handbooks, manuals, indexes, etc. which are frequently used for finding information. It also contains reference tools in other formats such as CD-ROM and computers for accessing the Internet and specialized electronic databases. The reference department typically has open shelves which are systematically arranged, although some materials such as indexes may be shelved on separate index tables to facilitate their use. Highly used reference books may also be shelved in a special area near the librarian's desk. Reference librarians familiar with this collection are available to help patrons find information in the reference area. As a rule, reference materials do not circulate and must be used in the reference area.

Reserve Materials

The reserve collection consists of materials that circulate for limited time periods, usually two hours or overnight. Most of the materials are for course assignments. Professors request that books which are needed for classes be placed together in the reserve area to ensure availability for the students.

Periodicals

In many libraries periodicals (magazines and journals) are shelved together in one area for convenience of use. Other libraries have found that it is more desirable to have only the current periodicals in one area with the bound volumes in a separate area or in the stacks with other books.

Newspapers

Current newspapers may be housed with other periodical literature or they may be kept in a separate area. Print copies of newspapers are kept for a limited period of time because they are printed on paper which does not last. Older copies are usually stored on microfilm.

Microforms

A microform is a photographic reproduction in a greatly reduced form. Microform materials include microfilm, microfiche, microcards, and microprints. These materials are not readable with the naked eye and require the use of special equipment or readers. Most of them are kept in a separate area with readers and copiers.

Audio/Visual Materials

Audio/visual materials consist of recordings, cassette tapes, video tapes, compact disks, films, and slides. These are usually kept in special areas which are designed to accommodate these types of materials.

Government Publications

Many university libraries serve as depositories for local, state, national, and international documents. These publications are usually shelved separately in a special area. Some libraries locate state and local government documents in a documents room with national and international documents, but it is also quite common to house these materials in a distinct "state" room designed to preserve materials dealing with the particular state. Documents housed in special areas are usually arranged by classification systems designed especially for those systems. For example, U.S. Government documents are usually shelved by the Superintendent of Documents system.

Archives and Manuscripts

Records and documents such as letters, manuscripts, diaries, personal journals, photographs, maps, and other materials which are of historical value are preserved in an archives department. This area is staffed by archivists who are specifically trained in methods of acquisition and preservation of historical materials.

Rare Books

Many college and university libraries have books that are valuable because of their artistic and/or unique qualities or because they are old and no longer printed. Such books need special protection and care in handling. They are shelved in specially designed areas and are not allowed to circulate.

Special Collections

In fulfilling its research mission, a university library frequently has a number of highly specialized collections. The advantage of such collections is that they support the university's effort to become a center for research in particular subject fields. Examples of such collections might be African-American history, women's studies, or Asian studies.

Branch Libraries

Branch libraries consist of subject collections such as agriculture, business, chemistry, engineering, music, law, or architecture in libraries located away from the central library. These are conveniently located in buildings which serve the needs of students and faculty in a particular discipline.

Library Services

As more and more materials accumulate in libraries, the task of accessing stored information becomes more complex. While the introduction of computer technology into information handling has resulted in more efficient and faster methods of storing and retrieving information, it has not done away with basic library services. It is still necessary for library users to become familiar with all the library services, regardless of whether or not these are automated, in order to use the library effectively. The services outlined below are representative of services offered in most academic libraries.

Circulation

Books and other materials are usually checked out from a centrally located desk which handles all matters dealing with the lending of library materials. In most libraries the circulation desk is located near the entrance or the exit of the library. Information regarding lending policies, fines, schedules, etc. is available at the circulation desk. Many tasks such as checking books out and in, verifying circulation status, and sending out overdue and recall notices, once performed manually at the circulation desk, are now automated.

Librarians

An important and indispensable resource in any library is the librarian. In order to acquire, maintain, and disseminate the vast amount of information which is stored in libraries, trained personnel are needed. Most libraries require that its professional librarians have a Master's degree or the equivalent from an American Library Association (ALA) accredited institution. Persons trained in librarianship or information sciences perform a variety of services: administrative, technical, and public. Administrators are concerned with the overall operation of the library and with the budget, staff, and physical plant. Technical service librarians are concerned with the acquisition, preparation, and maintenance of library materials. They are in charge of ordering and cataloging materials, serials check-in, sending materials to be bound, repairing damaged books, etc. Public service librarians are those who serve the patron directly as at a reference or circulation desk. Not everyone who works in a library is a librarian. Support staff such as clerks, paraprofessionals, and technicians help to maintain the library's services.

Library patrons are more familiar with public service librarians because these are the individuals with whom they come into contact when seeking assistance. Reference librarians are available to answer questions about the collection, to assist in using electronic reference tools, to help with search strategies, and generally to help locate and sort out information. A student seeking assistance with a research project will find that the librarian is better able to help if the student has some knowledge of basic library sources and services.

When reference librarians are approached for assistance with a question that involves research, they conduct an informal reference interview to determine the purpose of the research, the type of information desired (e.g., statistical, historical, etc.), specific questions to be answered, limitations (e.g., date, geographical, etc.), and extent and findings of preliminary research. It is important for students to learn to ask the appropriate questions during the reference interview. For example, a student might ask where the books on computers are located when he/she really wants to know about computer crimes among government workers. It is beneficial for the student to conduct a preliminary search, such as searching the catalog, browsing, or looking up material in reference books, before approaching the reference desk for help. This enables the student to focus on the type of information needed to deal with various aspects of the topic and then ask specific questions. It also gives the librarian a starting point from which to proceed in directing the student to appropriate sources.

Electronic Reference Services

Most libraries now provide access to information in electronic format as part of their reference services. Some of the information sources are located within the library; others are located in computers in distant locations. These include:

Online search services. These are searches that are done by means of a computer which is located in the library and linked by telecommunications to a computer data center in a distant location. The data center provides access to information that is stored in machine readable form and which can be searched as a unit. Reference librarians trained in search techniques usually conduct the searches, although some libraries allow patrons to conduct their own online searching. The library usually charges a fee for online searching in order to recover the cost charged by vendors.

CD-ROM databases. Many of the reference sources in libraries are now available in CD-ROM format. These include both bibliographic and full-text databases. The library provides computer workstations, usually with printers, to access these databases.

Internet. Some libraries provide access to the Internet, a worldwide information network, at public service workstations located in the reference area or in a computer lab.

Library Instruction

Library instruction is a service provided by the reference librarians. It might include formal (for credit) courses, general orientation sessions, subject-related instruction, and computer-assisted instruction. The reference librarians also prepare printed guides to the collection.

Interlibrary Loan

The rising costs of library operations and acquisitions have forced more and more libraries to seek cooperation with other institutions in order to serve their patrons. Libraries lend each other books and other materials which are unavailable at the local library. The loans are for limited periods, and the costs of borrowing material (postage, handling, and duplication) are generally borne by the patron. If a lending library does not circulate an item, it may send photocopies. Patrons borrowing books are required to fill out forms giving accurate and complete information on the item they would like to borrow. This usually includes the author, title, publication information and a reference showing where the citation was found. Interlibrary loan is for specific titles only and not for subject requests such as "all the works on the Cold War."

Document Delivery

Document delivery usually refers to the concept of "documents on demand." Rather than subscribing to costly, low-use journals, the library subscribes to services which promise fast delivery of the articles. One of the largest document delivery services is the Colorado Alliance for Research Libraries (CARL). CARL is a database containing the full text of articles from several thousand journals. There is no charge to search the database, but if an individual wants a copy of the article, there is a charge, which includes the cost of reproducing and sending the article plus a copyright fee. The articles are usually sent by facsimile transmission (fax) to the individual or library requesting it.

Library Cooperatives

A practice which is prevalent among libraries today is that of forming a cooperative for the purpose of making holdings and services available to members and their patrons on a reciprocal basis. These groups are known by various names: library networks, information centers, consortia, or library systems. Some groups share general printed materials while others share specialized materials such as computing facilities, periodicals, films, slides, and other audio-visual material.

Regional and state library systems, in which libraries in a geographical area share resources, are widespread throughout the United States. There are also national library networks in which members from different libraries all over the country cooperate to share resources. OCLC (Online Computer Library Center) is a national network with a variety of services ranging from shared cataloging to bibliographic searching. Members of OCLC may use its services to handle requests for interlibrary loan material, to catalog materials, and to help identify and locate materials.

Instructor: _____   Name: _____

Course/Section: _____   Date: _____

Review Questions for Chapter Two

1. What is the purpose of research?

2. What are the differences between open and closed stacks in a library?

    a.   What are the advantages and disadvantages of each?

    b.   What type of stack arrangement is used in your library?

3. What purpose does the reserve book department serve in the library?

4. What is the function of an audio/visual room? Name the different types of audio/visual materials found in your library.

5. What kinds of materials are found in an archives department?

6. Why is the reference librarian an important resource in the library?

7. What service does an interlibrary loan department perform for the library patron?

8. What are branch libraries? What are the branch libraries on your campus?

9. What is meant by the term "document delivery"?

10. What is online searching?

11. Name three electronic reference services one might find in libraries.

12. Which of the library services discussed in this chapter does your library provide?

Instructor: _____   Name: _____

Course/Section: _____   Date: _____

Library Tour Exercise

Take a tour of your library and complete the exercise below. Write NA for any items that are not applicable for your library.

1. Look in the card catalog and locate a book on heraldry and give the following information:

   a. Complete call number:

   b. Title of the book:

   c. Where in the library is the book located?

2. Look in the online catalog and locate a book on discrimination and give the following information:

   a. Complete call number:

   b. Title of the book:

   c. Where in the library is the book located?

3. Locate any reference book from the reference department and give the following information:

   a. Title of the book:

   b. Call number:

   c. Where in the reference area is the book located (e.g., reference stacks, ready reference, index tables)?

4. Locate any book that has been assigned as reading for a course and give the following information:

   a. Title of the book:

   b. Course name and number for which the book is assigned:

5. Locate the latest copy of *Newsweek* magazine and give the following information:

   a. Call number:

   b. Date of the issue and volume number:

   c. Title of one article from the issue:

   d. Inclusive pages of the article:

   e. Where in the library is it located?

6. Locate a copy of *Newsweek* magazine that is five years old and give the following information:

    a. Call number:

    b. Date of the issue:

    c. Volume no.:

    d. Title of one article from the issue:

    e. Inclusive pages of the article:

    f. Where in the library is it located?

7. Locate a recent issue of a newspaper from a city near your hometown or any large city and give the following information:

    a. Title of the newspaper:

    b. Date of the issue which you located:

    c. Call number:

    d. In which department or area is it located?

8. Locate a U.S. Government document and give the following information:

    a. Title of the document:

    b. Call number:

    c. In which department or area is it located?

9. Locate a recording of a musical work and give the following information:

    a. Title of the recording:

    b. Call number:

    c. In which department or area is it located?

UNDERSTANDING THE SOURCES FORMATS

A PREVIEW

Information sources, both within the library and beyond, have become so complex that one can hardly keep pace with them. In order to locate and retrieve information sources, it is essential for the researcher to have a basic understanding of the formats of the more commonly used materials. In this chapter the parts of the book are analyzed in detail. Other sources are treated with sufficient detail to provide the researcher with an understanding of their physical properties.

KEY TERMS AND CONCEPTS

Books
Serials
Dissertations and Theses
Archives
Vertical File
Audio-Visual Material
Electronic Sources

INTRODUCTION

The term *format* refers to the general physical quality or appearance of an information source. Thus, book format refers to printed pages of paper that are bound together. The book is still the most extensive way that information is stored, and it is the source that most of us find most "friendly." Other formats, such as photographs, magnetic recordings, video tapes, laser disks, CD-ROMs, online databases, and electronic catalogs, are being used with increasing frequency as a means of storing information. Some library users do not feel as comfortable with these sources as they do with books. Understanding the formats of the various information sources will help to dispel some of the fear users feel about unfamiliar formats. Beyond that, developing skills in the intelligent use of information sources will save time and result in a more effective use of the source. This chapter will explain in detail the book's content and give descriptions of other library materials both in printed and non-printed formats. Many of the elements found in books are basic to other sources of information.

Books

A book consists of written or printed pages fastened together at one edge and covered with a protective cover. The first printed books consisted only of the cover and the text of the work. There were no title or introductory pages as in modern books. As printing evolved, publishers developed a uniform way to arrange the contents of books which greatly enhanced their usability. The most significant features are discussed below. (Some books may not have all the different parts described, and the order of their appearance may vary.)

Book Cover

The cover of the book holds the pages of the book together and protects them. The edge of the cover where the pages are bound together is called the spine. On the spine are ordinarily printed the short-title of the book, the author's name, the publisher, and, in the case of library books, the call number. The front of the cover is often decorated. It may also give the author's name and the short-title of the book.

Title Page

The title page is the first significant page in the book. It gives the following information:

Title: The title page gives the full title of the book, including any subtitles or descriptive titles, e.g., *The Book: The Story of Printing and Bookmaking.* The title from the title page should be used in a bibliography.

Author: The author's name and sometimes a list of credentials such as degrees, academic position, and, occasionally, the names of other works.

Editor, Compiler, Illustrator, or Translator: The name of anyone other than the author who made a significant contribution to the book.

Edition: Given if the book is other than a first edition. All copies of a book printed from one set of type make up an edition. Reprints are copies of the same edition printed at a later time. When any changes are made, it is a revised edition or a new edition.

Imprint: The place of publication, the publisher, and the date of publication. These are usually found at the bottom of the title page, although the publication date is sometimes omitted. The publication date identifies when a book was published. Only the place of publication, publisher and date are needed for identification purposes in a bibliography. If there is no publication date, the copyright date is used in a bibliographic citation.

Copyright and Printing Information

The back of the title page contains the following information:

Copyright: The copyright grants legal rights to an author or publisher to sell, distribute, or reproduce a literary or artistic work. A small *c* before a date identifies it as the copyright date.

Printing history: A list of different editions and printings of the work.

Preface or Foreword

The *preface* or *foreword* gives the author's purpose in writing the book and acknowledges those persons who have helped in its preparation.

Introduction

The introduction differs from the preface or foreword in that it describes the subject matter of the book and gives a preliminary statement leading into the main contents of the book.

Table of Contents

The table of contents lists in order the chapters or parts of the book and gives the pages on which they begin. Some books include a brief summary of each chapter listed.

Illustrations

The list of illustrations gives the pages on which illustrative material can be found. Illustrations might include pictures, maps, charts, etc.

Text and Notes

The main body of printed matter is the text of the book. It is usually divided into chapters or separate parts and includes explanatory material and identification of reference sources in the form of notes at the bottoms of the pages (footnotes) or at the ends of chapters (endnotes). In some books notes appear at the end of the book.

Glossary

A list with definitions of the special words or unfamiliar terms used in the text, usually at the end of the text.

Appendix

Supplementary materials following the text such as tables, maps, questionnaires, or case studies.

Bibliography

A list of all books, articles, and other materials the author used in writing the book. It may also include other sources which are relevant to the subject. The bibliography may appear at the end of each chapter or at the end of the book.

Index

An alphabetical list of the subjects discussed in the book, along with the corresponding page numbers. Some books also include a separate name and/or author index.

Serials

A *serial* is a publication which is issued on a continuing basis at regularly stated intervals. The publication frequency varies: some serials are published each day (daily); others, once a week (weekly), every two weeks (biweekly), once a month (monthly), every two months (bimonthly), every three months (quarterly), twice a year (semiannually), or once a year (annually). Serials include periodicals (magazines and journals); newspapers; annuals and yearbooks; and the proceedings, transactions, memoirs, etc. of societies and associations.

Periodicals are numbered consecutively and given volume designations so that several issues make up a volume. In many libraries, when a complete volume of a periodical has been accumulated, the issues are bound together in hard covers. These bound volumes may be shelved with other books by classification number, or they may be shelved in a separate periodical area. Some libraries acquire the current copies of periodicals in paper and the back issues on microform.

Periodicals include *magazines* and *journals* which are issued at regular intervals, usually weekly, bi-weekly, monthly, bimonthly, or quarterly. *Magazines* contain popular reading, while *journals* are more scholarly.

Newspapers are usually published daily or weekly. They are printed on a type of paper called *newsprint* which does not last. For this reason, they are usually preserved on microfilm. The paper copies of newspapers are kept only until the microfilm copies arrive.

Annuals and *yearbooks* are treated much as other book materials and shelved in the general collection or in the reference collection. The proceedings, transactions, memoirs, etc. of a society or association are usually shelved in the stacks unless they are acquired on microform.

The serial titles owned by a library are usually listed in the library's catalog but may also appear in a separate serials list, which identifies those titles and issues which have been received in the library.

Dissertations and Theses

A *dissertation* is research that is conducted and written in partial fulfillment of the requirements for the doctoral degree at a university. A *thesis* is a research project completed in partial fulfillment of the requirements for the master's degree. At least one copy of the original of all the dissertations and theses written at a university are usually kept in the university library. Many libraries acquire microfilm copies of the theses and dissertations in order to preserve the original. Libraries may acquire dissertations and theses from other universities on microfilm.

Archives

Archives consist of both unpublished and published materials that have special historical value, such as the public and private papers of notable persons or the records of an institution. The format of archival materials varies: for example, archives might include original manuscripts, letters, photographs, diaries, legal records, books, etc. (See Figure 3.1.) The materials found in archives may be likened to the items one frequently finds in the attics of old family homes: birth and marriage certificates, letters, newspaper clippings, etc., which tell that family's story. Archives require special care and handling, and it is not unusual to find that access is limited to only serious researchers. Archival materials are also being preserved on microform, magnetic tapes, or CD-ROM.

Vertical File

The vertical file consists of pamphlets, brochures, newspaper and magazine clippings, pictures, maps, and other materials which are not suitable for cataloging and shelving along with the regular book collection. Vertical file materials are usually placed in manila folders and stored alphabetically by subjects in filing cabinets. The material placed in the vertical file is ephemeral in nature—that is, it has little, if any, lasting value and will soon be out-of-date. Therefore, the vertical file must be weeded, or cleared, from time to time to get rid of dated material. Much of the information kept in the vertical file might never appear in any other published form. Some libraries maintain a separate index of vertical file material.

Figure 3.1 *A fascimile of a manuscript from the National Archives.*

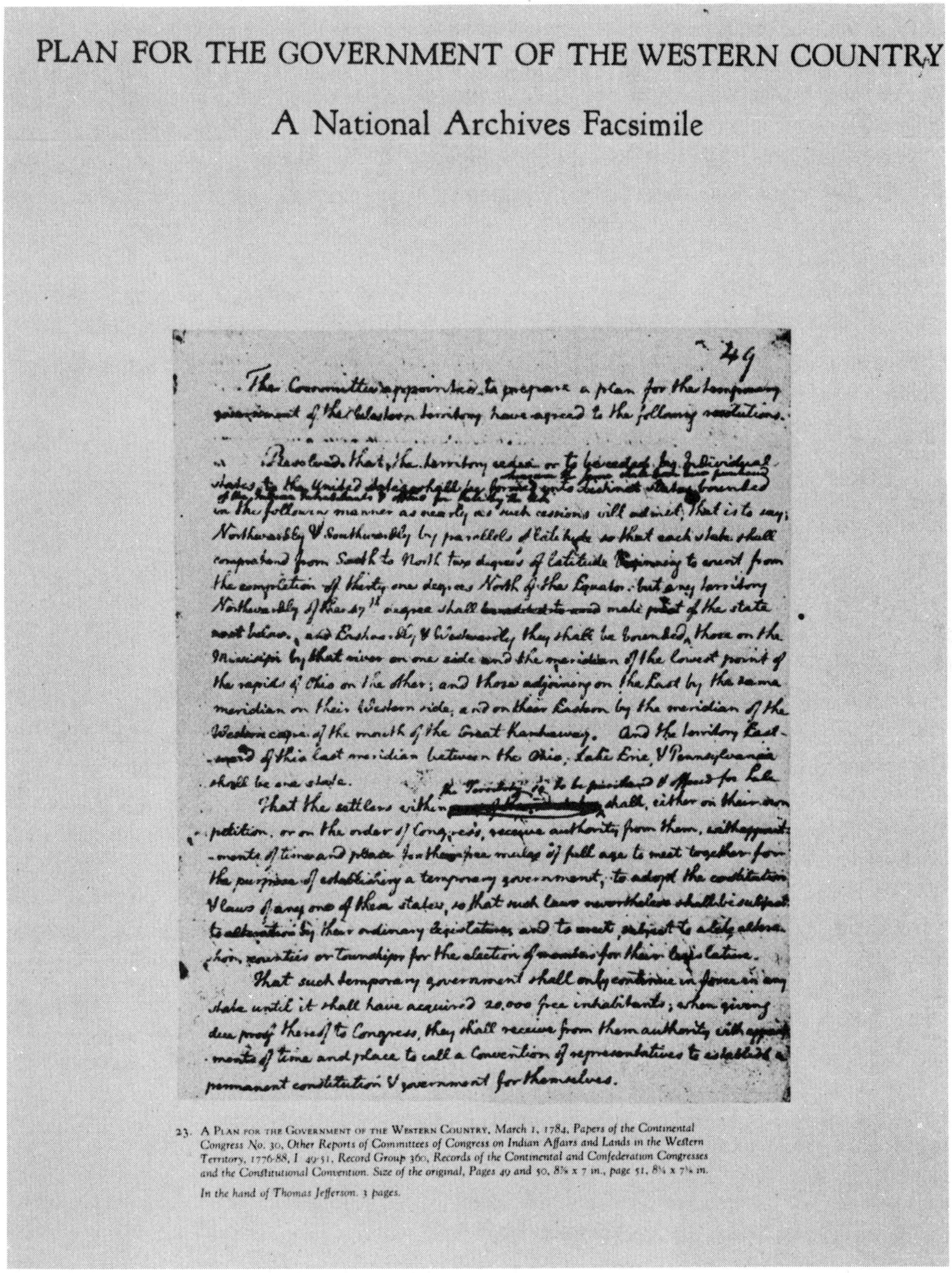

PLAN FOR THE GOVERNMENT OF THE WESTERN COUNTRY

A National Archives Facsimile

A-V (Audio-Visual) Materials

Audio-visual materials include audio, video, and microform formats. A-V materials require special equipment for their use and are usually housed in separate areas of the library. The types of A-V materials are:

Audio materials: records, audio cassettes, and reel-to-reel tapes. The audio materials in most libraries include musical as well as spoken records.

Video materials: microforms, video-cassettes, slides, and synchronized slide-tapes.

M*icroforms:* printed materials which are reduced in size by photographic means and which can only be read with special readers. (See Figures 3.2 and 3.3.) There are several types of these photographically reduced materials: (See Figure 3.4)

microfilm is print which is reproduced on a roll of 35 or 16 mm film;

microfiche is a flat sheet of film, usually measuring four by six inches, on which separate pages of text are reproduced;

microprint is the reproduction in positive form of a microphotograph. Microprint is printed on opaque paper, unlike microfilm and microfiche, which are printed or reproduced on film;

microcard is a form of microprint, but its reduction is greater.

Microprints and microcards are no longer being distributed because of the difficulty in reproducing them on paper.

Acquiring materials in microform permits libraries to save valuable space and perhaps to acquire material not available any other way. For instance, the census records containing the names of persons are available from the National Archives and Records Administration only on microfilm. While it is more likely that newspapers and periodicals are acquired in microform format, it is not unusual to find books, especially out-of-print ones, on microfiche or microfilm.

Electronic Sources

The sources of electronic information common to many libraries are: (1) online catalogs; (2) library networks; (3) online databases; (4) in-house databases; (5) magnetic tapes, (6) CD-ROM; (7) Internet. The kind of information available in electronic format includes bibliographic information such as descriptions of books, periodical articles, and other literary works; raw data (e.g., statistics, census data, voting records); the full text of periodicals, books, and reports; and illustrative material such as maps and photographs.

Online catalog, known as the OPAC (Online Public Access Catalog), is a computerized version of the card catalog. The records are in machine readable format and are accessible by computer both within and beyond the library walls.

Library networks are made up of libraries which are linked together via telecommunications facilities for the purpose of sharing resources. Such services as inter-library loan, cooperative cataloging, and bibliographic reference services are available to members of the network. Members may share cataloging records and agree to lend one another materials.

Online database is used to describe information which is stored in a computer and retrieved by other computers through telephone lines and communication networks. There are thousands of online databases, providing nearly every type of information, both bibliographic and full text. Although commercial vendors are still the major producers of online databases, government agencies and professional and scholarly organizations also produce and disseminate them. The costs of accessing online databases vary, but in general, the benefits outweigh the costs. And, of course, some databases, namely the federal government databases, are free. Some of the more well known vendors are: DIALOG, LEXIS/NEXIS, and First Search. (See Chapters 4 and 9.)

Figure 3.2
Microfilm reader.

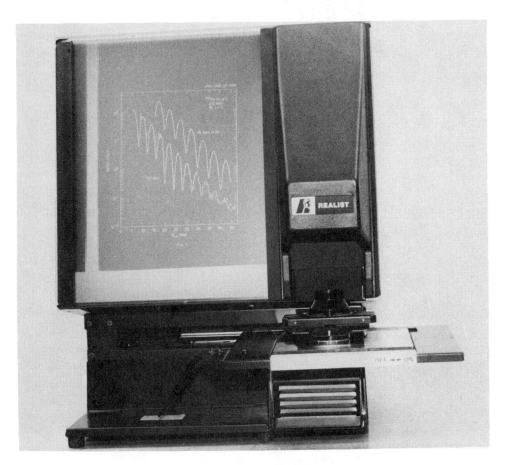

Figure 3.3
Microfiche reader.

***Figure* 3.4** *Microform material; clockwise: microfilm, microcard, microfiche, and microprint.*

***Figure* 3.5** *Information in electronic format; clockwise: magnetic tape, compact disks, floppy disks.*

In-house databases are those created within the library that can be stored on hard disks, floppy disks, or magnetic tapes. The kinds of information created may consist of community information, campus announcements, job listings, local statistics, research in progress, and vertical file type material.

CD-ROM is a small (4.75 inches in diameter) plastic coated optical disk on which information can be stored. One disk is equal in contents to approximately 250,000 printed pages, or about 300 books. The information stored on CD-ROM cannot be erased or altered, although it can be transferred to another utility such as a floppy disk or a magnetic tape. CD-ROM requires a microcomputer with appropriate software and a disk player to run the program. There are thousands of CD-ROM databases available. These include indexes, census data, corporation records, encyclopedias, government documents, statistics, maps, journal back files, and other literary works.

Internet is a network that connects computers to one another, allowing for the free flow of information among them. The Internet contains all types of information: online catalogs, electronic journals, in-house databases, CD-ROM databases, and, in fact, any information that is computer generated can be found on the Internet. (For a full discussion of the Internet, see Chapter 7.)

The equipment used to store and access information in electronic format consists of microcomputers, computer terminals, and disk players. Telecommunications equipment is required for online databases, online catalogs, and library networking. In addition, software (computer programs) are necessary to run the various programs.

The format of computer-generated material is different, at least in appearance although not in content, from traditional library sources. Computer technology is developing and changing at such a fast pace that it is not possible to predict what the format of electronic information will look like even in the very near future.

Instructor: _____   Name: _____

Course/Section: _____   Date: _____

Review Questions for Chapter Three

1. What is meant by the term "format" in reference to information sources?

2. What is the difference between the copyright date and the publishing date of a book? Where are the copyright date and publishing history usually found?

3. Name the items that are included in the imprint of a book.

4. What different purposes do the table of contents and the index serve?

5. What is the difference between the preface and the introduction?

6. What is the purpose of the bibliography in a book?

7. Serials include what kinds of publications?

8. What is the difference between a thesis and a dissertation?

9. What kinds of materials are included in audio-visual collections?

10. Name the forms of electronic information common to many libraries.

11. Which of the library materials discussed in this chapter are found in your library?

Instructor: _____   **Name:** _____

Course/Section: _____   **Date:** _____

Parts of a Book Exercise

Using the library catalog, select a book on a topic that interests you and examine its contents. Give the following information:

1. Locate a book in the library stacks and examine its contents.

Give the following about the book. If you do not find some of these items, write NA (not applicable) in the blank.

2. Call number:

3. Author's or authors' name(s). (If the book has editor instead of author, write "ed" after the name.)

4. Full title.

5. Place of publication. (Give first one listed.)

6. Publisher:

7. Edition (if given):

8. Date of latest copyright and publishing date.

9. Does the author state the purpose of the book? If so, state briefly what it is.

10. Is there an introduction? If so, identify two points made in the introduction.

11. Does the book have a table of contents?

12. Is there a list of maps or illustrations? If so, give pages.

13. Does it have a bibliography? If so, give pages.

14. Does the book have an appendix? If so, what does it contain?

15. Does the book contain an index? If so, how many pages make up the index? What is its purpose?

16. Is there a glossary in the book? What is the purpose of a glossary?

ELECTRONIC TOOLS
BASIC SEARCH TECHNIQUES

A PREVIEW

It has been said that access to information has never been so easy! Computer technology makes it possible to create, store, and retrieve information quickly and effectively. However, for the novice, the retrieval process can be daunting. We now have online catalogs, online databases, databases on CD-ROM, and information of all kinds on the Internet. To compound the confusion, there is very little uniformity even among the types of databases. This chapter acquaints researchers with the "whys" and "hows" of database searching. It outlines the steps in planning a search and shows some basic techniques for executing the steps. It is expected that the searching skills discussed here will be a springboard to use the myriad of electronic information sources which are now available.

KEY TERMS AND CONCEPTS

Format
Database
Bibliographic Database
Full-text Database
Entries
Fields
Author Search
Title Search
Subject Search
Keyword Search
Boolean Operators
CD-ROM
Online Databases

INTRODUCTION

We have heard the phrase "information in electronic format." That phrase refers to any information that is created by a computer, stored electronically (either on a hard drive on the computer, on a disk, or on magnetic tape), and which is accessed by computer. Information in electronic format is available on a wide variety of subjects in all disciplines—science, social sciences, and humanities. *Database* is the term usually used to refer to a body of information in electronic format. Just as with any information source stored in libraries, electronic databases are of two kinds: (1) *bibliographic*—citations to periodical articles, books, government reports, statistics, patents, research reports, conference proceedings, and dissertations—and (2) *full-text*—the complete text of newspapers and periodicals, court cases, encyclopedias, research reports, books, etc. The types of databases include online catalogs, online databases, CD-ROMs, and the Internet. The term *online* refers to databases stored on a remote computer and accessed locally; other databases, such as those on CD-ROM are usually housed in the library. Many of the online catalogs in libraries today are part of a network which share resources: mainframe computing services, and bibliographic and full-text databases.

In order to search electronic databases effectively, whether they are part of a network or available on a single workstation in a library, one should have some knowledge of the contents of the database, what information is included, how it is organized, and how it is accessed. One of the problems with electronic databases is that there is no standardization among the producers of all the different electronic products. The search commands in one database on CD-ROM might be completely different from those in another; the way that the information appears on the screen in one database may look altogether different on another screen, depending on the producer of the database. However, even with that caveat, it is possible to acquire some basic search skills that will enable one to do research effectively, regardless of the source or type of database.

Advantages of Information in Electronic Format

There are obvious advantages to searching information in electronic formats:

- It saves valuable research time. It takes minutes or even seconds to search an entire database or several databases covering multiple years. To search the same indexes in paper copy might take hours or even longer as each volume of the index would have to be searched separately.

- It is more effective than searching a printed source because it permits the searcher to link words and terms in a way that can never be done manually. Compare, for example, searching for a book in a card catalog. The search is limited to searching by the author's name, the title of the book, or the standardized subject heading. In an index to periodicals in paper format the access points are usually the same as in a card catalog—author, title, standardized subject heading. Information in electronic databases can be searched by keying in almost any element in the record, and "mixing and matching" keywords and terms.

- Electronic searching is more flexible than searching printed indexes and abstracts because it is possible to search for words regardless of where they appear in the record. This is called *free-text searching* or *keyword searching*.

- In some databases it is possible to truncate or shorten terms so that all the variations of a term can be located.

- Electronic searching provides access to many more databases than are available in the library. Online databases through DIALOG provide access to hundreds of databases; library networks provide access to the catalogs of other libraries in the network; LEXIS/NEXIS provides access to hundreds of full-text journals, newspapers, and legal material.

- Information is usually more up-to-date. In an online catalog, records can be entered for materials as soon as they are ordered. With online databases the records are updated frequently, sometimes daily. For example, in the LEXIS database information is available almost as soon as it is put into the computer.

- Acquiring a printout or a copy of material retrieved from an electronic database is more convenient than hand copying citations from the online catalog or from an index or abstract.

- Searching an electronic database can be done from computers both inside and beyond the library—from offices, dormitories, and homes.

And a few caveats:

- Sometimes the "logic" in database searching does not work. For example, a search for articles on apricots retrieved articles on the fruit as well as on a computer named "Apricot." This kind of result is called a "false hit"' or "false drop." Free-text searching is likely to yield more false drops than searching by controlled vocabulary. Full-text databases are more likely to yield false hits than are bibliographic databases.

- Many databases do not include older information. Most of the Wilson databases (see Chapter 9) go back to 1983. In many databases, the information does not go beyond the last five to ten years. For example, one could use a database for current studies showing the effects of advertising on consumer preferences, but to find articles about consumer preference in the 1950s, one should consult a printed index from that period.

- One of the problems with searching for information in electronic databases is the lack of standardization. The screens of an online catalog in one library may not look at all like those in another library. This is because the software which runs the online system is different. Some libraries use NOTIS software (a product of Ameritech Library Services); others use DRA (Data Research Associates), Innovative Interfaces, or some other system from a commercial vendor. A number of academic libraries have developed their own systems. CD-ROM databases also vary greatly in the way they are searched. For example, the CD-ROM database for *Readers' Guide to Periodical Literature,* available from SilverPlatter, does not use the same search commands as the database available directly from the H.W. Wilson Company, its producer.

- Not all of a library's databases are available beyond the library walls. Many, especially those in CD-ROM formats, are available only in the library.

Database Records

In many ways bibliographic databases in electronic format can be compared to the printed materials in libraries: card catalogs, indexes, and abstracts. They provide access to information in other sources: magazines, journals, and books; they organize the information in a systematic way; and they provide several access points by which to locate the source. As with access tools in paper format, each entry points to an individual source. The individual entries are called *records*. A bibliographic record in an electronic database has many of the same elements as its counterpart in paper format. The elements are divided into *fields*, each of which is labeled. The fields serve as access points by which to retrieve the record. A typical record in an OPAC (Online Public Access Catalog) might contain the following labeled fields:

AUTHOR: [of the work being cited]

TITLE: [Title of the work cited]

EDITION:

PUBLISHER:

DATE:

PHYSICAL DESCRIPTION:

NOTES:

SUBJECTS:

(There may be other fields which are indexed, but they might not appear in the OPAC.)

A typical bibliographic record for a journal article in a periodical database might contain the following labeled fields:

AN: [Accession number]

TI: [Title of article]

AU: [Author of article]

IN: [Author's institutional affiliation]

JN: [Journal title or SO in some databases]

IS: [International Standard Serial Number]

LA: [Language of the article]

PY: [Publication year]

AB: [Abstract]

DE: [Subject descriptors or terms]

Full-text databases usually contain the following fields: database accession number (unique number assigned to that record in the database), author, title, issuing source or publisher, date, and the complete text of the item.

Search Basics

Following are some basic techniques which are common to most electronic databases.

Commands

While the computer is a powerful information storage and retrieval tool, it is also a very exacting one. To retrieve information, the searcher selects the appropriate database and then types in a search request or a *command*. The computer then scans the database looking for an exact match of the search statement. If the searcher misspells a word, the computer will look for a match on the misspelled word. If the search query is: "find standard of living among people of Appalachia during the Great Depression," the search is not likely to yield anything because the computer is searching for an exact match on that statement. It does not understand natural language. Rather, the software programs that run databases are designed in such a way as to be able to search on certain access points, to combine terms, and to limit terms. For example, if you want to search for books *by* Hemingway in the online catalog you would search in the author field. If you want works *about* Hemingway, you would search in the subject fields. If you wants all works both **by** and **about** Hemingway you would search all the fields.

Access Points

The key to access in any database is identifying the concepts and terms you wish to search, designing a search strategy, and applying basic search skills to achieve the desired results. The four basic access points are: author, title, subject and keyword. Each of these is discussed below.

Author Search

An author search is restricted to searching only the author field. It necessarily involves a known element—either an author's name or part of the author's name. Some databases allow you to truncate or shorten the author's name if you do not know the complete first name or correct spelling.

Title Search

A title search is also a known element—you know the title of a work, or enough of the title to make it distinctive. To retrieve a title you must key in the title exactly as it appears in the title field (except that initial articles are omitted). If the first part of a title is sufficiently distinctive, it is not necessary to type in the full title.

Subject Search

A subject search here refers to using *controlled vocabulary* to search a record. That is, a subject search must be keyed in exactly as it is entered in the subject field(s). The subject headings used in online catalogs are established by the Library of Congress or the National Library of Medicine (in the case of medical terms). In electronic databases, the subject headings or descriptors (as they are called in many databases) are listed in a *thesaurus* or an index. Lists of subject headings, such as the *Library of Congress List of Subject Headings (LCSH)* and the various online and printed thesauri which accompany electronic databases should be consulted to determine appropriate terminology to use in searching. The lists give alternative terms (refers from a term that is not used to one that is used), related terms, and terms used to broaden or narrow a search. Subject searching is usually recommended whenever possible because it gives a more precise search than free-text searching.

Keyword Search

Keyword searching is the term used to refer to free-text searching, or searching all the fields in a record. Keyword searching is used when:

- you are unsure about the order or spelling of all words in the title;

- you don't know the author's name;

- you don't know the precise subject heading used;

- you want to link terms from different parts of a record such as an author's name with a word from a title;

- you want to combine terms to narrow a topic or to limit a topic.

Keyword searching allows for flexibility in searching which you do not have with author, title, or subject searches. Below are outlined some of the facets of keyword searching used to limit or broaden a search.

Truncating Search Terms

In keyword searching it is possible to shorten a term by using a "?" or, in some databases, an asterisk [*]. This allows one search to retrieve singular or plural forms or different spellings of a word or name:

For example: k=colleg? will match "college," "colleges," "collegial," and "collegiate."

Avoid "over-truncating" search terms. Do not enter k=const? if you're searching for the term "constitution" as it will pull up too many terms.

Boolean Operators

Boolean operators are words used to make a logical search query. They enable you to broaden or narrow your search or link terms. Most databases use three basic boolean operators: **and, or, not**. When using any database you should verify whether or not boolean operators are used. (See Figure 4.1.)

- **AND** searches for occurrences of all of the search terms in a single record.
  Example:
  conservative **and** liberal **and** moderate (All three terms must be present.)

- **OR** searches for records that contain any of the terms.
  Example:
  conservative **or** liberal **or** moderate.

- **NOT** searches for records that contain the first term but not the second term.
  Example:
  liberal **not** conservative

Nested Searches

Nesting is used to specify the order of the search. With nesting parentheses are placed around words so that it makes a single search statement.
Example: (fraud or evasion) and income tax

Positional Operators

Positional operators are used to refer to the order in which words appear in a record:

- **ADJ** searches for terms in the exact order in which they are typed. In many databases ADJ is the default operator, so there is no need to type it in.

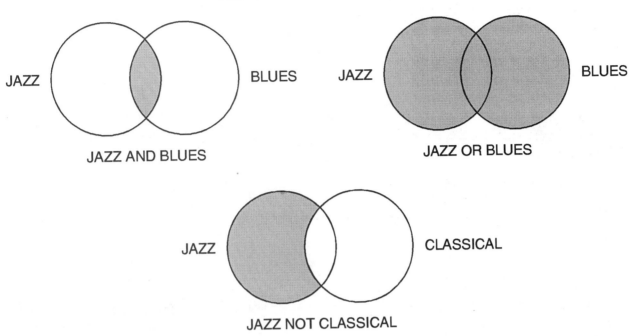

**How the Boolean Operators AND, OR, and NOT
Affect the Records Retrieved**

JAZZ AND BLUES

JAZZ OR BLUES

JAZZ NOT CLASSICAL

Figure 4.1 *Example of Boolean operators.*

Example:
Liberal democrat or liberal adj democrat

- **ADJ#** finds terms in the order typed within a specified number of words of each other.
  Example:
  k=conservative adj3 politics
  (Finds records that contain the word "conservative" within three words of the word "politics.")

- **WITH** searches for records that contain the search terms in the same field, and in the same record, such as the title field, the subject field, etc.
  Example:
  k=ultraviolet with radiation

- **SAME** searches for terms in the same group of fields (subjects, titles, etc.) in any record.
  Example:
  k=ultraviolet same radiation

Limiting a Search to a Field

In keyword searching it is possible to limit a search to a field or a group of fields in a record, such as author, title, or subject. For example, if you recall that there is an article on the Surma tribe in Africa that was published in *National Geographic* but you do not recall the date , you could narrow your search to certain fields to locate it:

Example:
Surma in ti and National Geographic in so

Note: In this case "ti" refers to the title field of the article, "so" refers to the source in which the article appears.

Qualifying a Search Term

Search terms may be further qualified by format, language, or date. For example, in an online catalog if one only wants works in French by Moliere one could do a keyword search on Molière in the author field and French in the language field.

Stopwords

Some words and abbreviations appear so frequently in records that a keyword search system does not search for them. Some common stopwords are:

- A BY FROM OF TO AN FOR IN THE WITH AND NOT OR SAME

  Avoid use of all stopwords when constructing your keyword search statement.

- AND, NOT, OR, and SAME may be used only as boolean or positional operators in a search.

The Search Strategy

In order to search a particular topic it is first necessary to prepare a search strategy which consists of the following steps:

1. Consider the appropriate discipline or large subject area for your topic.
    What aspect of the topic are you looking for? Under what discipline does it fall?
    What are some concepts related to the topic which might cross disciplines?

2. Identify standardized subject headings.
    Look in *LCSH* (*Library of Congress Subject Headings*).
    Check a printed thesaurus for the database.
    Look for a known item, such as an author in a field, and use the subject headings you locate.

3. Identify keywords and terms which are not standardized subject headings.
    What words or terms most nearly describe the subject you are searching?
    What are some synonyms?

4. Combine subject headings or keywords to narrow or broaden your search.

5. Select the appropriate database(s) to use.
    Look at the menu in the library's online catalog to see if indexes and abstracts are available.
    Look at the menu on the library's LAN.
    Search the library's online catalog.
    Check any guides to bibliographic databases.
    Ask a reference librarian.

6. Execute the search by typing in the commands on the computer's keyboard.

7. Evaluate the search results for appropriateness.
    The search results are sometimes called *hits*. If your search yields too many, or too little hits, you might need to go back and modify it.

8. Revise the search in light of your results:
    consult a thesaurus or index in the database;
    narrow the search by combining search terms;
    broaden the search if the results are too limited.

Searching Online Catalogs

The online catalogs in most libraries use software that embraces all or most of the search techniques described above. They also include help screens to assist in understanding how to search.

Searching CD-ROM Databases

CD-ROMs may be available on a LAN (Local Area Network), a server connected to computers within a building or a small geographical area like a campus. Databases on a LAN can be accessed by a number of simultaneous users, depending on the licensing agreement with the database producer. In some libraries the CD-ROMs are mounted on a WAN (Wide Area Network) which allows access to a wide area. CD-ROMs may also be mounted on *stand-alone workstations*, available only to one user at a time. A library usually keeps low demand databases on stand-alone machines and high demand on a LAN or a WAN.

Boolean and positional operators are used in searching most of the bibliographic databases. What is different is the search commands and the structure of the database. New users of CD-ROM databases should consult the *help* screens or the printed guides if any are available. Some libraries have tried to get all of their databases from a single producer, or vendor, such as SilverPlatter, in order to make it easier for their users to learn different search commands and database structure. (See Chapter 9 for a sample search in a CD-ROM database.)

Searching Online Databases

The term *online databases* is used here to describe databases which are stored in the mainframe of large computer data centers. Libraries and research centers, rather than purchasing subscriptions to a multitude of databases, subscribe to services which enable them to select those databases they wish to access. The computer data center also arranges for the telecommunications services between the database user and the data center. Computer data centers do not usually produce the databases themselves; rather, they acquire them from organizations or businesses to whom they pay a lease and/or royalty fee. Thus, the computer data center is known as a *vendor*. Some producers who market their products to vendors are H. W. Wilson Co., producer of WILSONLINE; the National Library of Medicine, producer of MEDLINE; and University Microfilms, Inc. (UMI), producers of ABI/INFORM. The major vendors of online services are DIALOG, BRS, and ORBIT. Online databases are available on a wide variety of subjects in the areas of science, social sciences, and humanities. In most libraries, the search is done by a reference librarian who has been trained in search techniques. The results of the search may be printed online or offline. Online printouts are generated immediately and printed on a local printer. Offline printouts are requested while the computer is linked to the vendor's information system; these are then printed by the vendor and sent by mail or other delivery service to the library. Online searching can be expensive as the costs include the fees charged by the vendor for use of the database, telecommunications charges, and printing costs.

Search techniques

The illustration below shows a hypothetical search in one of the DIALOG databases. The searcher wanted to find out all the information in the database relating to how artificial intelligence is used to write poetry or music.

Example:

        ? s (music or poetry) and artificial intelligence
        6946 music
        3958 poetry
        574 artificial intelligence
S4   **317** (music or poetry) and artificial intelligence

Searching Full-Text Databases

Unlike bibliographic databases, full-text databases do not have labeled fields. They are usually searched by free-text or keyword method. Free-text searching is not as precise as searching by controlled vocabulary or standardized subject headings. The words in the search statement are taken from titles, abstracts, headings, notes, and the complete text. Although it is possible to use boolean and position operators in full-text databases, the search may not be as precise as searching a database that has controlled vocabulary. On the other hand, obscure terms may show up in full-text searching, which may not have been included in a bibliographic citation.

Instructor: _____   Name: _____

Course/Section: _____   Date: _____

Review Questions for Chapter Four

1. What is meant by the term "information in electronic format"?

2. Define database as it is used in this chapter.

3. What is the difference between a bibliographic database and a full-text database?

4. Name four advantages of using an electronic database.

5. Name three things you need to watch for with regard to searching electronic databases.

6. Explain what is meant by "records" as applied to an electronic database.

7. What are "fields" in an electronic database?

8. Name four basic access points for retrieving information in an electronic database.

9. Explain the difference between a subject search and a keyword search.

10. What is meant by the term "truncating" as applied to searching?

11. What are Boolean operators?

12. Name the three Boolean operators and define each.

13. What is meant by the term "nesting" as applied to searching an online database?

14. What are "positional operators"? Name three positional operators.

15. What is meant by the term limiting a search?

16. Name three ways you can qualify a search.

Instructor: _____   **Name:** _____

Course/Section: _____   **Date:** _____

═══

Electronic Searching Exercise

In the hypothetical problems below state the command you would use to execute the search:

Use: a=   for author searches

             t=   for title searches

             s=   for subject searches

             k=   for keyword search

             ?   to truncate

For Nos. 1-6 use Boolean or positional operators to state your commands:

For example:

Find all the information on using animals in experimentation.

Command:

                                 k=animal and experimentation

Find all the records with information on importing perfume from France.

Command:

                                 k=perfume and import? and France

1. Find any records dealing with vitamins in the diet.
   Command:

2. Find all the records that have information on diets and all the records that have information on exercise.
   Command:

3. Find the records that have information on diets, but eliminate those dealing with exercise.
   Command:

4. Find all the records that have heart in the same fields as exercise.
   Command:

5. Find all the records that have solar and energy in the same field and in the same record.
   Command:

6. Find all the records where country appears within five words of music.
   Command:

Assume that you are using the OPAC in your library for problems 7-13.

7. Find the periodical: *The New Yorker*.
   Command:

8. Find all the works on the subject of folk dancing.
   Command:

9. Find all the books by Flannery O'Connor.
   Command:

10. Find all the books about Flannery O'Connor.
    Command:

11. Find all books that have the word earthquakes in the record.
    Command:

12. Find all books with earthquakes as the approved subject.
    Command:

13. Find a book about the Civil War by an author whose last name is Williams.
    Command:

ORGANIZATION OF LIBRARY MATERIALS

A PREVIEW

Libraries have large numbers of materials in a wide variety of formats, making retrieval complex. In order to provide access to its collections, libraries organize materials by classifying and assigning specific location numbers. Library organization systems are based on classification schemes which group related materials together. This rationale has resulted in the development of uniform classification systems. This chapter surveys the major classification schemes used by libraries and introduces the user to the effective use of these systems.

KEY TERMS AND CONCEPTS

Classification Systems
Dewey Decimal Classification System (DC)
Library of Congress Classification System (LC)
Superintendent of Documents Classification System (SuDocs)
United Nations Symbols (UN)
Call Numbers

INTRODUCTION

The purpose of any classification system is to bring together comparable materials so they can be found easily and the library will have some logical arrangement. In addition, library patrons should be able to browse the shelves in a given subject classification number or letter in order to find materials on that subject grouped together. Reference materials, and in some libraries, serials, may be shelved in a different area but will have the same call number ranges. For example, books on sociology would be found in the stacks under HM while encyclopedias on sociology would be found in the HM section of the reference stacks.

Early libraries sometimes arranged materials by author, color, or even size. Modern libraries have stack areas in which materials are arranged by subject, but often these may be grouped according to format such as microforms, CD-ROMs, and audio-visual materials.

Classification Systems

The two most commonly used classification systems in American libraries are the Dewey Decimal Classification System (commonly called Dewey or DC) and the Library of Congress Classification System (referred to as LC). (See Figure 5.1.) Most public libraries use the Dewey system while colleges and universities use the Library of Congress system.

All classification systems start with a general classification and then proceed to a more specific classification. Note that in Figure 5.2 Dewey classifies all engineering in 620, while Library of Congress subdivides it into several branches. The Library of Congress system is used in large libraries because its broader base allows room for expansion as new subjects are added to the fields of knowledge.

Materials covering one particular subject can be classified easily under that subject. However, when the item deals with more than one subject, it is classified under the largest subject covered or under what the catalogers feel is the most important subject. Subjects covered in the book which are not reflected in the call number selected by the cataloger are brought out by means of *subject headings*. For example, the book described in Figure 6.10, *Affirmative Action for Women: A Practical Guide,* is classified under HD 6058, the Library of Congress Classification number for women—employment—United States. It is assigned the additional subject heading, "discrimination in employment—United States."

Libraries which have extensive collections of materials published by the United States Government often use the *Superintendent of Documents* or SuDocs System to classify their publications. This system was devised by the Superintendent of Documents to organize the thousands of publications it issues.

In addition to the three major systems discussed above, libraries may also use other systems for classifying smaller special collections such as state documents, United Nations documents, or archives. For most library users it is not necessary to learn all the details of the classification systems. In order to make effective use of the library's resources, however, the researcher needs to know which classification systems are being used and to understand the basic principles on which each system rests.

Dewey Decimal Classification System

The Dewey Decimal Classification system was originated by Melvil Dewey in the latter part of the 19th century. The system divides all knowledge into ten different classes. These ten primary classes are further subdivided into subclasses. Decimals are used to subdivide further.

900	Geography and History
970	General history of North America
973	United States history
973.2	Colonial period 1607-1775
973.7	Civil War 1861-1865
973.71	Political and economic history (Civil War period)
973.73	Military operations
973.7349	Battle of Gettysburg
973.9	20th century 1901-
973.92	Later 20th century 1953-

The example above illustrates how the addition of each decimal number to the whole number makes the classification more precise.

Library of Congress Classification System

The Library of Congress Classification system was designed by the Library of Congress in the latter part of the 19th century solely for its own use. Because it is so comprehensive, it has been adopted by many other large libraries both in the United States and in other parts of the world.

MAJOR LIBRARY CLASSIFICATION SYSTEMS

DEWEY DECIMAL (D.C.)	LIBRARY OF CONGRESS (LC)	SUPERINTENDENT OF DOCUMENTS (SuDocs)	UNITED NATIONS SYMBOLS (UN)
ex: 635.05 B35	ex: B358 C.57 1985	ex: L3.134/2:C83/2/983	ex: ST/ESA/165
000 Generalities	A General Works	A Agriculture	A/ General Assembly
100 Philosophy/Psychology	B Philosophy/ Psychology/Religion	AE Archives/Records	E/ Economic & Social Council
200 Religion			
	C History-General	C Commerce	S/ Security Council
300 Social Sciences	D History-World	C.3 Census	
400 Language	E American History	D Defense	T/ Trusteeship Council
	F Local American History	E Energy	
500 Natural Science/ Mathematics	G Geography/Anthropology/Sports	ED Education	ST/ Secretariat
		EP Environmental Protection	
	H Social Sciences	FR Federal Reserve	Other:
600 Technology	HA Statistics	GS General Administration	
700 The Arts	HM Sociology	HE Health & Human Services	CCPR/ Human Rights Committee
		HH Housing & Urban Development	
800 Literature/Rhetoric	J Political Science	I Interior	DP/ UN Development Program
	K Law	I19 US Geological Survey	
900 Geography/History	L Education	J Justice	
	M Music	JU Judiciary	
	N Fine Arts		
		L Labor	
	P Language/Literature	LC Library of Congress	
	PR English/Literature		
	PS American Literature	NAS National Aeronautics/Space	
		PR President's Office	
	Q Science		
	R Medicine	S State Department	
	S Agriculture	SI Smithsonian Institute	
	T Technology		
	U Military Science	T Treasury	
	V Naval Science	T22 Internal Revenue	
	Z Bibliography/Library Science	TD Transportation	
		VA Veterans Administration	
		Y Congress	
		Y4 Congressional Hearings	

Figure 5.1 Comparison of Major Library Classification Systems

DEWEY DECIMAL

000	GENERALITIES
010	Bibliography
020	Library & Info Sciences
030	Gen Encyc Works
040	Gen Serials & Indexes
050	Gen Organiz & Museology
060	News Media, Jl, Publishing
070	General Collections
080	Manuscripts, Rare Books
100	PHIL & PSYCHOLOGY
110	Metaphysics
120	Epistemology, Creation
130	Paranormal Phen.
150	Psychology
160	Logic
170	Ethics
180	Ancient, Medieval, Oriental
190	Modern Western Phil.
200	RELIGION
210	Natural Theology
220	Bible
230	Christian Theology
240	Christian Moral/Devotional
250	Christ.Orders, Local Church
260	Christian Social Theology
270	Christian Church History
280	Christian Denom & Sects
290	Other, Comp. Religion
300	SOCIAL SCIENCES
310	General Statistics
320	Political Science
330	Economics
340	Law
350	Public Administration
360	Social Services, Admin.
370	Education
380	Commerce, Comm., Transp.
390	Customs, Etiquette, Folklore
400	LANGUAGE
410	Linguistics
420	English & Old English
430	Germanic Lang, German
440	Romance Languages, Fr
450	Italian, Rumanian
460	Spanish, Portuguese
470	Italic Languages, Latin
480	Hellenic Lang, Class. Greek
500	NATURAL SCIENCE
510	Mathematics
520	Astronomy & Allied Sci.
530	Physics
540	Chemistry & Applied Sci.
550	Earth Sciences
560	Paleontology, Paleozoology
570	Life Sciences
580	Botanical Sciences
590	Zoological Sciences
600	TECHNOLOGY
610	Medicine
620	Engineering
630	Agriculture
640	Home Economics
660	Chemical Engineering
670	Manufacturing
690	Buildings
700	THE ARTS
710	Civic & Landscape Art
720	Architecture
730	Plastic Arts, Sculpture
740	Drawing & Decorative Art
750	Painting & Paintings
760	Graphic Arts, Printmaking
770	Photography & Photographs
780	Music
790	Recreational & Perfm Art
800	LITERATURE
810	American
820	English & Old English
830	Germanic Languages
840	Romance Languages
860	Spanish & Portuguese
870	Italic; Latin
880	Hellenic, Classical Greek
890	Literature of Other Lang.
900	GEOG & HISTORY
910	Geography & Travel
920	Biography, Genealogy
930	Ancient History
940	Gen History of Europe
950	Gen Hist of Asia, Far East
960	Gen Hist of Africa
970	Gen Hist of North America
980	Gen Hist of South America
990	Gen Hist of Other Areas

LIBRARY OF CONGRESS

A	GENERAL WORKS
	Gen. Encyc, Ref Works
B	PHILOSOPHY/ RELIGION
C	HISTORY
CB	History of Civilization
CC	Archaeology
CD	Archives
CR	Heraldry
CS	Genealogy
CT	Biography (General)
D	HISTORY, World History
DA	Great Britain
DB	Austria
DC	France
DD	Other countries
E-F	HISTORY OF AMERICA
G	GEOG, ANTHRO, FOLK.
G	Geography
GB	Physical Geography
GC	Oceanography
GN	Anthropology
GR	Folklore
GV	Recreation
H	SOCIAL SCIENCES
HA	Statistics
HB	Economics
HM-HX	Sociology
J	POLITICAL SCIENCE
JC	Political Theory
JF-JQ	Constitutional History/ Public Administration
JS	Local Government
JX	International Law
K	LAW
L	EDUCATION
M	MUSIC
ML	Literature of Music
MT	Musical Instruction
N	FINE ARTS
NA	Architecture
NB	Sculpture
NC	Graphic Arts
ND	Painting
NK	Decorative Arts
P	LANGUAGE, LITERATURE
PA	Classical Languages
PC	Romance Languages
PD-PF	German Language
PJ-PL	Oriental Language
PN	Gen. and comparative
PQ	Romance literature
PR	English Literature
PS	American Literature
PT	Germanic Literature
PZ	Fiction in English, Juvenile
Q	SCIENCE
QA	Mathematics
QB	Astronomy
QC	Physics
QD	Chemistry
QE	Geology
QH	Natural History
QK	Botany
QL	Zoology
QM	Human Anatomy
QP	Physiology
R	MEDICINE
S	AGRICULTURE
SB	Plant Culture/Horticulture
SD	Forestry
SF	Animal Culture
SH	Fish Culture/Fisheries
SK	Hunting Sports
T	TECHNOLOGY
TA	Gen Engineering
TC	Hydraulic Engineering
TD	Sanitary/Municipal Engr.
TE	Highway Engineering
TF	Railroad Engineering
TH	Building Construction
TJ	Mechanical Engineering
TK	Electrical, Nuclear Engr.
TP	Chemical Technology
TR	Photography
TS	Manufactures
TT	Handicrafts, arts and crafts
TX	Home Economics
U	MILITARY SCIENCE
V	NAVAL SCIENCE
Z	BIBLIOG LIBR. SCIENCE

Figure 5.2 Comparison of Dewey Decimal and Library of Congress Classification Systems

The LC system has 21 different classes with numerous subdivisions under each class. Each primary class is designated by a single letter as illustrated in Figure 5.2. Following the first letter or group of letters there will be a whole number which indicates a subdivision.

H	**Social sciences (General)**
HA	Statistics
Economics	
HB	Economic Theory. Demography
HC-HD	Economic history and conditions
HE	Transportation and communications
HF	Commerce
HJ	Finance
Sociology	
HM	Sociology (General and theoretical)
HN	Social history. Social problems. Social reform
HQ	The family. Marriage. Woman
HS	Societies: Secret, benevolent, etc. Clubs
HT	Communities. Classes. Races
HV	Social pathology. Social and public welfare. Criminology
HX	Socialism. Communism. Anarchism

The initial classification number can be subdivided further as shown in the three call numbers below:

HF	HF	HF
5686	5686	5686
.D7	.P3	.S75

HF	=	commerce
5686	=	accounting
.D7	=	drug stores
.P3	=	petroleum industry
.S75	=	steel industry

Although the system is based on the alphabet, not all of the letters have been used in either the main classes or the subclasses. These letters are reserved for new subjects or for the expansion of older subjects, or in the case of I and O, to avoid confusion with the numbers one and zero.

Superintendent of Documents Classification System

The SuDocs system is used by the United States Government Printing Office to assign call numbers to government documents before they are sent to depository libraries. Libraries which serve as depositories for government publications usually establish separate collections arranged by SuDocs number. This system is an alphanumeric scheme based on the agency which issues the publication rather than on subjects, as in the case of Dewey or LC. The initial letter or letters designate the government agency, bureau, or department responsible for the publication. The letters are subdivided further to indicate sub-agencies.

Publications which are part of a series are assigned a number which designates a particular series. Each individual publication in the series is assigned a number or letter/number combination which identifies the individual title, volume, year, or issue number. This number follows a colon. The following example illustrates the elements in a typical SuDocs number:

C 3.134/2:C 83/2/994

C	=	Issuing Department	Commerce Department
3	=	Subagency	Bureau of the Census
134/2	=	Series	Statistical Abstract Supplement
C 83/2/994	=	Title and date	County and City Data Book, 1995

United Nations Symbol Numbers

United Nations publications are classified by series/symbol number designed by the UN library. Figure 5.1 shows the top level of the classification scheme. The numbers are divided further to indicate departments and series. The series symbol numbers are composed of capital letters in combination with numerical notations. The elements in the numbers are separated by slash marks.

The *Report on the World Social Situation* has the classification number ST/ESA/165.

ST	=	United Nations Secretariat
ESA	=	Department of International and Social Affairs
165	=	series number

CALL NUMBERS

The *call number* assigned to an item usually indicates its subject matter, author, and title. The call number, either alone or in conjunction with an added location symbol, determines the location of the item in the library.

For example: This book would be shelved in the stacks: DS 69 .5 C5; a book with this call number would be located in the reference area: Ref BF 311.G3.

In research it is important to record a complete call number, including any location symbols, in order to locate the item.

The example below identifies each element in a Dewey Decimal number:

Classification number: _____ 976.3
Book number: _____ D261 Lo3

    author's initial and number _____

    first two letters of book title _____

    edition number _____

The example below identifies each element in a Library of Congress number:

Classification number _____ F
    369
Author and Book number _____ .D24
Date of edition_____ 1971

The following illustration demonstrates how several books by the same author are classified in both the Dewey and LC systems.

Dewey Decimal		Library of Congress
976.3 D261Lo3	Davis, Edwin Adams Louisiana; a narrative history...1971	F 369 .D24 1971
976.3 D261Lo2	Davis, Edwin Adams Louisiana; a narrative history...1965	F 369 .D24 1965
976.3 D261Lo	Davis, Edwin Adams Louisiana; a narrative history...1961	F 369 .D24 1961
976.3 D261L4	Davis, Edwin Adams Louisiana, the Pelican state...1975	F 369 .D25 1975
976.3 D261L3	Davis, Edwin Adams Louisiana, the Pelican state...1969	F 369 .D25 1969
976.3 D261L	Davis, Edwin Adams Louisiana, the Pelican state...1959	F 369 .D25
976.3 D261s	Davis, Edwin Adams The story of Louisiana...1960	F 369 .D26

In both the Dewey and LC systems, it is necessary to read the numbers/letters in the call numbers sequentially in order to locate books on the shelves. In Dewey, the number before the decimal point is always treated as a whole number or integer, while all of the numbers following the decimal point are treated as decimals. Although the decimal point may not appear physically in the call number, the book number is nevertheless treated as a decimal.

For example:

	338	would be shelved before	338
	A221i		A36

The following call numbers are arranged in correct order as they would stand on the shelf.

338	338	338.908	338.91	338.917	338.94
A22li	A36	F911r	B138e	R896y	R31c

When locating a call number in LC, it is necessary to start with the letter combination and then proceed to the numbers. As with Dewey, the first set of numbers is treated as a whole number. The whole number or integer is followed either by a decimal point and numbers and/or one or more letter/number combinations. The remaining numbers are all treated as decimals.

For example:

PN	would be shelved before	PN
6		6
.S55		.S6

The next consideration when reading the call number is the letter/number combination which, in many cases, is followed by a third letter/number combination. All parts of the book numbers are read first alphabetically and then numerically as decimals. In many call numbers, the date of the book is added. When call numbers are exactly the same except for dates, as in the case with multiple editions, the books are arranged in chronological order. Notice in the second and third examples that the call numbers are exactly alike except for the 1967. The call number without the date is shelved before the one with the date. The following call numbers are arranged in correct order as they would stand on the shelf.

PN	PN	PN	PN	PN
6	56	56	56	57
.S55	.H63T5	H63T5	.3	.A43L5
		1967	.N4J6	
			1971	

The call numbers for documents are usually written horizontally unless there is not space on the spine of the book to write the numbers. In that case, the numbers are written vertically, with the break occurring at a punctuation mark.

For example:

A 13.106/2-2:C 35

Documents with SuDocs call numbers are shelved in alphanumeric sequence. The numbers following periods are whole numbers as are the numbers following slashes or colons.

The following SuDocs numbers are in shelf order:

A 2.113:C 35   A 13.92:R 59   A 13.92/2:F 29   A 13.103:163

Many libraries have books housed in areas other than the regular stacks, and these areas are usually indicated by a symbol over the call number. For example, books on the reference shelves often will have the symbols R, Ref, or X. It is necessary to check the library handbook or a chart of symbols to determine their meaning and location.

Instructor: _____   Name: _____

Course/Section: _____   Date: _____

Review Questions for Chapter Five

1. Which classification system is used in most academic libraries in the United States?

2. How many main classes are found in the:

    a. Dewey Decimal classification system?

    b. Library of Congress classification system?

3. What does the class or classification number stand for in the call number in either the Dewey or the LC system?

4. What are the main differences between the Dewey Decimal and Library of Congress classification systems?

5. What is the SuDocs classification system? How does it differ from the Dewey and LC classification systems?

6. What is the main difference between the SuDocs classification system and the UN symbols?

7. Why is it useful for researchers to become familiar with class letters and numbers in their subjects of interest?

8. What determines the location of a book in the library's collection?

9. Why are location symbols used in some libraries?

Instructor: _____   Name: _____

Course/Section: _____   Date: _____

===

Classification Exercise

1. Use Figure 5.2 to answer these questions for the Dewey Decimal classification system:

   a. What number range would include works on psychology?

   b. What number range would you use to find books on zoology?

   c. What number range would you use to find books written in the German language?

2. Use Figure 5.2 to answer these questions for the Library of Congress (LC) classification system:

   a. What general number would you use to find sociology books?

   b. What general number would you use to find reference books on medicine?

   c. In what call number range would you find periodicals on American History?

3. Use Figure 5.1 to answer these questions about the Superintendent of Documents (SuDocs) classification system:

   a. Give the names of three government agencies which are likely to publish information on drug abuse.

   b. Which agency of the government produces the census?

Instructor: _____   **Name:** _____

Course/Section: _____   **Date:** _____

Call Number Exercise

Listed below are two sets of call numbers. For each set, identify the classification system used and arrange each group of numbers within the set in shelf order.

Classification system: _____

PS	PR	PR	PQ	PR
559	5219	132	3939	5219
.R87R8	.R26Q3	.T8	.D37E4	.R26L5
	1856			1865

HT	HT	HT	HT	HT
393	393	393	393	393
.L616	.L62R323	.L62L52	.L62R52	.L6R52

KFL	KFL	KFL	KFL	KFL
112	45.1	45	211	30
.A2	.W35	.A212	.Z9L68	.5
1820				.N48A3
				1910

TD	TD	TD	TD	TD
525	194.5	624	195	525
.L6S4	.E58	.L8A53	.P4U555	.L3J48
			1978	

Classification system: _____

261	261	261	261	261
R51k	R6h	R13p	R13pr	R519g

828	828	828	828	828
M57p	M57	M57b	M5655	M152g

973.016	973.7349	973.41	973.8	973.8
W93	Ev26a	W277	G767ca	G767

341.6016	341.7	341.6016	341.63	341.67
W93	Am26	Am4	Am14c	Am35a

Classification system: _____

D301.6:177-19/988	D5.350:96943	D301.6:177-19/989
Y4.Ap6/6:L11/990/pt.2	Y3.T25: 2 W53	Y3 Ad6: 2F31
Al3.13:F39	Al3.13: W36/2/989	Al3.2: Si 3/7
HE20.3038:G28/988	HH1.108/a:N81c	HH1.2:R26/11
EP1.8:Su7/5	ED1.17:D84	E3.45:988
ED1.308:D84	E3.2:Ut3/2	

LIBRARY CATALOGS

A PREVIEW

One may think of the library's catalog as a massive index to virtually all the contents of the library. It is the goal of this chapter to describe the library catalog and guide the library user in a systematic way to a mastery of its use. The researcher will be introduced to traditional card catalogs and to online catalog systems.

KEY TERMS AND CONCEPTS

Library Catalogs
Book Catalogs
COM Catalogs
CD-ROM Catalogs
Card Catalogs
Online Catalogs
Author Search
Title Search
Subject Search
LCSH
Cross References
Keyword Search

INTRODUCTION

The catalog is the key to the collections of any library. Library users will be able to access the materials in a library through its catalog. It is also important to be able to interpret the information on the catalog record. The catalog record gives the location of each item and provides a full description, including name of the author, complete title, edition, number of pages, size, publisher, place of publication, date of publication, etc. Thus, it is possible to learn a great deal about the item even before it is located in the library. The catalog record also suggests other related subject headings under which additional material can be found.

Types of Library Catalogs

Traditional library catalogs consisted of index cards arranged alphabetically, but today most library catalogs are online. A few libraries might still maintain catalogs in other formats which include book catalogs and COM (Computer Output Microform), CD-ROM (Compact Disk-Read Only Memory) catalogs, and online catalogs.

Some libraries, because of the expense involved, cannot afford to change all of their records when they convert from one type of catalog to another; therefore, records for older materials are left in one system, while those for newer materials are entered into the new system. For example, a library changing from a card catalog to an online catalog might leave all of its records for materials cataloged before a certain date in the card catalog and enter only records for materials processed after that date into the online catalog. The user needs to determine which type or types of catalogs the library is using in order to locate materials. This information is generally available in the library's handbook or from a reference librarian.

Book Catalogs

Early libraries often used *book catalogs* which listed the library's holdings in book form. It was difficult to keep these catalogs up-to-date, and therefore, it was necessary to issue frequent supplements. With a book catalog, it is rather easy to maintain several catalogs at the same time in different locations. The "updates" are kept in a separate volume until complete revisions are made. Library patrons must consult several different volumes to be sure that they are getting all the references available.

COM Catalogs

A COM catalog (Computer Output Microform) lists the library's holdings on microfiche and may be accessed by author, title, subject, and sometimes by keyword and classification number.

CD-ROM Catalogs

The CD-ROM catalog is a catalog on compact disk and requires a workstation consisting of a microcomputer with a monitor and compact disk drive. Usually there is a printer attached. The CD-ROM catalog looks and works like an online catalog, but instead of being operated from a mainframe computer, it runs on a microcomputer.

Card Catalogs

Card catalogs consist of multiple drawers containing 3 X 5 cards arranged alphabetically by author, title, subject, and added entries. Added entries consist of cards for such things as editors, compilers, translators, illustrators, arrangers of music, and series. Catalogs that are divided into sections and are referred to as divided catalogs. Divided catalogs may consist of three sections—author, title, and subject—or two sections: author/title and subject. The cards in each section are filed alphabetically word-by-word. Practically every book, with the exception of fiction, has at least three cards in the catalog. These are: author, or main entry card; title card; and one or more subject cards. With printed cards, except for the top line, all the cards are identical. Figures 6.1- 6.5 illustrate a set of cards found in the card catalog for a particular work. The access points for this book are: author, joint author, title and two LC established subject headings.

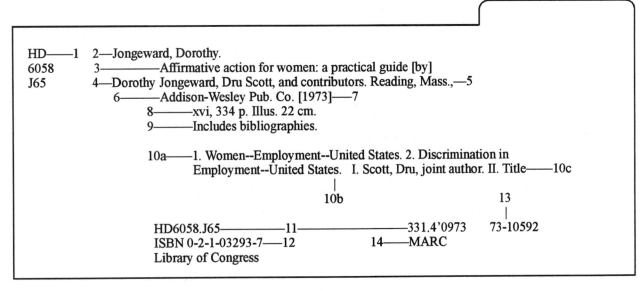

Figure 6.1 *Author or main entry card from a printed card catalog.*

1. *Call number (Library of Congress class number and author number)*

2. *Author (first one listed on the title page)*

3. *Title of the book*

4. *Restatement of the Authors' names*

5. *Place of publication*

6. *Publisher*

7. *Publication date*

8. *Physical description (preliminary paging, textual paging, note that it contains illustrations, size of book.)*

9. *Notes: book includes bibliographies*

10. *Tracings (Traces cards in catalog for this book)*

   10a   Subject headings

   10b   Joint author

   10c   Title

11. *Classification numbers assigned by the Library of Congress*

12. *International Standard Book Number*

13. *Library of Congress catalog number*

14. *MARC note (Record available in Machine Readable Catalog (MARC) format*

Figure 6.2 *Title card from a printed card catalog.*

WOMEN--EMPLOYMENT--UNITED STATES
HD   Jongeward, Dorothy.
6058   Affirmative action for women: a practical guide [by]
J65   Dorothy Jongeward, Dru Scott, and contributors. Reading, Mass.,
                  Addison-Wesley Pub. Co. [1973]
                       xvi, 334 p. Illus. 22 cm.
                       Includes bibliographies.

                  1. Women--Employment--United States. 2. Discrimination in
                  Employment--United States. I. Scott, Dru, joint author. II. Title

            HD6058.J65   331.4'0973   73-10592
            ISBN 0-2-1-03293-7   MARC
            Library of Congress

*Figure 6.3 Subject card from a printed card catalog. (Subjects are typed in upper case or in red on the
    top line.)*

DISCRIMINATION IN EMPLOYMENT--UNITED STATES
HD   Jongeward, Dorothy.
6058   Affirmative action for women: a practical guide [by]
J65   Dorothy Jongeward, Dru Scott, and contributors. Reading, Mass.,
                  Addison-Wesley Pub. Co. [1973]
                       xvi, 334 p. Illus. 22 cm.
                       Includes bibliographies.

                  1. Women--Employment--United States. 2. Discrimination in
                  Employment--United States. I. Scott, Dru, joint author. II. Title

            HD6058.J65   331.4'0973   73-10592
            ISBN 0-2-1-03293-7   MARC
            Library of Congress

Figure 6.4 Subject card from a printed card catalog.

Additional cards may be used for a joint author, titles in series, or other entries. Figure 6.5 illustrates a joint author card for the work described above.

HD
6058
J65

Scott, Dru, joint author.
Jongeward, Dorothy.
    Affirmative action for women: a practical guide [by]
Dorothy Jongeward, Dru Scott, and contributors. Reading, Mass.,
    Addison-Wesley Pub. Co. [1973]
    xvi, 334 p. Illus. 22 cm.
    Includes bibliographies.

    1. Women--Employment--United States. 2. Discrimination in
Employment--United States. I. Scott, Dru, joint author. II. Title

HD6058.J65   331.4'0973   73-10592
ISBN 0-2-1-03293-7   MARC
Library of Congress

Figure 6.5 Joint Author card from a printed card catalog.

Cross reference cards are used to direct the card catalog user to the proper terminology or to additional sources of information. There are two kinds of cross reference cards—*see* and *see also*. The *see* reference directs the card catalog user from a subject heading or term that is not used to the synonymous term that is used. The *see also* reference card lists related subject headings under which more information can be found.

DISCRIMINATION AGAINST WOMEN

see

SEX DISCRIMINATION AGAINST WOMEN

Figure 6.6 Subject cross reference.

DISCRIMINATION

see also: Age discrimination; Civil rights; Discrimination in education; Discrimination in employment; Discrimination in housing; Discrimination in public accommodation; Minorities; Race discrimination; Sex discrimination; Toleration.

Figure 6.7 See also cross reference.

Arrangement of the Card Catalog

There are two methods of alphabetizing commonly used in filing—*letter by letter* and *word by word*. Dictionaries use letter-by-letter filing as do some indexes and encyclopedias. Cards in the card catalog are filed word by word. Library users should be aware of differences in the two methods so that they will not miss entries in reference sources. The word-by-word method treats each word in a name, title, or subject heading as a separate unit, while the letter-by-letter method treats all the words in a name, title, or subject heading as if they were one unit. In other words, in the letter-by-letter method all the words in the heading are run together as if they were one word.

For example:

Word by Word	*Letter by Letter*
San Antonio	San Antonio
San Diego	Sanctuary
San Pedro	Sandalwood
Sanctuary	Sandblasting
Sand blasting	Sand, George
Sand, George	San Diego
Sandalwood	San Pedro

Online Catalogs

Today most libraries have replaced the card catalog either entirely or in part by an automated catalog, usually referred to as an OPAC (Online Public Access Catalog). Online catalogs were made possible with the advent of MARC (machine readable catalog) records in 1965.

The Library of Congress developed the MARC format as a means of improving access to library information. Since that time it has been universally adopted by libraries throughout the world as a means for cataloging library materials. MARC records are stored on computer tapes (or in other electronic format) and retrieved by the use of a computer.

The greatest advantage of an online catalog is that it provides access to library materials in ways not possible with a card catalog. Note that with the card catalog the access points are limited to author, title, and subject. The online catalog provides all of those access points plus keyword search capabilities. In addition to the public catalog, online systems may have other capabilities. These include the ability to:

1. update the catalog on a daily basis;

2. provide information concerning materials on order;

3. provide circulation information, such as whether or not material has been checked out;

4. provide information on periodical "holdings;"

5. access the database from remote locations, such as a faculty office, dormitory room, or home.

Library Catalogs: The Key to Access

Format of Cataloged Materials

When looking at catalog records one should recall that format is a consideration. The online catalog does not list only the books in the collection. It identifies materials in a variety of formats. These include films, microfilm, microfiche, microprint, sound recordings, reel-to-reel tapes, video cassettes, scores, maps, musical scores, CD-ROMs, online databases, and, most recently, information found on the Internet.

The locations of material with special formats will be indicated on the catalog record. They usually have a location symbol such as "Film," "LP," "Recording," or "Tape" plus a sequence number instead of a classification number as a means of locating them. The number given with the location symbol is often an *accession* number. This means that as the materials are received by the library, they are assigned a number indicating their order of receipt. Sometimes a classification number and a location symbol are assigned to non-book materials.

Access Points

The purpose of cataloging materials in a library is to describe certain elements of the work so that it can be identified, classified according to its subject, and shelved or stored. The elements used in describing the work are also the key to access. In card catalogs the access points are called *entries*. In online records, they are called *fields*. The main access points in any cataloging record are: author, title, subject, and keyword. Each of these is discussed below.

Author Search

Usually an author search is for a "known item." To find information or a specific work in the library if you know the author of a work, look in the library catalog under author's name.

The author might be an individual, or two or more individuals (joint author(s)). The author could also be a *corporate author* which refers to an organization such as a governmental agency, an association, a company, or other corporate body that issues a publication in its name rather than in the name of the individuals who did the actual writing. There might also be access points for editor, compiler, composer, arranger (music), translator, or illustrator.

Title Search

The title search is also for a known item, although if only some words in the title are known it might be necessary to do a keyword rather than a title search. The title found on the title page of the work is the main access point, although there could be other title-related access points. Other records for titles might include:

- *series* titles. *A series* is a set of volumes which are published successively and have some connection, such as a common subject, author, or publisher.

- individual selections within *anthologies* (or collections). Although the contents of anthologies are not always included in the catalog, it is not unusual to have records for each individual work within a collection. For example, a collection of short stories might have entries for each individual title within the work.

- *periodical* titles. There is usually no author of a periodical, so the main entry in the card catalog will be the title. There is no field for author in the online record.

Subject Search

To find information on a specific topic when you know the correct subject heading, check the library catalog under that subject heading.

To find material in the library's catalog on a topic when the subject is not known, consult the *Library of Congress Subject Headings* (*LCSH*). It lists standardized or approved terms used by the Library of Congress to describe the subject matter in cataloged materials. It also lists *see* references for terms not used, and *see also* references for related topics. The standardized subject headings are used as subject headings in entries in both card catalogs and online catalogs. They must be searched exactly as they appear in *LCSH*. One advantage of subject searching is that the search results are likely to be much more on target than keyword searching. This is because professional catalogers have assigned the subject headings after examining the work and determining that the work is about the subject listed.

A sample page from the *Library of Congress Subject Headings* is shown in Figure 6.8. It identifies standardized subject headings that can be used to find information on a specific topic. It also suggests terms to use to broaden or narrow a topic. It sometimes suggests classification numbers that might be used to search the online catalog for materials on the topic, or it can serve as a guide to browsing the stacks for other materials to the topic.

Sex discrimination (May Subd Geog)
    UF Discrimination, Sexual
          Gender discrimination
          Sexual discrimination
    BT Discrimination
          Sexism
    NT Radical therapy
          Sex discrimination against men
          Sex discrimination against women
          Sex discrimination in employment
          Sex of children, Parental preferences for
    --Law and legislation (May Subd Geog)
Sex discrimination against men
    (May Subd Geog)
    UF Discrimination against men
          Men, Discrimination against
    BT Sex discrimination
Sex discrimination against women
    (May Subd Geog)
    UF Discrimination against women
          Subordination of women
          Women, Discrimination against
    BT Feminism
          Sex discrimination
          Women's rights
    NT Purdah
    --Law and legislation (May Subd Geog)

Sex discrimination in consumer credit
    (May Subd Geog)
Here are entered works on the difficulties
encountered in obtaining consumer credit
due to sex discrimination.
    BT Consumer credit
    --Law and Legislation (May Subd Geog)
**Sex discrimination in criminal justice
administration** (May Subd Geog)
    BT Criminal justice, Administration of
          Discrimination in criminal justice
          administration
Sex discrimination in education
    (May Subd Geog) [LC212.8-LC212.83]
    UF Education, Sex discrimination in
    BT Discrimination in education
    NT Sex discrimination in medical education
Sex discrimination in employment
    (May Subd Geog) [HD6060-HD6060.5]
    BT Discrimination in employment
          Sex discrimination
    RT Sex role in the work environment
          Sexual division of labor
          Women--Employment

Figure 6.8 Library of Congress Subject Headings, 1995, p. 1710.

Primary subject heading. *This is the approved or
standardized term for this subject. These headings
are always in* **bold.**

UF = Used for

BT = Broad term

*RT = other terms that might be related to the
primary term.*

*NT = narrower terms which relate to the primary
term but are more limited in scope.*

Scope note *= the range of material included under a
subject heading.*

Subdivisions of the subject *= more specific subject
headings or subheadings.*

*May Subd Geog = a geographical subdivision may
be added to this subject*

for example:

Sex discrimination in education--United States.

***Library of Congress Classification System class
number*** *= letters or number combinations appropriate for the subject (useful for browsing the shelves).*

Keyword Search

Keyword searching is used to:

1. find information when the user has incomplete or partial information. For example, only part of a title is known, or the word order is incorrect, or the correct subject heading is not known. If you knew that an author named Brown had written a book with gender in the title:

> k= brown and gender
> would retrieve Clair Brown's book entitled *Gender in the Workplace*

2. find terms using "common language" or "free-text" searching. Unlike subject searching which searches only the approved subject heading fields for terms listed in *LCSH*, keyword searching allows the researcher to scan all fields of each catalog record. The keywords will retrieve any item which has the requested search term(s) anywhere in its record.
   For example:

s= guns	shows no records
k= guns	retrieves multiple records. In this case, the word "guns" occurs in a field other than the subject.

3. narrow or refine a search in ways that are not possible with a catalog which permits searching only by controlled terms. Logical (Boolean logic) and positional operators are used to link terms in order to specify the exact search desired.
   For example:

and	k= fitness and women	finds all occurrences in a single record
or	k= golf or tennis	finds any of the terms in any record
not	k= skiing not water	finds records that contain the first term *but not* the second

In keyword searching one must guard against the possibility of "false" hits or records. For example, if the searcher wants to search "apple" as a keyword, the search will result in entries on the fruit, on Apple computers and on persons with the name Apple.

Keyword searching is performed by a series of commands which may vary from system to system. However, the basics of keyword searching and logical operators are standard for most systems.

Searching the Online Catalog

To retrieve the materials in an online catalog one conducts a search using the basic access points: author, title, subject, keyword. The search is executed by typing a command on the "command line." The command line is also called the "prompt." A command, or prompt, instructs the computer to perform a search using the query that is typed on the command line.

The command structure of the online catalog is governed by the software which is used to run the online system. The following search instructions were developed for the online catalog, LOLA, at Louisiana State University Libraries. The system uses the NOTIS (Northwestern Online Totally Integrated System) software which is common to many academic libraries. LOLA is part of a statewide network, Louisiana Online University System (LOUIS). The catalogs of other academic libraries in the state, as well as some online periodical indexes, are available through LOUIS. All of the libraries' catalogs and the periodical indexes are searched using the same command structure.

HOW TO SEARCH THE ONLINE CATALOG

Author Search:

Type   a= followed by the author's last name or a portion of the last name.

  a=Shakespeare   or   a=solzhen

  a=james hen   (For more common names, include at least some of the first name.)

  a=oneill eugene   (Omit accent marks and all other punctuation in the author's name.)

  a=unesco   (An organization as author)

Title Search:

Type   t= followed by as much of the title of which you are certain.

  t=red badge of cour   (You need not include the entire title: *Red Badge of Courage.*)

  t=man for all seasons   (Omit initial articles **a, an, the** and foreign equivalents: *A Man for All Seasons.*)

  t=red white black   (Omit all punctuation in the title: *Red, White, and Black.*)

  t=2 minutes to noon   (Write numbers in numeric form or spell out.)

  t=part time teacher   (Do not use hyphens; try as separate words or one word.)

Subject Search:

Type   s=followed by a standardized subject heading

  s=afro american inventors

Standardized subject headings may be divided into parts, called subdivisions. To search for a subject heading with subdivisions, separate each part of the heading with two hyphens (--).

  s=france--history   s=migraine--therapy   s=Georgia--fiction

Use the *LCSH* to determine the authorized subject heading.

Keyword Search:

Type k=followed by a word, phrase, date, etc. found in any indexed field within a record.

Truncating Search Terms

A search term can be shortened by using a "?"

k=nation? (Will retrieve nations, nationality, nationhood, etc.)

Avoid "over-truncating" search terms. Do not enter k=const? if you're searching for the term "constitution" as it will pull up too many terms.

Boolean and Positional Operators

Boolean and positional operators enable you to broaden or narrow your search or link terms.

- **AND**   k=bees and wasps   finds all occurrences of both words in a single record
- **OR**   k=bees or wasps   finds any records that contain either of the terms
- **NOT**   k=bees not wasps   finds records that contain the first term, but not the second
- **ADJ**   k=killer bees   finds records that have the words "killer bees" in that order
                                 (ADJ is the default operator, so there is no need to type it in.)

Limiting a Search to a Field

To limit a search to a field or group of fields in a record, such as author, title, or subject, a period must precede and follow the field code. Some of the qualifiers used in the system are:

- .su.-- to limit the search term to subject fields only;
- .ti.--to limit the search term to title fields only;
- .au.-- to limit the search term to author fields only.

  bennett.au. and virtues.ti.

(A search for Bennett in the author field and virtues in the title field. Useful when only partial information is known.)

Qualifying a Search Term
Search terms may be further qualified by format, language, or date.

- **.fmt.**--to limit a search to a particular format:

b.fmt.=book	**m.fmt.**=music	**s.fmt.**=serials
p.fmt.=maps	**f.fmt.**=visuals	**d.fmt.**=computer file
u.fmt.=archives		

  k=plantations and u.fmt. (archival materials on plantations)

- **.lng.**-- to limit a search to items written in a particular language:

  eng.lng.=English   **spa.lng.**=Spanish   **fre.lng.**=French

  k=intelligence testing and eng.lng. (materials on intelligence testing in English).

- **.DT1.**--to limit a search to a specific publication year:

  k=politics and 1995.DT1. (materials on politics published in 1995)

Call Number:
Type   c= to search Library of Congress call numbers (always begin with alphabetic characters).
c=pn3321c7

cd= to search Dewey Decimal Call numbers (always begin with three digit numbers);
cd=817h477m

cs= to search SuDocs call numbers (usually begin with alphabetic characters);
cs=d301.26/6:b38

In any call number search, if you aren't certain of the entire call number, enter as much as you know. The system will place you in the Call Number Browsing Index at the nearest match. From there, you may page forward and backward using F and B.

Each index entry includes the call number and an abbreviated title. To display additional information for any entry, type the line number to the left of the entry. You can return to the Index by typing *I*.

Displaying Records
Your search results will be displayed as a single record if there is one hit. If there is more than one record it will display as one of the following:

Guide Screen
When the search results in a large number of matches, the entries that match your search term are segmented into groups, with the first entry from each group appearing as an entry on the GUIDE screen. The numbers to the right of each GUIDE entry represent the matches in the group. The numbers to the left of each GUIDE entry are line numbers. Select the GUIDE entry that most closely matches or precedes the term you are searching for, and enter its line number (from the left).

Index Screen
The system will display the INDEX, beginning with the entry you selected from the GUIDE. To see the entries, select the line number for the appropriate group.

To move to the next screen press F8 or type *for*; to move back a screen press F7 or type *bac*.

Brief View (**br**) gives only the basic retrieval information for each item, including the call number.

Long View (**lo**) gives the subject headings for this work as well as the basic retrieval information.

Use the NEXT or **N** command to display the next record. N with a number will jump forward more than one record. For example, next 4 or n4 will jump forward four records.

Use the BACK or **B** command to page backwards. Back3 or B3 will page backwards.
Type Index or **I** on the command line to return to the INDEX Screen from a record.

Holdings

If the item you are displaying is multi-volume (like a magazine or journal), **HOL** will appear in the footer of the display. Type **hol** to display Holdings Detail for the item. Holdings Detail information includes a summary of all volumes owned by the library, as well as volumes that may be missing. The following information is also commonly displayed:

- the latest issue(s) received;
- any volumes that are charged to another library user;
- the location of the material.

If you want to display holdings for one particular location, type **hol** followed by the location number.

Periodical Indexes in the Online System

One of the capabilities of some of the software for online systems is the ability to manage bibliographic records for periodical indexes in the same database as the online catalog. The NOTIS system's InfoShare software provides this capability. There are several advantages to having periodical indexes available through the same system as the library's online catalog:

1. It provides the ability to do "one stop shopping." The user can search one system for both books and periodical articles on a topic.

2. Many of the systems provide a "hook to holdings." That is, after retrieving a citation, one can query the database to see if the library owns the periodical.

3. The search techniques for the periodical articles are the same as those for books in the online catalog, thus providing a measure of standardization.

4. The databases can be shared by members of library networks, who, in turn, share the costs of the databases.

The following screen reproductions are from the LOUIS system.

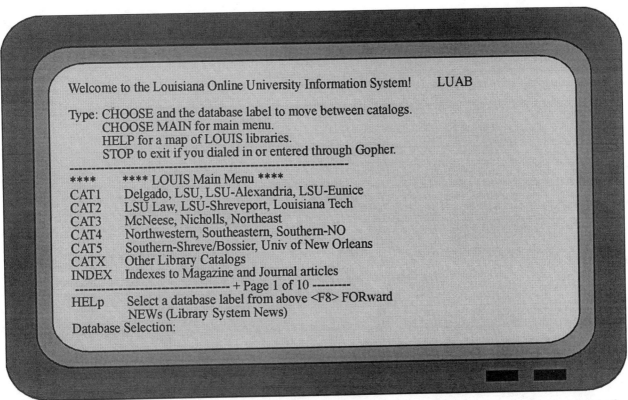

Figure 6.9 *Introductory OPAC screen showing available databases. CAT# refers to the online catalogs of the member institutions. INDEX refers to a selection of indexes to periodicals.*

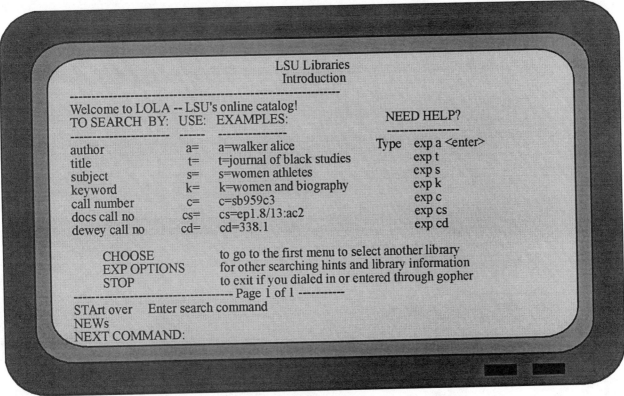

Figure 6.10 *Introductory screen for LOLA, the LSU Libraries Online catalog.*

All LOUIS, LOLA, and other LSU screens reprinted by permission of Louisiana State University and Louisiana State University Libraries.

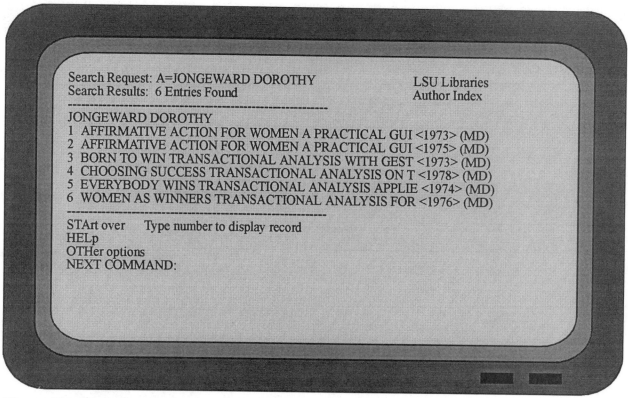

Figure 6.11 *Shows the results of an author search: a=jongeward dorothy. Notice that there are six entries under this author's name.*

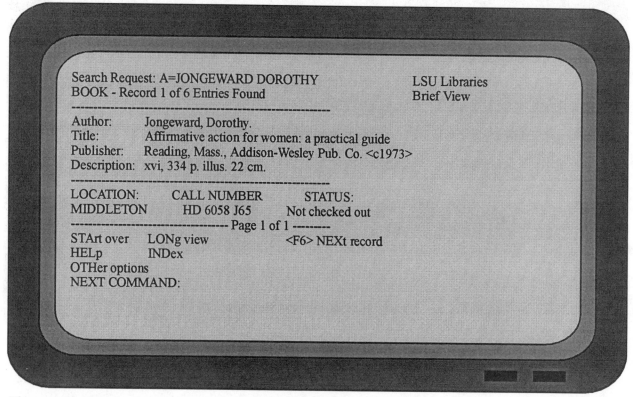

Figure 6.12 *Shows a brief view of the catalog record. This was retrieved by typing the desired line number from the index screen shown in Figure 6.11.*

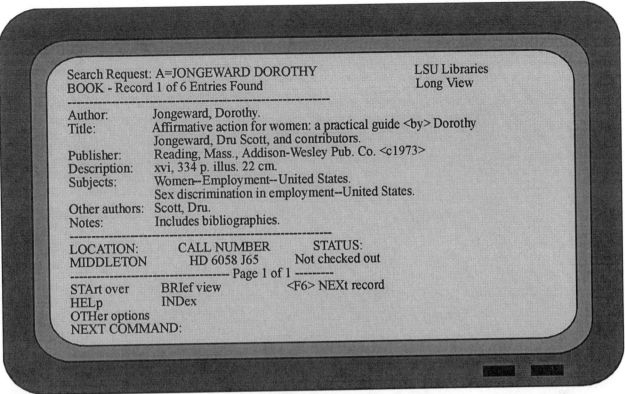

Figure 6.13 *Shows a long view of the record in Figure 6.12. This was retrieved by typing l in the command line of the previous screen. Notice that it shows the approved subject headings.*

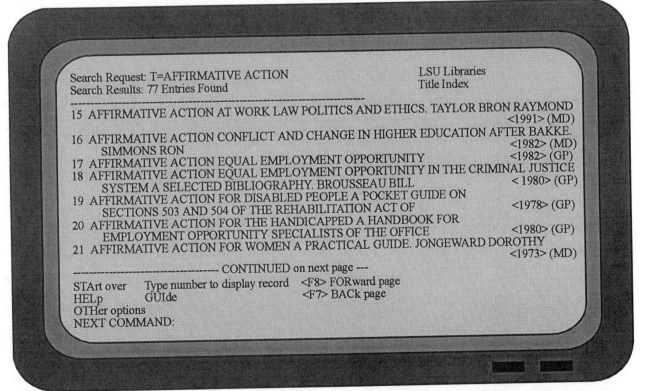

Figure 6.14 *Title Index search screen. Shows the results of a title search: t=affirmative action for women. The screen displays the Title Index which lists the title, author, and publication date. The Title Index screen lists titles in alphabetical order and includes the library location. Typing the line number shown will pull up the same record as in Figure 6.12.*

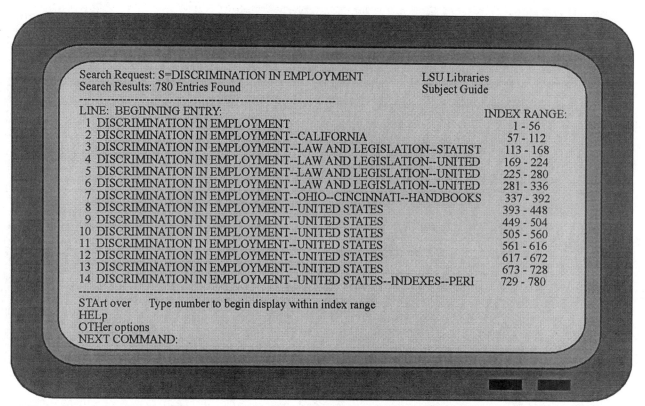

Figure 6.15 *Shows the results of a subject search: s=discrimination in employment. The* **Subject Guide** *screen indicates general works first, then the subheadings divide the topic into subdivisions.*

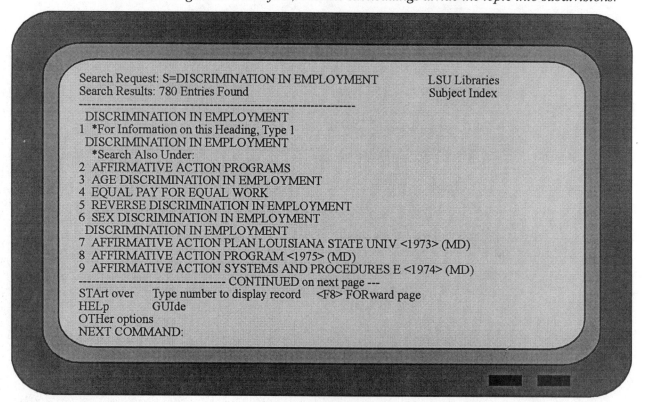

Figure 6.16 *The* **Subject Index** *screen retrieved by selecting line one from Figure 6.15. The screen gives information about this topic. Lines two-six suggest other subject headings appropriate for this topic. Entries for the topic, discrimination in employment, begin with line seven. Notice that lines one-six do not have dates after the entries. The entries beginning with line seven have publication dates.*

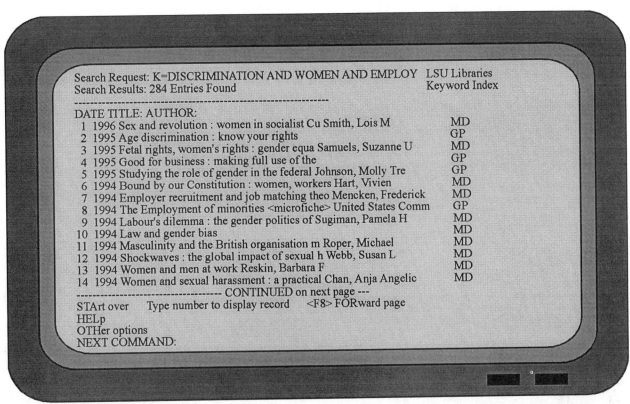

Figure 6.17 *Shows the results of a keyword search: k=discrimination and women and employment. Notice that it retrieved 284 entries. The subject search (s=discrimination in employment) shown in Figure 6.15 retrieved 780 entries.*

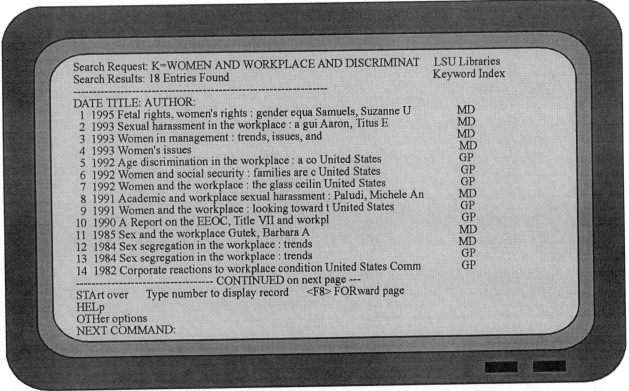

Figure 6.18 *Results of the search: k=women and workplace and discrimination. Notice on the screen the initials **MD** or **GP** following the entries. These indicate specific library locations.*

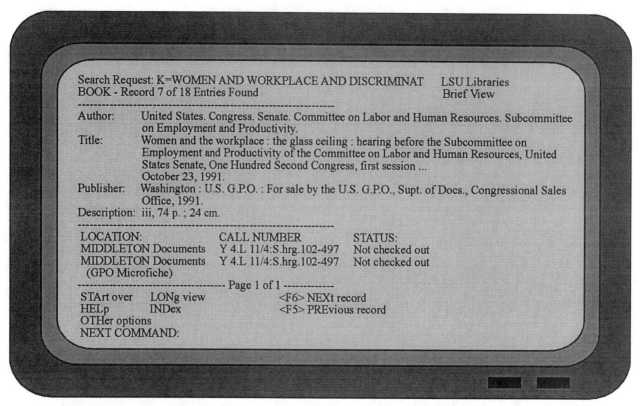

Figure 6.19 *The record retrieved by selecting line seven from the screen shown in Figure 6.18. This item is a Federal document, which is located in the Documents collection of the library and is available both in microfiche and print.*

```
Search Request: T=TIME                                    LSU Libraries
Search Results: 1417 Entries Found                        Title Guide
-----------------------------------------------------------------
LINE: BEGINNING ENTRY:                                    INDEX RANGE:
  1 TIME                                                     1 - 102
  2 TIME AND PLACE CONDITIONS OF GROUP IDENTITY 1989. TOPIC  103 - 204
  3 TIME CAPSULE HISTORY OF THE WAR YEARS 1939 1945          205 - 306
  4 TIME EXPOSURE THE AUTOBIOGRAPHY OF WILLIAM HENRY JACKSON W  307 - 408
  5 TIME GOODS AND WELL BEING                                409 - 510
  6 TIME LIMITED DYNAMIC PSYCHOTHERAPY. STRUPP HANS H        511 - 612
  7 TIME OF THE DRAGON. EDEN DOROTHY                         613 - 714
  8 TIME PLACE. MARK TWAIN OVERSEAS A BIOGRAPHICAL ACCOUNT O  715 - 816
  9 TIME SERIES FOR SOFA. STATE OF FOOD AND AGRICULTURE DISKET  817 - 918
 10 TIME TO BUILD INTERRELATED INVESTMENTS AND LABOUR        919 - 1020
 11 TIME TO WRITE REPORT OF THE US IEA STUDY OF WRITTEN COMPOS  1021 - 1122
 12 TIMELINESS AND QUALITY OF PROCESSING CLAIMS FOR COMPENSATI  1123 - 1224
 13 TIMES LITERARY SUPPLEMENT. PURPOSE AND PLACE ESSAYS ON AME  1225 - 1326
 14 TIMES PICAYUNE. WHOS WHO IN LOUISIANA AND MISSISSIPPI BIOG  1327 - 1417
-----------------------------------------------------------------
STArt over    Type number to begin display within index range
HELp
OTHer options
NEXT COMMAND:
```

Figure 6.20 *Title Guide Screen, t=time. To retrieve the entry for the magazine,* Time, *select line no. 1.*

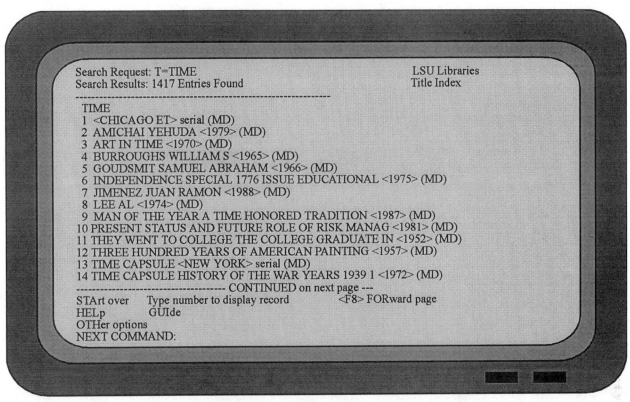

```
Search Request: T=TIME                                      LSU Libraries
Search Results: 1417 Entries Found                         Title Index
-------------------------------------------------------------
TIME
 1 <CHICAGO ET> serial (MD)
 2 AMICHAI YEHUDA <1979> (MD)
 3 ART IN TIME <1970> (MD)
 4 BURROUGHS WILLIAM S <1965> (MD)
 5 GOUDSMIT SAMUEL ABRAHAM <1966> (MD)
 6 INDEPENDENCE SPECIAL 1776 ISSUE EDUCATIONAL <1975> (MD)
 7 JIMENEZ JUAN RAMON <1988> (MD)
 8 LEE AL <1974> (MD)
 9 MAN OF THE YEAR A TIME HONORED TRADITION <1987> (MD)
10 PRESENT STATUS AND FUTURE ROLE OF RISK MANAG <1981> (MD)
11 THEY WENT TO COLLEGE THE COLLEGE GRADUATE IN <1952> (MD)
12 THREE HUNDRED YEARS OF AMERICAN PAINTING <1957> (MD)
13 TIME CAPSULE <NEW YORK> serial (MD)
14 TIME CAPSULE HISTORY OF THE WAR YEARS 1939 1 <1972> (MD)
------------------------------- CONTINUED on next page ---
STArt over    Type number to display record         <F8> FORward page
HELp          GUIde
OTHer options
NEXT COMMAND:
```

Figure 6.21 *Title Index Screen, result of selecting line 1 from screen shown in Figure 6.20. Notice that entry one has a place of publication (Chicago) and the word "serial." Entry two is also called Time, but has a date of publication (1979) indicting that it is a book.*

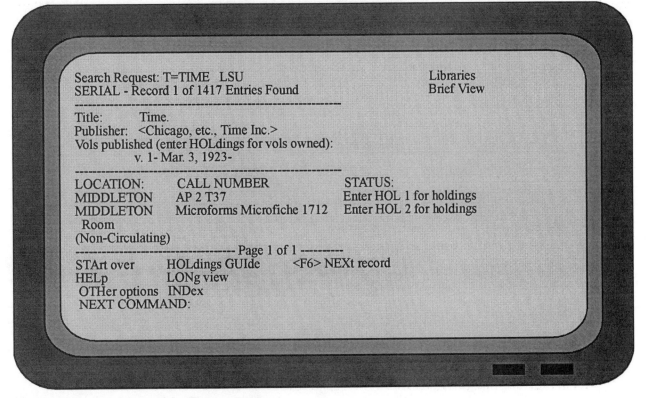

```
Search Request: T=TIME   LSU                               Libraries
SERIAL - Record 1 of 1417 Entries Found                    Brief View
-------------------------------------------------------------
Title:      Time.
Publisher:  <Chicago, etc., Time Inc.>
Vols published (enter HOLdings for vols owned):
            v. 1- Mar. 3, 1923-
-------------------------------------------------------------
LOCATION:         CALL NUMBER              STATUS:
MIDDLETON         AP 2 T37                 Enter HOL 1 for holdings
MIDDLETON         Microforms Microfiche 1712   Enter HOL 2 for holdings
 Room
(Non-Circulating)
------------------------------ Page 1 of 1 ----------
STArt over        HOLdings GUIde    <F6> NEXt record
HELp              LONg view
 OTHer options    INDex
 NEXT COMMAND:
```

Figure 6.22 *Brief Record for* Time *magazine.*

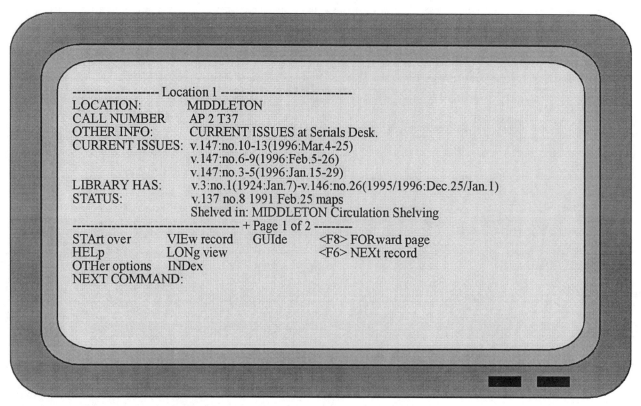

```
-------------------- Location 1 ----------------------------
LOCATION:        MIDDLETON
CALL NUMBER      AP 2 T37
OTHER INFO:      CURRENT ISSUES at Serials Desk.
CURRENT ISSUES:  v.147:no.10-13(1996:Mar.4-25)
                 v.147:no.6-9(1996:Feb.5-26)
                 v.147:no.3-5(1996:Jan.15-29)
LIBRARY HAS:     v.3:no.1(1924:Jan.7)-v.146:no.26(1995/1996:Dec.25/Jan.1)
STATUS:          v.137 no.8 1991 Feb.25 maps
                 Shelved in: MIDDLETON Circulation Shelving
------------------------------------- + Page 1 of 2 ---------
STArt over       VIEw record    GUIde       <F8> FORward page
HELp             LONg view                  <F6> NEXt record
OTHer options    INDex
NEXT COMMAND:
```

Figure 6.23 *Holdings Screen,* Time *magazine.*

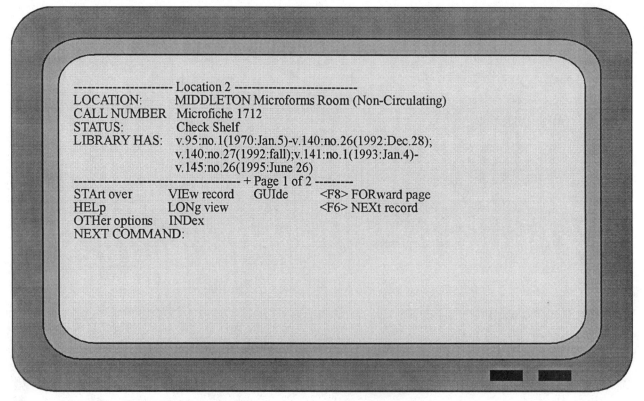

```
--------------------- Location 2 ----------------------------
LOCATION:        MIDDLETON Microforms Room (Non-Circulating)
CALL NUMBER      Microfiche 1712
STATUS:          Check Shelf
LIBRARY HAS:     v.95:no.1(1970:Jan.5)-v.140:no.26(1992:Dec.28);
                 v.140:no.27(1992:fall);v.141:no.1(1993:Jan.4)-
                 v.145:no.26(1995:June 26)
------------------------------------- + Page 1 of 2 ---------
STArt over       VIEw record    GUIde       <F8> FORward page
HELp             LONg view                  <F6> NEXt record
OTHer options    INDex
NEXT COMMAND:
```

Figure 6.24 *Microforms Holdings for* Time.

The following screens illustrate searches done in VICTOR, the University of Maryland's online catalog.

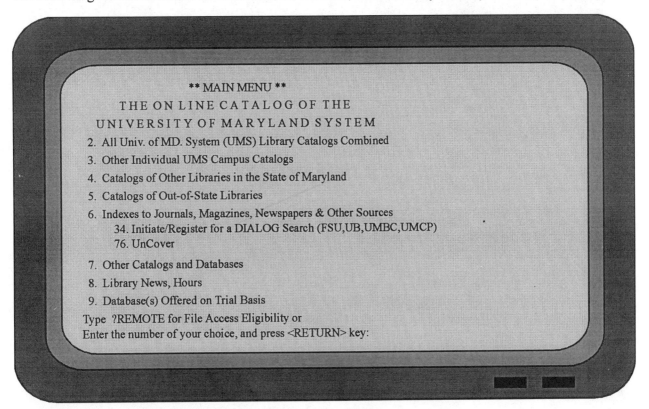

** MAIN MENU **

THE ON LINE CATALOG OF THE
UNIVERSITY OF MARYLAND SYSTEM

2. All Univ. of MD. System (UMS) Library Catalogs Combined

3. Other Individual UMS Campus Catalogs

4. Catalogs of Other Libraries in the State of Maryland

5. Catalogs of Out-of-State Libraries

6. Indexes to Journals, Magazines, Newspapers & Other Sources
     34. Initiate/Register for a DIALOG Search (FSU,UB,UMBC,UMCP)
     76. UnCover

7. Other Catalogs and Databases

8. Library News, Hours

9. Database(s) Offered on Trial Basis

Type ?REMOTE for File Access Eligibility or
Enter the number of your choice, and press <RETURN> key:

Figure 6.25 Main Menu, University of Maryland Online Catalog.

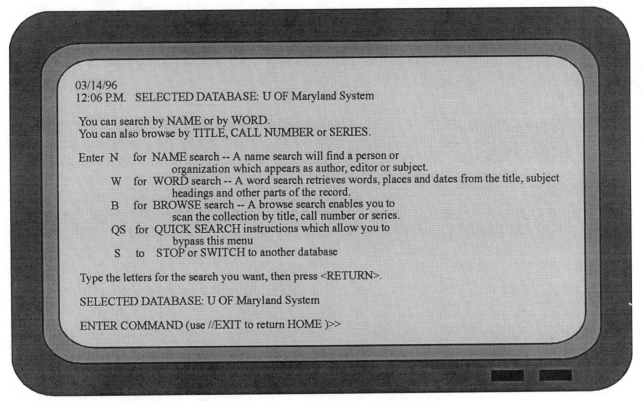

03/14/96
12:06 P.M. SELECTED DATABASE: U OF Maryland System

You can search by NAME or by WORD.
You can also browse by TITLE, CALL NUMBER or SERIES.

Enter N   for NAME search -- A name search will find a person or
                    organization which appears as author, editor or subject.
       W   for WORD search -- A word search retrieves words, places and dates from the title, subject
                    headings and other parts of the record.
       B   for BROWSE search -- A browse search enables you to
                    scan the collection by title, call number or series.
       QS for QUICK SEARCH instructions which allow you to
                    bypass this menu
       S   to   STOP or SWITCH to another database

Type the letters for the search you want, then press <RETURN>.

SELECTED DATABASE: U OF Maryland System

ENTER COMMAND (use //EXIT to return HOME)>>

Figure 6.26 Command Screen, University of Maryland Online Catalog.

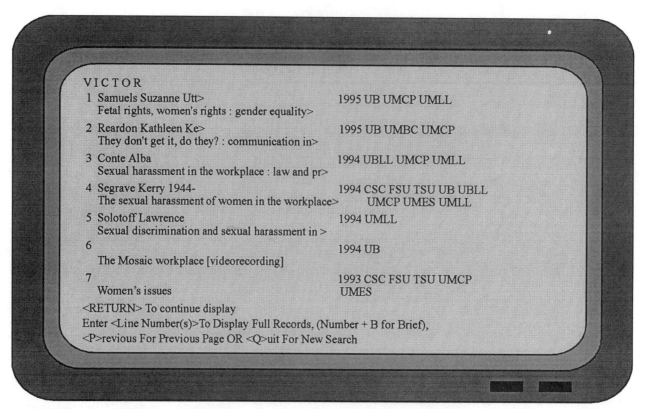

Figure 6.27 List of titles received from University of Maryland Online Catalog.

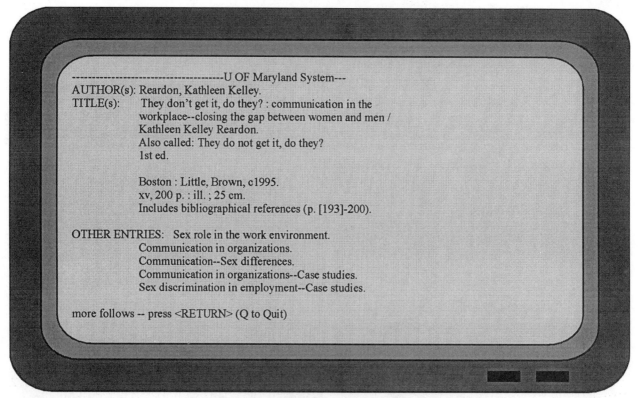

Figure 6.28 Item record, University of Maryland Online Catalog.

Materials That Might Not Be Found in Library Catalogs

To use the library catalogs efficiently, library users must know what they cannot expect to find there as well as what they can.

- individual articles from magazines, journals, and newspapers

- individual titles in series (although some individual titles may be cataloged)

- individual titles from anthologies

- government publications (varies with individual libraries)

Instructor: _____   **Name:** _____

Course/Section: _____   **Date:** _____

Review Questions for Chapter Six

1. What is the purpose of the library catalog?

2. Name one outstanding feature of each of the following:

    a. Book catalog

    b. COM catalog

    c. CD-ROM catalog

    d. Card catalog

    e. Online catalog

3. Name the three different kinds of catalog cards found for most material.

4. What is a corporate entry or corporate author?

5. Which form of alphabetizing is used in a card catalog? In most dictionaries?

6. Name four access points to library resources in an online catalog.

7. Define "commands" as it applies to the online catalog.

8. How does keyword searching differ from subject searching?

9. What is the purpose of the *Library of Congress Subject Headings*?

Instructor: _____   **Name:** _____

Course/Section: _____   **Date:** _____

Card Catalog Exercise

```
                        ARTIFICIAL INTELLIGENCE
P           Moyne, John A.
37               Understanding language: man or machine / John A.Moyne.
.M69        --New York: Plenum Press, c1985.
1985             xvi, 357 p. ; ill. 24 cm. --(Foundations of computer science)
                 Bibliography: p. 325-345.
                 Includes index.
                 ISBN 0-306-41970-X

            1. Psycholinguistics. 2. Linguistics--Data processing. 3. Comprehension.
            4. Artificial intelligence. 5. Grammar, Comparative and general. 6. Formal
            Languages. I. Title. II. Series.
            P37.M69 1985                    401.9              85-12341
                                                               AACR 2 MARC

Library of Congress
```

1. Use the information on the catalog card reproduced above to identify each of the following:

    a. call number of this book:

    b. classification system used:

    c. author/authors:

    d. complete title of the work:

    e. physical description of the work:

2. Is the work illustrated? How do you know?

3. Does it have a list of sources or references? How do you know?

4   List the subject headings used for this book.

5. How are the assigned subject headings used in the research process?

6. Name four other entries you could look under in the card catalog to find this work. Give the exact words you would use.

7. Which type of record does this card represent:

    a. Author entry
    b. Title entry
    c. Subject entry
    d. Joint author
    e. Corporate author
    f. Series

8. Use the bibliographic citations example at the end of Chapter 14. Write a complete bibliographic citation for this work.

Instructor: _____   Name: _____

Course/Section: _____   Date: _____

Library of Congress Subject Headings Exercise

Use the latest edition of the *LCSH* available in your library. List the subject headings and possible subheadings which are appropriate for the topic you have chosen. Write N/A (not applicable) for any term which does not apply.

1. Subject heading or headings:

2. Was there a classification letter or number following any of the subject headings? If so, list them here.

3. List up to three subdivisions found under the topic.

4. Copy any Used For **(UF)** terms.

5. Copy one related term **(RT)**.

6. Copy one broad term **(BT)**.

7. Copy one narrow term **(NT)**.

Use the sample *LCSH* page shown in Figure 6.8 to respond to the following questions:

8. Give two broad terms which could be used for "sex discrimination."

9. Are either "gender discrimination" or "sexual discrimination" correct terms to use in a subject search?

10. Give two related terms for "sex discrimination in employment."

11. If your topic is "discrimination against men" what subject heading would you use?

Instructor: _____   Name: _____

Course/Section: _____   Date: _____

Library Catalog Exercise

1. Select any five of the following subjects. Use your library catalog to determine whether or not the library has any books on these subjects. Use a separate sheet of paper to record the titles and dates of the most recent books found and the commands or search terms used to find them.

DRUG ABUSE	MICROCOMPUTERS	AMERICAN FICTION
AVIATION ACCIDENTS	ANIMAL RIGHTS	INDUSTRIAL SAFETY
MEXICAN POLITICS	VIET NAM	CHILD DEVELOPMENT
NUCLEAR POWER	JOURNALISM	HISTORY OF CHINA
SOCIAL SECURITY	POLITICS	AUTOMOBILES
SPORTS	CRIME & CRIMINALS	CANADIAN POLITICS

2. Look up the authors below in your library's catalog. If the library has any of their works, record the titles and dates of the most recent ones found, and the commands or search term used.

John Grisham	Ann Rice	Virginia Woolf	John Donne
Samuel Johnson	Stephen King	Maya Angelou	Michael Crichton
Sidney Sheldon	James Joyce	Walt Whitman	Oscar Wilde
Benjamin Franklin	Robert Herrick	Robert Browning	Ernest Hemingway

3. Use the following sample screen from the OPAC at the LSU Libraries to respond to the questions below:

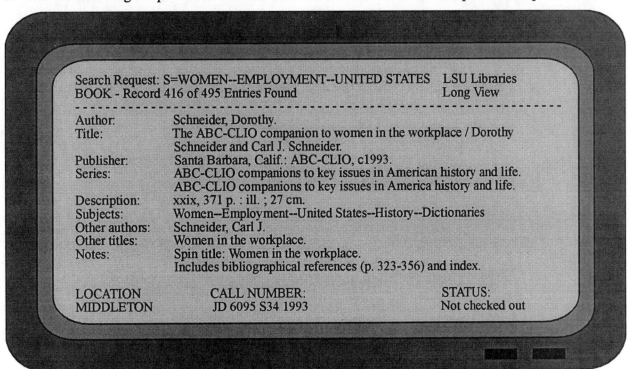

Search Request: S=WOMEN--EMPLOYMENT--UNITED STATES   LSU Libraries
BOOK - Record 416 of 495 Entries Found   Long View
- -
Author: Schneider, Dorothy.
Title: The ABC-CLIO companion to women in the workplace / Dorothy
                Schneider and Carl J. Schneider.
Publisher: Santa Barbara, Calif.: ABC-CLIO, c1993.
Series: ABC-CLIO companions to key issues in American history and life.
                ABC-CLIO companions to key issues in America history and life.
Description: xxix, 371 p. : ill. ; 27 cm.
Subjects: Women--Employment--United States--History--Dictionaries
Other authors: Schneider, Carl J.
Other titles: Women in the workplace.
Notes: Spin title: Women in the workplace.
                Includes bibliographical references (p. 323-356) and index.

LOCATION   CALL NUMBER: STATUS:
MIDDLETON   JD 6095 S34 1993   Not checked out

a.   Who is the author of this work?

b.   Name the publisher and the place of publication.

c.   What is the date of publication?

d.   Is the work illustrated? Justify your answer.

e.   What subject headings are used for this work?

f.   Is this work part of a series? How do you know?

g.   Would this be an appropriate source for the topic "equal employment for women"? Explain your answer.

4.   Use the following subject guide screen to answer the questions below:

```
Search Request: S=SEX DISCRIMINATION                    LSU LIBRARIES
Search Requests: 816 Entries Found                      Subject Guide
- - - - - - - - - - - - - - - - - - - - - - - - - - - - - - - - - - - -
LINE: BEGINNING ENTRY:                                  INDEX RANGE:
   1 SEX DISCRIMINATION                                     1 - 59
   2 SEX DISCRIMINATION--UNITED STATES--CONGRESSES         60 - 118
   3 SEX DISCRIMINATION AGAINST WOMEN                     119 - 177
   4 SEX DISCRIMINATION AGAINST WOMEN--LAW AND LEGISLATION--GRE  178 - 236
   5 SEX DISCRIMINATION AGAINST WOMEN--LAW AND LEGISLATION--UNI  237 - 295
   6 SEX DISCRIMINATION AGAINST WOMEN--UNITED STATES      296 - 354
   7 SEX DISCRIMINATION AGAINST WOMEN--UNITED STATES--CONGRESSES  355 - 413
   8 SEX DISCRIMINATION IN EDUCATION                      414 - 472
   9 SEX DISCRIMINATION IN EDUCATION--UNITED STATES       473 - 531
  10 SEX DISCRIMINATION IN EDUCATION--UNITED STATES       532 - 590
  11 SEX DISCRIMINATION IN EMPLOYMENT                     591 - 649
  12 SEX DISCRIMINATION IN EMPLOYMENT--LAW AND LEGISLATION--UNI  650 - 708
  13 SEX DISCRIMINATION IN EMPLOYMENT--UNITED STATES      709 - 767
  14 SEX DISCRIMINATION IN EMPLOYMENT--UNITED STATES--CONGRESSES  768 - 816
```

a. How many entries were found for the search s=sex discrimination?

b. Which line number would be the most appropriate for the following:

    (1) legal aspects of this topic?

    (2) for entries on sex discrimination in education?

    (3) for sex discrimination in education only in the United States?

    (4) for employment law regarding sex discrimination?

    (5) for conferences on sex discrimination in the United States?

    (6) for general books on sex discrimination?

5. Look up any three of the following titles in your library catalog. If the library has any of them, record the title, author, and copyright date, and the commands or search term used.

    Boswell's Life of Samuel Johnson   *Modern Man in Search of a Soul*

    Silent Spring   *Webster's Dictionary*

    MLA Handbook of Writers of Research Papers   *Great Dialog of Plato*

    Dead Man Walking: An Eye Witness Account
        of the Death Penalty in the United States

6. Conduct a keyword search in your online library catalog to find books on the following topics:

    the relationship between drugs and crime   crawfish and crayfish

    abortion statistics   an education encyclopedia

    books on any computer except IBM   sexual harassment of women

THE INTERNET
AN INTRODUCTION

A PREVIEW

In many respects the Internet mirrors the way that information has been processed through the ages. In a domain that we have come to call cyberspace, we find people from all walks of life and from throughout the globe talking to one another, storing information, retrieving information, and producing new information. This chapter answers some basic questions about the Internet: what the Internet is, how it got started, why it is used, and how it works. It provides an introduction to exploring its services and resources. The Internet is a complex system requiring many levels of expertise to tap its full range of capabilities. This chapter is only an introduction to get you launched. The list of Internet reference sources at the end of the chapter includes how-to manuals and lists of sources to get you further along.

KEY TERMS AND CONCEPTS

Internet	E-Mail
Virtual Library	Newsnet News
ARPAnet	Telnet
Cyber Village	Hypertext
Networks	Browser
Information Transfer	Lynx
Dialup Access	Mosaic
Information Provider	Netscape
FTP	URL
Gopher	Home Page
WAIS	Links
World Wide Web	

INTRODUCTION

The Internet contains information from millions of sources, created by people from all over the world. This information is available to anyone with a computer and connections to an Internet provider. While it is possible to retrieve useful information with minimal skills, it is also true that the more skills you have, the more successful you will be in retrieving information. To become skilled in retrieving information on the Internet, one should understand how the Internet works, how information resources are constructed, and how they are retrieved.

What Is the Internet?

The Internet is a vast network of networks connected via telephone lines, cables, and communications satellites. The metaphor that is often used for the Internet is "information superhighway." That image is meant to convey a superhighway over which information travels. It is similar to the Interstate system in the U.S., which criss-crosses the country connecting states and major cities. Connected to the super highways are smaller highways which are linked to rural roads and city streets. The "Interstate" highway of the Internet is a system of regional networks, which constitute the "backbone" of the system. Connected to the backbone are smaller networks serving particular geographic areas or organizations. Leading into these are small local networks and individual computers.

How It Began

The story of the beginning of the Internet helps one to understand how it has evolved. In the 1960s, researchers began linking computers to each other through telephone hook-ups, using funds from the U.S. Defense Department's Advanced Research Projects Agency (ARPA). ARPA was interested in designing a system that would support military research and at the same time provide a measure of security against partial cable outages. Previous computer networking efforts had required a single line between two computers. If something were to go wrong with the system, the entire network would be out of operation. The new system used a software program called Internet Protocol (IP) to send data in packets along a network of communication lines. Each piece of information was split into packets and transmitted from one network node to another until it reached its destination. There it could be reassembled by the computer into a readable message. With this system, researchers could exchange electronic mail (e-mail) and later were able to form discussion groups. Much of the early research for ARPANet was done at universities, where researchers soon realized what a powerful tool it was. They found ways to use ARPANet connections in order to communicate and exchange information with other researchers throughout the country.[1]

How It Grew

In 1986, the National Science Foundation provided funding for the creation of five supercomputing networks. As more and more researchers connected to the networks, the system became overloaded. NSF again stepped in, upgrading the system to faster communications lines and faster computers. It promoted the widespread use of the Internet by providing funding to those institutions which planned to expand the development and use of the Internet. Until this time access to the Internet had been limited to researchers in universities and a few government agencies. The five original networks were expanded to fifteen and use was extended to include thousands of colleges, research companies, and government agencies. By 1988 the NSFNET had replaced ARPANet. In 1991, Vice President (then Senator) Al Gore introduced the National Research and Educational Network (NREN) legislation which expanded NSFNET by extending use to K-12 schools, junior colleges, and community colleges. It also included provisions for businesses to purchase part of the network for commercial use.[2]

---

[1] Ed Krol. *The Whole Internet: User's Guide and Catalog* (Sebastopol, CA: O'Reilly, 1992) 13-29.

[2] "Computers: The Internet," *The World Almanac and Book of Facts 1996*, 167.

And What It's Like Today

There has been tremendous growth of the Internet since 1991. We do not know exactly how many individual users access the Internet in a year, but in early 1996 it was estimated that there were over 93,000 networks and over 9.4 million host computers. Approximately 96 countries were connected to the Internet as of June 1995.[3] At the end of 1995, according to one source, the annual rate of growth of traffic on the World Wide Web was 341,000%.[4]

The academic community and research organizations once dominated the use and development of the Internet. Today, commercial networks such as America Online, CompuServe, and Prodigy are major providers of Internet services. They are experiencing competition from a growing number of smaller companies—some local, others nationwide—which are working to provide subscribers direct access to Internet services. Software developers are constantly introducing new products to provide access to the Internet. And as it becomes easier to use, it is expected that more and more people will join the worldwide community known as the Internet.

Who Owns the Internet?

By mid-1994, the U.S. government had removed itself from any day-to-day control over the Internet. The Internet does not "belong" to anyone or any company. Anyone can connect to the Internet and anyone who wishes to can "publish" on the Internet. The only "authority" rests with the Internet Society (ISOC). This is a non-governmental, international organization with voluntary membership whose purpose is to promote global cooperation for the Internet and its working technologies. It is governed by a board which is responsible for setting policy and planning for the future.

Who pays for it?

Some portions of the Internet are subsidized, but each network is usually self-supporting and each pays for its connection. Commercial providers pass their costs on to the user. Colleges and universities which provide access to their faculty and students not only pay the costs of network connections, they also incur large costs for hardware and software.

Why Use the Internet?

The millions of people who access the Internet do so for a variety of reasons: access to information, international communications, research, education, recreation, business, self-improvement. Some of the information on the Internet duplicates print sources; much of it is unique. One important aspect of information on the Internet is its currency. Newspapers become available almost as soon as they are printed; court cases are available within twenty-four hours; federal regulations, previously unavailable until after they were out-dated are now available almost as soon as they are produced.

The Internet as Virtual Library

The Internet is considered a virtual library, or a library without walls, because of all the information it contains. It has full texts of books, journal articles, music, images, manuscripts, radio and television transcripts, software programs, maps, weather bulletins, business reports, etc. It is the access point for thousands of

---

[3] Robert H. Zakon, *Hobbes Internet Timelines*, v.2.4a. Online. Internet Society. Available HTTP: Http://info.isoc.org/guest/zakon/Internet/History/HIT.html, updated February 1996.

[4] "Computers: The Internet," 167.

library catalogs, text files, images, graphics, and video. It is used in teaching at all levels—from Kindergarten to graduate programs. It is also a gigantic shopping mall, where merchants advertise their products, and shoppers with credit cards place orders.

Tools are available to help users search for information. If you are looking for information on a particular subject or a particular fact, you can query the system for assistance. It is possible to search by keyword or by broad topic just as you would in a library's online catalog.

Unlike libraries, where materials are selected according to a set of criteria, there is no control over the materials on the Internet. It is the unbridled nature of the Internet that represents its best and its worse features. The quantity of information on the Internet is enormous. It is of every stripe and hue, and runs the gamut from pure nonsense to the most highly respected research. In any research process, one must pay careful attention to selection and evaluation criteria. This is especially important with information on the Internet. The same strict criteria used in evaluating the appropriateness of print sources to research should be applied to information on the Internet.

The Internet as Cyber Village

The Internet is both a virtual library and a "cyber" village. It provides information and the means to access and retrieve information; but it serves as more than a library—it resembles more closely a community where people socialize, exchange ideas, engage in commerce, and participate in educational, cultural, and recreational activities. Unlike the traditional village, the cyber village is not limited by space. It encompasses the entire globe and provides communications and informational capabilities that probably never were dreamed of when the first messages were sent over the ARPANet in the 1960s. The Internet has a variety of forums for making this possible. It provides access to thousands of discussion groups (listserv and news groups) where users exchange information. And, of course, individuals and businesses all over the world can communicate via electronic mail (e-mail).

How the Internet Works

Networks

The basic element of the Internet is the network. A network consists of computers that are connected one to another through a communications channel. The channel may be an ordinary telephone wire, a fiber optic cable, or a high-speed microwave or satellite communications device. The two types of networks are Local Area Networks (LAN) and Wide Area Networks (WAN). The LAN connects computers in a small geographic area over a single channel. A WAN connects LANs, one to another over a wide geographic area. The Internet is a WAN. It is composed of three levels of networks: national, regional and local. To send or receive information over the Internet an individual must be connected to a local network which, in turn, is connected to the other levels as shown in Figure 7.1. If an individual wishes to send a message to someone within the local area, the message will be routed directly to the local computer on the local network. If the message is being sent to a computer at a distant location, it will be routed through the appropriate local and regional networks until it reaches its destination.

Information Transfer

The software used to send and receive information is called Transmission Control Protocol/ Internet Protocol suite (TCP/IP). The Internet is often called a TCP/IP network and for users to connect to the Internet, they must connect to what is known as an IP address. The other key to information sharing on the Internet is the use of the client/server model of data transfer. In the client/server model one computer serves as "host" machine that distributes information to a "client" machine that receives information. With the client/server model, client software is installed on a personal computer to perform such tasks as displaying menus to the screen,

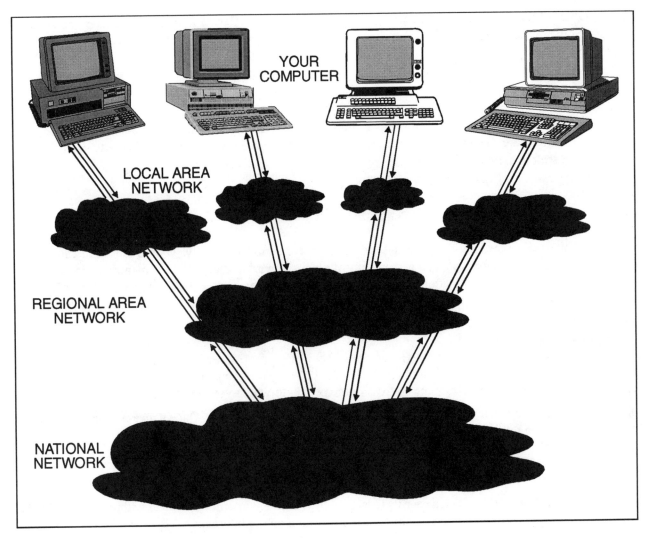

Figure 7.1 *The Internet, a network of networks*

connecting to a remote computer, and saving files. The server or remote host computer performs tasks such as searching a database and transmitting the results to the client. All of the major Internet tools use the TCP/IP and the client/server model.

How to Connect to the Internet

The two most common ways to connect to the Internet are: 1) direct network connection, and 2) dialup to an Internet provider. Direct network connections are usually available on college or university campuses and in large companies. With direct access, individual computers are wired directly, using high-speed network cables, to the main campus or company network, which in turn is connected to a regional or national network. The service is usually available around the clock and provides text, images, sound, and video. Usually the organization pays the costs for networking services and there are no charges to the individual users for connect time.

With dialup access, the user dials in through a regular telephone connection to an Internet provider. This requires a computer equipped with a modem. Typically, the transmission is slower than with direct cabling. Most direct providers charge for connection time and many have a monthly fee. College campuses may provide dialup access to its users at no charge. In some cases, the dialup services through college campuses might provide access to text browsers only. To use Internet services via a dialup modem, campus users need a validated account from the campus computing center.

There are a growing number of commercial Internet providers, offering a wide range of services to subscribers. Some of the better known are America Online, CompuServe, Delphi, Netcom, and Prodigy. A list of Internet providers may be found on the Internet at: http://thelist.com.

Internet Tools

The term, Internet tools, refers to special programs that provide access to the services of the Internet. The major Internet tools are: electronic mail (e-mail), Telnet, FTP, Gopher, WAIS, and World Wide Web. Each of these is discussed in more detail below.

Electronic Mail (E-Mail)

Electronic mail (e-mail) allows you to send or receive mail electronically. With e-mail you can send a message to any person with a computer account anywhere in the world. Mail delivered in this way is extremely fast, usually arriving at its destination within seconds of having been sent. E-mail functions support Listserv discussion groups where you can share information with people around the world interested in the same topics that you are.

E-Mail Procedures:

1. Logon to the computer and activate the e-mail software.

2. The system will prompt you for the address of the person to whom you are sending mail.

3. Create the message. (Be sure to proofread the message before sending it. Once a message has been sent it is impossible to retrieve it.)

4. Send the message.

E-Mail Addresses:

The e-mail address is based on a user ID (assigned to you by the Internet provider) within the domain at a specific institution. The domain defines the type of institution on the Internet:

EDU=	educational institution
COM=	commercial organization or a business
GOV=	government agency
ORG=	organization
MIL=	military organization
NET=	network resources

The authors' e-mail addresses are: notmsb@unix1.sncc.lsu.edu and notgap@unix1.sncc.lsu.edu.

E-Mail Etiquette:

Avoid inflammatory statements (called flames).
Use ordinary capitalization—use of all caps is regarded as shouting.
Read mail promptly.
Keep your mailbox cleared in order to avoid filling up your allocated space on the system.

Listservs

Listservs are a combination of e-mail and Discussion Groups. You must formally subscribe to a listserv in order to receive and send mail. Once you have subscribed you will automatically receive mail that is sent by any other member of the list. To subscribe to a listserv you must first find the address of the list to which you wish to subscribe. Then send a message to that address. Place the following message in the body:

subscribe [name of listserv] [your real name (not your e-mail ID)]

Usenet News

There are thousands of Usenet Newsgroups which are designed to serve as electronic forums for discussion, debate, questions, talk, and distribution of software, images, sounds, and other information. The Newsgroups' messages are distributed to computer sites all over the world. Each computer site accumulates the messages and redistributes them to its own subscribers. Subscribers can read the articles posted to the Usenet Newsgroups, reply to articles, post new articles, save articles, or forward them via e-mail to others. Newsgroups are listed by categories which define the subject. For example, soc.culture.Fr deals with social issues related to French culture.

TELNET

Telnet is a program that allows you to log in to a host computer on the Internet. Once you have logged in to the host computer, the session emulates the host. For example, if you "telnet" into the Library of Congress, your screen will be identical to the screen of a computer in the library. With Telnet you can log into online databases, library catalogs, and thousands of specialized and useful information servers around the world. Many host sites are restricted and will allow you to have access only to certain of its databases. Logging in as "guest" or "anonymous" might allow you access to only parts of the database.

To "telnet" to the Library of Congress from a UNIX account, use the following commands:

> telnet locis.loc.gov

FTP

File transfer protocol (FTP) allows you to transfer data files of all kinds over the Internet. Ordinarily you use the FTP command to copy computer files from a host computer to your own computer, but you may also copy files from your computer to a remote computer.

To FTP a file from a remote host:

1. Make the FTP connection by logging in to the host computer:
   > ftp   [name of remote host]

2. Determine the type of file—binary or ASCII—and type the command at the prompt:
   ftp>ASCII

3. You will be asked for a login ID and password. Use anonymous for your ID and your full e-mail address for your password. If the host site permits anonymous login you will be given access to the files.

4. Move to the subdirectory where the desired file is stored:
   ftp>cd   [to change directory]
   ftp>cd..   [to go to the parent directory]
   ftp>dir   [to list directories]
   ftp>ls   [to list files]
   ftp>pwd   [to tell you which directory you are currently in]
   ftp>help   [for a list of commands]

5. Locate the name of the file you want to FTP.

6. After you have identified the file you want, begin the transfer:
   ftp>get   [filename]

7. When you have finished the session, type:
   ftp> bye   [or quit]

Gopher

The Gopher program is useful for retrieving text-based documents. Gopher was developed at the University of Minnesota. Although it is named after the school's mascot, the name is appropriate because it will "go for" information that is requested. When someone sets up a Gopher site, menus are created with pointers so that the information is retrievable. Gopher burrows through the various Internet "tunnels" until it reaches the menu that has the requested item. It then retrieves the information. In effect, Gopher combines FTP, Telnet, and other search programs. Although some servers are moving away from Gophers, they are still useful and still have lots of information. Through Gopher you can connect to online databases, library catalogs, WAIS databases, World Wide Web sites, FTP sites, Usenet Newsgroups, and more. Gopher allows for a Graphical User Interface (GUI) which will display images and allow access to WWW pages. You can create your own personal Gopher menus (called bookmarks) of frequently used Gopher items. Although it is possible to search Gopher by tunneling through the menus, there are several specialized search tools for searching Gopher menus: **Archie** is a database of FTP files located on Gopher menus; **Veronica** is an index of menu titles found on Gopher servers; **Jughead** is an index to titles on Gopher servers, but, unlike Veronica, it searches only the indexes currently displayed on your screen.

WAIS

WAIS stands for Wide Area Information Server. It is a program that allows you to search a string or keyword using Boolean operators. The WAIS search engine is more generalized than Jughead and Veronica which search only Gopher menus. WAIS operates on a client/server basis. If you do not have a WAIS on your server you would have to telnet to a server that does and conduct your search from there. Data retrieved in a WAIS search is ranked according to how relevant it is to your search statement. WAIS databases are located on a variety of different remote computers. They can also be accessed via Gopher or World Wide Web.

World Wide Web

What is it?

The World Wide Web (WWW or Web) is an interconnected system of information resources and services available on the Internet. The Web was developed by scientists at CERN, a research institute located in Switzerland. The idea was to develop a tool that would make sharing information easier than with Gopher. With the Web, a searcher can follow a thread that will lead to documents and files wherever they might be. The World Wide Web is the fastest growing and the most popular way to exploit the Internet. This is, no doubt, due to the fact that it is easy to use and extremely effective as a search tool.

How the Web Is Created

The World Wide Web is created by the use of *hypertext* to link documents and files located on servers anywhere on the Internet. In a hypertext document, words, phrases, or images are highlighted in order to point to a different document where more information can be found. When the user selects a highlighted word or phrase, a second document is opened. (To select a highlighted word or phrase using a mouse interface, the user would place the mouse over the highlighted section and click the mouse button.) The second document may contain links to other related documents. The linked documents may all be located at different sites, all of which will be transparent to the user as he/she moves through the Web. Hypertext documents are created by using Hypertext Markup Language (HTML). With HTML the words and phrases are written as normal text but special format codes, called tags, are used to activate the terms that are highlighted for creating links. It is not necessary to be able to write HTML to retrieve documents. This is used only by those individuals who wish to create their own links to information.

How Information Gets on the Web

As you begin to browse the World Wide Web you might wonder how information gets there. The Web may be thought of as a gigantic broadcast service, with no central authority—anyone with a server can make information available on the Internet. The main way that this is done is through Home Pages or Web pages. A *Home Page* on the World Wide Web may be thought of as the Webmaster's (the page creator's) menu of hypertext links. The Home Page must be readable by a browser, so it must be written in HTML. Since a graphics Web browser is capable of "reading" colors, fonts, graphics, and video and audio files, talented Webmasters with imagination and resources can create pages which are extremely complex and artistic.

The links on a Home Page may reference files which are located on the Webmaster's own server or which are located anywhere on the Internet. It is this feature (the ability to reference files located on other computers) which makes the Internet such a powerful tool. The speed in retrieving linked files located on a server on the other side of the earth virtually matches the speed of retrieving a file on one's own server.

Searching the World Wide Web

The way to search the Web is with a browser—a powerful tool that allows you to navigate the Web by pointing and clicking on highlighted words or images (hot links or hyperlinks). The browser then retrieves the selected information from a remote computer and displays it on your screen. This information might be a picture, a movie, text, or sound, or it might be a connection to a Gopher, WAIS database, Usenet Newsgroup, or a Telnet or FTP site. The browser uses the address and protocol information (URL) which is in the script for the link you selected. There are two types of browsers—text-based and graphical user interface (GUI). With a text-based browser, you can view only the text, while with a GUI browser you can see images.

Lynx is a text-based browser for WWW using arrows and tab keys to access highlighted links on hypertext documents. Lynx has no image or sound capabilities: any images or sounds are replaced by a bracketed note indicating the placement of an image. One advantage of using Lynx is that in downloading documents, the embedded characters are automatically excluded. Lynx is a good alternative for users without a graphical user interface.

Mosaic is the first browser to use a graphical interface. It was widely used during the late 1980s and early 1990s, but lately has been outscored by Netscape as the most popular browser. With Mosaic it is possible to point to hypertext links, display images, and play sounds. It is an easy to use, intuitive system. Mosaic also provides an interface to the other information systems (WAIS, Gopher, etc.) thus giving access to all Internet resources from a single interface.

Netscape is the most widely used of Web browsers. It is easy to use and highly versatile. Figure 7.2 shows the Netscape Home Page. At the top of the screen is a standard menu bar and tool bar buttons with frequently used commands. The block just below the toolbar shows the Internet address (URL) of the document that is currently displayed. A new address can be typed in at any time to change the page. Beneath that is the screen showing the Netscape graphics and hypertext links. A Home Page is the top-level menu document for a particular Web site. It contains jumping off points in the form of highlighted text or graphic images on the screen. At the bottom of the page is the status bar. It provides messages about what information is being transferred. At the far right is a progress bar that fills with color as a document is being retrieved. The key at the lower left indicates whether security has been implemented for this page: a broken key means that transactions are sent across the Internet as plain text, whereas a solid key indicates the transmissions are encoded for security.

Figure 7.2 Netscape Home Page (Netscape Communications, the Netscape Communications logo, Netscape, and Netscape Navigator are trademarks of Netscape Communications Corporation. Netscape has not endorsed or otherwise sponsored the advertised product or service.)

Moving Around in the World Wide Web

To move around in the Web you can:

1. go directly to a specific Internet resource from a known address;

2. browse Home Pages and select certain links to explore;

3. use subject related and keyword search engines.

URL

To go directly to a specific source you must know the URL (Uniform Resource Locator). This is a unique global Internet identifier used by World Wide Web. It allows any document anywhere on the Internet to be accessed by any browser. The URL is comparable to someone's address giving the country, state, city, street, and house number. URLs are composed of several parts including the Internet access protocol, the location, and the file.

For example:

http://www.lib.lsu.edu/weblio.html#Search

http stands for hyperText Transfer Protocol.
//www etc. is the domain address for the Web server at Louisiana State University
/ is the specific page—Webliography: A Guide to Internet Resources

Listings of URLs can be found in a great number of places, including guides and directories on the Internet. You can create a special directory on your computer of addresses to frequently visited sites. This is called a bookmark. To save the address of a site which is currently displayed on the screen:

- click on the bookmarks button on the menu bar;
- click on ADD BOOKMARK;
  The location and description of that site will be placed at the bottom of your bookmark list.

  To retrieve a bookmark in your bookmark site:

- click on the bookmark button on the menu bar;
- move to the bookmark you want to activate, and it will be automatically retrieved.

  Note: You should create bookmarks only on your own computer. Public access computers, such as those available in libraries, would soon become cluttered if each user added his/her own bookmarks.

  Keep in mind that URLs may change and even disappear.

Home Page Links

A *Webmaster* is one who maintains a Home Page to offer links to the users of the Internet. He/she must, therefore, design the page to be of some utilitarian or recreational value for other users and must publicize the existence of the page so that users will know about it. There are numerous free Internet services whose sole function is to announce new sites to Internet users. Many sites have a "Site of the Day," featuring a new site each day (or almost each day) which, in the judgment of the Webmaster, merits being publicized. Since the "Site of the Day" sites archive their announcements, they are valuable indices of what's new (or what was new at one time) on the Internet.

Once a Home Page "address" is known—remember that the unique Uniform Resource Locator or URL assigned to each computer on the Internet which operates a Home Page—to any Internet user, that user may access the contents of the Webmaster's Home Page. Once the page is accessed, of course, it becomes (for as long as the user accesses it) the menu of the user, and he/she can connect to other links or move around freely. Figure 7.3 shows the LSU Libraries Home Page.

Subject and Keyword Search Engines

There are dozens of subject related and keyword search tools (called search engines) available on the Web and each one works differently. They allow you to input keyword and retrieve a listing of links to WWW resources. Most of the Web search tools are compiled by robot software programs that roam the Web creating indexes that are searchable. Many libraries have Home Pages which include pointers to search engines.

Retrieving Information: Five Easy Steps

The following beginning search procedures are based on using a Netscape browser to find information on a particular topic.

1. Connect to the Internet with direct connection:

   click on the Netscape icon.

   (With dialup connection, dial into the Internet provider and follow the instructions until you get to the introductory [default] page.)

2. From the default page (this will be the default page from Netscape or whatever page has been set up as the default page on the computer you are using):

   type the URL in the open location bar below the menu bar.

   http://www.yahoo.com

LSU Virtual Library

Compendex, the engineering database, joins the <u>LOUIS databases</u> searchable from your desktop.
Also added to LSU's LOUIS databases are <u>Art Index</u>, <u>Applied Science and Technology Index</u>, and <u>sociofile</u>.

<u>LSU Libraries Information and Services</u>
<u>LSU and Louisiana Electronic Publications</u>
<u>Webliography: A Guide to Internet Resources</u>

<u>About this Site</u> | <u>Usage Stats</u> | <u>Search this Site</u> | <u>Comments and Questions</u>

<u>LSU Libraries Gopher</u>
<u>Text Menu</u>

<u>LSU Home Page</u>

Copyright © 1995 Louisiana State University Libraries
Last Update: Monday, 17-Jun-96 14:35:28 CDT

Figure 7.3 *LSU Libraries Home Page (Reprinted by permission of Middleton Library, Louisiana State University.)*

3. Following links

    From the Yahoo main page, select a topic and click on it.

    Type a search statement in the box that is displayed on the Yahoo page. When it returns the results, click on a site which is described. This will take you to the next Web page. Links will be displayed in blue or underlined; previously followed links are displayed in purple (or red). This helps the user to avoid clicking on previously searched links.

    Return to Yahoo's main page by clicking on BACK on the menu bar until you get to the page.

4. Printing information

    To print a file, click the print button in the toolbar or click on the File button and select **Print**.

5. To exit Netscape and return to the main menu:

Click on FILE in the menu bar;
Click on Exit.

Some Useful URLs

The list below is current as of Spring 1996. Recall that the Internet is fluid—anything listed here is subject to change.

Find Information: Top Internet Search Engines

Newer and better search engines are coming out everyday. The following is a selected list of some that are currently available.

http://www.yahoo.com/

Yahoo: A hierarchical subject-oriented guide for the World Wide Web and the Internet. Provides Links to Internet resources with brief descriptions. Supports Boolean operators (**and, or**) and string searching. Displays the links along with descriptive text and the subject hierarchy under which it can be found in Yahoo. Updated daily. Figure 7.4 shows the Yahoo Home Page.

Stock Quotes   Web Launch

Options

- **Arts** - - *Humanities, Photography, Architecture, ...*
- **Business and Economy** **[Xtra!]** - - *Directory, Investments, Classifieds, ...*
- **Computers and Internet** **[Xtra!]** - - *Internet, WWW, Software, Multimedia, ...*
- **Education** - - *Universities, K-12, Courses, ...*
- **Entertainment** **[Xtra!]** - - *TV, Movies, Music, Magazines, ...*
- **Government** - - *Politics* **[Xtra!]**, *Agencies, Law, Military, ...*
- **Health** - - *Medicine, Drugs, Diseases, Fitness, ...*
- **News** **[Xtra!]** - - *World* **[Xtra!]**, *Daily, Current Events, ...*
- **Recreation and Sports** **[Xtra!]** - - *Olympics, Sports, Games, Travel, Autos, ...*
- **Reference** - - *Libraries, Dictionaries, Phone Numbers, ...*
- **Regional** - - *Countries, Regions, U.S. States, ...*
- **Science** - - *CS, Biology, Astronomy, Engineering, ...*
- **Social Science** - - *Anthropology, Sociology, Economics, ...*
- **Society and Culture** - - *People, Environment, Religion, ...*

Yahoo! Shop - Yahooligans! - Yahoo! Japan - Yahoo! Internet Life - Yahoo! San Francisco

Figure 7.4 Yahoo Home Page (Text and artwork copyright © 1996 by YAHOO!, Inc.. All rights reserved. YAHOO! and the YAHOO! logo are trademarks of YAHOO!, Inc.)

http://galaxy.einet.net

Galaxy: Indexes the Galaxy subject directory to Internet resources, Web pages, Gopher titles, and Telnet resources. Supports Boolean **and** and **or** operators, which can be limited to full-text, title text only, or link text only, or across all fields. Results are returned with one line per page that matches the search terms. Each entry is scored and listed in rank order, with the highest score being 100. Clicking on a linked result will take you to the Galaxy page of that title.

http://altavista.digital.com

AltaVista: Searches World Wide Web pages and Usenet News. Offers simple search or advanced query mode. Advanced query mode offers Boolean (**and, or, not**) and simple positional (**near**) operators. Results are returned ten items at a time. Updated constantly by Web robot.

http://guide.infoseek.com

infoseek: Searches Web pages, Newsgroups, and Internet Frequently Asked Questions (FAQs.) Displays include document title, type (Web, Gopher, FTP, News, etc.), file size, URL, and a brief abstract of the document. Updated constantly by Web robot.

http://www.opentext.com:8080

Open Text Web Index: Indexes words of text and hyperlinks found in World Wide Web document abstracts and pointers. Offers Simple Search Power Search, and Weighted Search options. Power searching allows users to specify Boolean operators (**and, or, not**), adjacency, and fields (title, URL, etc.). Weighted searching allows the assignment of relative term weights to the power searching options. Retrieves document title, the size of the document in bytes, the score, last update date, an excerpt, and links to the document, the search terms in context, and an option to find similar pages. Updated constantly by Web robot.

http://www.lycos.com

Lycos: Index to over 10 million Uniform Resource Locators (URLs). Indexes abstracts, titles, headings, sub-headings, 100 most significant words and first 20 lines of each file. There is no way to specify **adjacency**. Results are listed in ranked order. Displays include document address (URL), title, file size, and an excerpt from the file. Updated weekly. (An automated Web roaming process samples the network continuously for more information to add, but the database is rebuilt once a week.) Figure 7.5 shows the Lycos Home Page.

http://webcrawler.com/

WebCrawler: This search engine is owned by America OnLine. It offers a basic word or phrase searching. The results are displayed in groups of 25. Results are displayed in ranked order with the relevancy displayed in the line with the document link. Figure 7.6 shows the WebCrawler Home Page.

Find Telephone Numbers and E-Mail Addresses

http://www2.switchboard.com

> Switchboard—Find anyone in the United States

http://www.whowhere.com/

> WhoWhere? - Search for people on the Internet

http://okra.ucr.edu/okra/

> OKRA: Net.Citizen Directory Service

http://www.four11.com/

> Four11 Internet Directory Services

http://www.iaf.net/

> Internet address finder

http://www.mailbox.co.uk/esp

> ESP—e-mail search program

***Figure* 7.5** *Lycos Home Page (Copyright © 1996 Lycos, Inc. All Rights Reserved. The Lycos™ "Catalog of the Internet" Copyright © 1994, 1995, 1996 Carnegie Mellon University. All Rights Reserved. Used by permission.)*

Search the web and show for results

Example: diving swimming **NOT** (pool **OR** "hot tub")   Search tips

---

SEARCHING FOR CASH? $ CRAWL HERE.

Win a million dollars! Play the Million Dollar WebCrawl today.

---

reviews the Best of the Net

Arts & Entertainment	Government & Politics	Personal Finance
Business	Health & Medicine	Recreation & Hobbies
Computers	Humanities	Science & Technology
Daily News	Internet	Sports
Education	Life & Culture	Travel

Featuring the best of The 1996 Summer Olympics

Figure 7.6 *WebCrawler Home Page (Reprinted by permission of America Online, Inc.)*

Find out Who Was Born on [date]

http://www.eb.com/bio.html
   Who Was Born Today? - From *Encyclopedia Britannica*

Find ZIP Codes

http://www.usps.gov/ncsc/aq-zip.html
   Find ZIP codes and postal abbreviations

Find Phrases

http://www.shu.ac.uk/web-admin/phrases/
   The phrase finder

Find Books

http://www.press.uchicago.edu/#aaup
   The American Association of University Presses Home Page

http://www.ambook.org/bookweb/
   The Web page of the American Booksellers Association

Find Businesses

http://www.bigbook.com/
   The BigBook - A guide to businesses on the Internet

http://www.tollfree.att.net/index.html
   AT&T Internet Toll Free 800 Directory

Find Some Good Gophers

gopher://liberty.uc.wlu.edu:3002/7
   Jughead server at Washington & Lee University

gopher://gopher.scs.unr.edu/11/veronica
   Index of Veronica servers

http://hoohoo.ncsa.uiuc.edu/ftp/
   Monster FTP Site List

http://riceinfo.rice.edu/Internet/
   RiceInfo's Internet navigation tools

Find Library Catalogs

http://www.loc.gov/
   Bibliographical searching across many platforms

Find Out What's New

http://www.dejanews.com/forms/dnquery.html
   Search Usenet with Dejanew

Find Full-text Reference Sources on Just about Anything

http://k12.oit.umass.edu/rref.html
   Full-text ready reference using the Internet

Find Government Information

http://www.law.vill.edu/Fed-Agency/fedwebloc.html
   Links to government information at all levels

http://Thomas.loc.gov/
   Legislative information on the Internet

Find the Weather

http://www.nws.noaa.gov/climate.htm
   Weather and climate data from NOAA.

EVALUATING INTERNET SOURCES

When using information from the Internet in the research process, it is important to keep in mind that the sources on the Internet are almost totally without standards, and that anyone with a computer and access to a remote connection can "publish" on the Internet. Any of the criteria applied to evaluating print sources of information should be applied to the Internet. Some aspects to consider are:

- *Reliability*: Examine the source by checking the domain in the URL. Is it from an educational institution (edu), a government agency (gov), a commercial enterprise (com)? If the source is from an educational institution, is there a disclaimer saying that the institution is not responsible for the contents? Is the site a commercial one designed to sell products or services? Is the site a government agency?

- *Authoritative*: Is the information solely reflective of the one individual's opinion? (If there is a tilde (~) in the address it usually indicates that an individual, acting alone, is responsible for the contents.) Do you detect individual biases in the writing? What is the motive of the author? Is the author someone who is well known or who might be considered an authority? Examine the contents carefully to see if the author's credentials are noted.

- *Currency*: When was the information posted or updated? What are the inclusive dates of the information?

- *Completeness*: Is the information the most complete available? It is not unusual to find postings that are just excerpts or summaries of another work in a printed source.

- *Relevancy*: Does the information fit your research needs? Do not let the attraction to the medium obscure the message. Simply because something is on the Internet, it is not necessarily the best source.

Print Guides to the Internet

Bang, Steve, Martin Moore, Rick Gates, et al. *The Internet Unleashed*. Indianapolis: Sams, 1994.

Bruce, Maxwell. *Washington Online: How to Access the Government's Electronic Bulletin Boards*. Washington: Congressional Quarterly, 1995.

Cady, Glee H. and Pat McGregor. *Mastering the Internet*. San Francisco: Sybex, 1995.

Clark, David. *Student's Guide to the Internet*. Indianapolis: Alpha Books, 1995.

December, John and Neil Randall. *World Wide Web Unleashed*. Indianapolis: Sams, 1994.

Glossary of Internet Terms

Acceptable Use Policy (AUP) A policy which defines the accepted use of the server and the network. Internet providers, both commercial and non-commercial, frequently have AUPs.

address Internet address which refers to the e-mail address or the IP (Internet Protocol) address.

American Standard Code for Information Interchange (ASCII) A standard character- to-number encoding widely used in the computer industry.

Archie A program which automatically gathers, indexes, and retrieves information on the Internet.

backbone The top level in a hierarchical network. It connects regional and local networks.

binary A code used in computing based on numbers. Binary files require special viewers to read. When transferring a file you must indicate whether it is ASCII or binary.

bit Binary digit, the smallest amount of information which may be stored in a computer.

Bitnet An academic computer network that provides interactive electronic mail and file transfer services.

browser The software that allows you to locate, display, and use WWW documents. Lynx, Netscape, and Mosaic are the most widely used browsers.

Bulletin Board Service (BBS) A computer service which typically provides electronic mail services, exchange of ideas, data files, and any other services or activities of interest to the bulletin board system's operator. May be operated by hobbyists, government agencies, or educational and research institutions.

byte one character of information, usually eight bits wide.

Chat (Internet Relay Chat) A world-wide "party line" protocol that allows individuals to converse with others in real time. See also: talk.

client A computer system or process that requests a service of another computer system or process.

client-server A common way to describe the relationship between the computer that requests information (client) and the computer that houses the information (server).

cyberspace A term used to refer to the universe of computers and networks. Originally coined by William Gibson in his fantasy novel *Neuromancer*.

Dialup A temporary, as opposed to dedicated, connection between computers established over a standard phone line.

domain Used in the context of Domain Name System, refers to the host IP address.

Electronic Mail (e-mail) A system whereby a computer user can exchange messages with other computer users (or groups of users) via a communications network.

File Transfer Protocol (FTP) A protocol which allows a user on one host to access and transfer files to and from another host over a network.

finger A program that displays information about a particular user, or all users, logged on the local system or on a remote system. It typically shows full name, last login time, idle time, terminal line, and terminal location (where applicable).

flame A strong opinion and/or criticism of something, usually as a frank inflammatory statement, in an electronic mail message.

FTP See: File Transfer Protocol

gateway Currently, a gateway is a communications device/program which passes data between networks.

Gopher A menu-driven client-server information system. Gopher uses a simple protocol that allows a single Gopher client to access information from any accessible Gopher server.

hacker A person who is skilled in the internal workings of computers and networks. The term usually refers to individuals who use this knowledge to penetrate systems to cause mischief.

Home Page The first screen you see when you go to a site on the WWW.

host A computer that allows users to communicate with other host computers on a network, such as by electronic mail, Telnet, and FTP.

HTML (Hypertext Markup Language) A standardized document formatting language used in creating documents on the World Wide Web. With HTML, tags are embedded in the text to instruct the client how to display the document.

HTTP (Hypertext Transfer Protocol) The client-server protocol used to transfer HTML documents from one site to another on the Web.

hypertext Text that contains pointers, or links, to documents on other servers or to parts of the same document. Words or phrases in the document are highlighted, or underlined, to indicate links. The user can click on the highlighted word to display the document.

Internet Refers to the largest collection of networks in the world: a three level hierarchy consisting of national (backbone) networks, regional networks, and local networks.

Internet Protocol (IP) The protocol which allows a packet to travel through multiple networks on its way to its final destination.

IP address The address identifying the host computer.

Jughead A search program that searches a specific set of Gophers.

Kermit A popular file transfer protocol developed by Columbia University, which provides an easy method of file transfer.

LAN (Local Area Network) A data network intended to serve a small area, usually users in close proximity.

listserv An e-mail distribution system in which mail is automatically distributed to all subscribers.

logon The process of identifying yourself and connecting to a computer system.

Lynx A text only browser designed to be used with DOS (Disk Operating System) and UNIX systems.

Mosaic A graphics browser developed at the University of Illinois for use with MacIntosh, Windows, and UNIX operating systems.

MUD (Multi-User Dungeon) An Internet version of Dungeons and Dragons. Players interact in real time.

Netscape The most widely used of the graphics browsers developed for the WWW.

netiquette Used for network "etiquette," meaning proper behavior on a network.

network A communications system which interconnects computers at different sites.

packet A small parcel of data that is sent over the Internet. Before information is sent over the Internet, it is automatically divided into small "packets" to expedite transfer over the networks.

route The path that a message takes from its source to its destination.

router A device which forwards traffic between networks.

search engine A search tool for finding information on the Internet.

snail mail A pejorative term referring to the U.S. postal service.

surfing Exploring sites on the Internet.

talk A protocol which allows two people on remote computers to communicate in real-time fashion.

TCP See: Transmission Control Protocol

TCP/IP (Transmission Control Protocol over Internet Protocol). The abbreviation which refers to the suite of transmission and application protocols which runs over IP.

Telnet The Internet standard protocol for logging in to remote computers.

Transmission Control Protocol (TCP) An Internet standard transport protocol.

tunneling Refers to the process in which data is transferred between administrative domains.

UNIX An operating system designed to be used by many people at the same time ("multi-user"). It is the most common operating system for servers on the Internet.

URL (Uniform Resource Locator) The address of any resource on the Internet that is part of the World Wide Web (WWW).

Usenet A collection of thousands of topically named Newsgroups, to which people contribute. Not all Internet hosts subscribe to Usenet.

Veronica (Very Easy Rodent Oriented Net-wide Index to Computerized Archives) A search program for Gophers.

virus A program which is spread by replicating itself on any computer system with which it comes in contact.

W3 See: World Wide Web

WAIS See: Wide Area Information Servers

WAN See: Wide Area Network

Web site A location on any server that contains WWW documents.

Wide Area Information Servers (WAIS) A search/retrieval information service which uses keywords to query a source. The search results are ranked according to relevancy.

Wide Area Network (WAN) A network which covers a large geographic area.

World Wide Web (WWW, Web, or W3) A hypertext-based, distributed information system that allows users to view, create, or edit hypertext documents. Documents are viewed using a browser such as Netscape or Mosaic.

worm A computer program which replicates itself and is self-propagating. Worms, as opposed to viruses, are meant to spawn in network environments.

WWW See: World Wide Web.

Definitions were adapted from Gary Scott Malkin and Tracy LaQuey Parker, "Internet User Glossary." Online. Available HTTP://http://www.kanren.net/kanren/internet_user_glossary.html; and David Wuolu, "Basic Internet Terminology." Unpublished paper (Baton Rouge: Louisiana State University), 1995. An excellent, frequently updated, glossary of Internet terms is available from Internet Literacy Consultants at: http://www.matisse.net/files/glossary.html.

Instructor: _____   **Name:** _____

Course/Section: _____   **Date:** _____

Review Questions for Chapter Seven

1. Why is the Internet referred to as the "Information Superhighway"?

2. How did the Internet originate?

3. Who owns the Internet?

4. Who pays for the Internet?

5. Explain why the Internet is considered to be a "virtual library."

6. What are networks?

7. What is an information provider? Name three major information providers.

8. Name the major tools used to access the Internet.

9. What is a listserv?

10. What is a Gopher?

11. What is the World Wide Web?

12. Who can "publish" on the Internet?

13. How does Lynx differ from Mosaic and Netscape?

14. Explain what is meant by URL.

15. What is a Home Page?

Instructor: _____   **Name:** _____

Course/Section: _____   **Date:** _____

Internet Exercise

The Internet provides current news sources as well as information on many subjects. Use an Internet terminal in your library to find the following:

Searching for Current News

1. Type the URL **HTTP://www.lib.lsu.edu,** then click on WEBLIOGRAPHY.
   - Select **WEBLIOGRAPHY from the LSU Library's home page.**
   - Scroll down to **News Sources,** then find **NANDO TIMES,** or another news source of interest.
   - Click on a category of news you might be interested in.

2. Give the title of one article you find.

3. Briefly summarize the article.

4. Read another entry you are interested in. Give the Internet URL (http:// address) for this entry.

Searching by Subject

Return to the WEBLIOGRAPHY page, then select "**YAHOO**— a Guide to the WWW" and click for a subject approach to the Internet.

5. Select a **subject** category from their list, or type in your own in the search box. Give the subject you select here.

6. Describe what you find and give the Internet address of one entry. It should begin **http://**

Return to the **WEBLIOGRAPHY** page.

Searching by Keyword

Scroll down to **WEB CRAWLER, Lycos, WWW Worm,** or another search engine and Enter.

At the "search" prompt, type a keyword for a topic of your choice. (You can then combine terms in the same manner you use on the online catalog. Try "drugs and crime" as an example.)

7. Give the exact command you type.

8. Give the Internet address of one source you find on your topic, or describe the document you find.

Now that you've seen how the Internet can be accessed by subject and keyword, explore a few URL's on your own. Use the list in the text as an example, or discover your own.

9. List five people who were also born on your birthday.
    (Search http://www.eb.com.bio.html)

10. What is the local weather report for today?

11. Find a full-text source on a subject of your choice. Identify the search engine you used.

REFERENCE SOURCES

A PREVIEW

Reference sources are useful in the research process for a number of reasons: they provide background information; they provide facts or specific details on a subject; they point to other sources of information. This chapter seeks to identify the major relevant reference works in a variety of areas and to instruct the library user in effective methods of retrieving information from them. A second objective of this chapter is to develop the researcher's ability to make critical judgements in the selection and use of reference materials.

KEY TERMS AND CONCEPTS

Reference Sources
Using Reference Sources
Direct Access
Indirect Access
Finding Reference Sources
Selected General Reference Sources
Selected Subject Reference Sources

INTRODUCTION

Reference books are housed in a separate area in the library. They usually provide quick answers to questions or specific facts, such as the address of the local Congressional representatives, the number of alcohol-related deaths in a given year, a short biography of Malcolm X, or a brief interpretation of the poem "The Love Song of J. Alfred Prufrock" by T.S. Eliot.

Certain non-book materials are also used for reference. These include information in electronic format such as CD-ROMs, online catalogs, online databases, and information in other formats such as microforms, video tapes, and the Internet.

What are Reference Sources?

- They are designed to be consulted rather than being read straight through (**refer**ence).

- They may provide facts and figures in an easy-to-find format.

- They may provide concise information to frequently asked questions.

- They may contain valuable information for particular subject areas.

- They may serve as guides to information.

Using Reference Sources

Reference works can serve a variety of purposes. In the beginning of the research process, general encyclopedias and dictionaries can highlight specific major aspects of a topic which might be explored. A subject bibliography might be found which would provide valuable information that has already been gathered on the topic. The *United States Government Documents on Women, 1800-1990: A Comprehensive Bibliography* by Mary Ellen Huls would be useful in reviewing the topic of women and discrimination in employment. An article in *Compton's Encyclopedia* entitled "Women's Rights" gives a nice narrative of the history of women in the workforce, and highlights the inequality in wages which continues to exist. Most encyclopedias give bibliographies for further reading. The entries listed in these sources can be quickly researched in the library catalog, saving time and effort on the student's part.

Subject reference books provide more in-depth information on a particular aspect of a topic. Statistics and facts are often found in one-volume reference works such as almanacs or yearbooks. Indexes and abstracts to periodical articles are usually available only in the reference area.

Some characteristics of reference works that one should look for to determine their suitability for research are:

- *Scope of coverage.* The scope of the reference work must match that of the research question. Does the work include sufficient material to answer the question? Is there sufficient detail to cover all the points needed for an answer? There are several ways to determine the scope of a work:

  (a) The introduction, the preface, and the table of contents all tell something about the scope or coverage of the work and about the author's intent. Manuals or instruction books which accompany non-book materials serve the same purpose as the introductory pages of books.

  (b) The title of a work will help to determine its scope. Subject reference works tend to give greater coverage to the topics which they cover than more general works. The title of the work often provides clues to the contents. The text itself might be perused to determine the extent of details and the type of coverage. Periodical articles from a subject index such as *ABI/Inform* tend to be more scholarly than those in a general index such as *InfoTrac*. Therefore, for a more scholarly approach to current information on women and wages, the user would select *ABI/Inform*. Sometimes it might be necessary to make comparisons to determine which sources match the reference need.

- *Timeliness.* The *copyright date* should be used to determine whether or not the information contained in a book is current. The contents of a reference book are about a year older than the copyright date since it takes approximately a year before a book is published. The publication date and any revised edition dates are found on the reverse side of the title page of a work. A revised edition with a new copyright may indicate only minor changes. The terms "completely revised edition" or "enlarged edition" are indicative of more extensive revisions.

■ *Arrangement.* Reference books may be arranged or organized in three ways:

alphabetically: subjects or words appear in simple alphabetical order. Dictionaries are typically arranged in this fashion. Some reference books arranged in alphabetical order often include a separate index to help locate subtopics within the work. For example, *Webster's New World* Dictionary has a single alphabetical arrangement without a separate index while *World Book Encyclopedia* includes a separate index volume.

topically: subjects are listed in order by broad categories. Reference works arranged by topics almost always have a separate index which is used to find specific subjects within the broad categories. *The Encyclopedia of Crime and Justice* and *Sociological Abstracts* are examples of this type of arrangement.

chronologically: by date or time periods. Historical works such as Langer's *Encyclopedia of World History,* for example, are arranged by time periods.

■ *Author.* Knowing something about the author can be useful for determining the reliability of information. Occasionally reference books are written by one author, but more often, they are the work of several authors under the direction of an editor. Individual articles are usually signed by the author or authors responsible. Often the author's full name is given along with a brief biographical note indicating education, professional position, and a list of the author's other works. Sometimes that information appears elsewhere in the book or even in a separate volume if the work is a multi-volume one. In *The New Encyclopaedia Britannica*, for example, only the author's initials appear at the end of the article; the full name and biographical information are found in a separate volume.

■ *Bibliographies.* Bibliographies are helpful in providing the researcher with a list of materials for further consideration. They also tell the reader that the author has researched the topic, which is an indication of the reliability of the information. Bibliographies may be found at the end of each article, at the end of a section in some topically arranged works, at the end of the entire work, or perhaps as an appendix to the work.

■ *Cross references.* Cross references include the *see* and *see also* references which direct the reader to similar or related topics. The see reference guides the reader from a term that is not used to one that is used. A see also reference suggests other terms to consult for additional information. Both of these are useful in gathering information.

Types of Reference Sources

Reference sources fall into two broad categories: (1) general and (2) subject. Materials that are general in scope provide information in one source on a wide variety of topics. *The New Encyclopaedia Britannica* and *World Almanac* are examples of general reference sources. Subject reference sources cover a single subject field or a group of related subjects. The *New Grove Dictionary of Musical Instruments* and *Black's Law Dictionary* are examples of reference works which are devoted to single subject areas. *The Encyclopedia of the Social Sciences* covers education, psychology, sociology, business and other subjects.

Both general and subject reference sources can be further categorized as being direct or indirect sources of information. A *direct source* provides the information in such a way that it is not necessary to consult another source. An *indirect source* serves as a guide to information which is located in other sources.

Direct Sources	**Indirect Sources**
almanacs	
atlases	abstracts
biographical dictionaries	
dictionaries	
directories	bibliographies
encyclopedias	
gazetteers	
guidebooks	concordances
handbooks	
manuals	
yearbooks	indexes

Each year thousands of reference materials are published. Librarians select those sources which will be of greatest value to their library users. The reference collection is necessarily diverse, consisting of various types of reference sources designed to yield different kinds of information. Whether looking for quick facts or conducting extensive research, it is helpful to know the types of reference sources which are available and which will be most useful for the particular reference need. Figure 8.1 briefly defines the various types of reference sources available.

TYPES OF REFERENCE SOURCES

ABSTRACT an index that lists citations of works as well as a summary of each item (ex. *Psychological Abstracts, ERIC, ABI/INFORM*)

ALMANAC usually a one-volume work with statistics and a compilation of specific facts (ex. *World Almanac and Book of Facts,* and *Information Please Almanac, Atlas and Yearbook*)

ATLAS a book of maps and geographical information (ex. *Atlas of American History*)

BIBLIOGRAPHY a compilation of sources of information; provides literature on a specific subject or by a specific author (ex. *Books in Print* and *Bibliography of Nursing*)

BIOGRAPHICAL DICTIONARY sources of information about the lives of people; short entries (ex. *Current Biography* and *Who's Who in America*)

CONCORDANCE an alphabetical listing of keywords or phrases found in the work of an author or work in a collection of writings (ex. *Strong's Exhaustive Concordance of the Bible*)

DICTIONARY defines words and terms; confirms spelling, definition, and pronunciation; used to find out how words are used; helps to locate synonyms and antonyms and to trace the origin of words (ex. *Webster's Dictionary* and *Black's Law Dictionary*)

DIRECTORY lists names and addresses of individuals, companies, organizations, institutions, etc. (ex. *Encyclopedia of Associations,* and *Foundation Directory*)

ENCYCLOPEDIA covers knowledge or branches of knowledge in a comprehensive, but summary fashion; useful for providing facts and giving a broad survey of a topic; written by specialists (ex. *Encyclopedia Americana* and *World Book Encyclopedia*)

GAZETTEER a dictionary of geographical places (no maps) (ex. *Webster's New Geographical Dictionary*)

GUIDEBOOK provides detailed descriptions of places; intended primarily for the traveler; geographical facts plus maps (ex. *Baedeker's guidebooks to various countries*)

HANDBOOK treats one broad subject in brief, or gives a brief survey of a subject (ex. *Handbook of Literature* and *Benet's Reader's Encyclopedia*)

INDEX lists citations to periodical articles, books, proceedings, etc. and tells where they can be found (See Chapter 9) (ex. *Readers' Guide to Periodical Literature, New York Times Index,* and *Biography Index*)

MANUAL a specific work which tells how-to-do something, such as how something operates; descriptions of the inner workings of an organization (ex. *Chilton's Car Repair, MLA Handbook,* and *U.S. Government Organizational Manual*)

YEARBOOK covers the trends and events of the previous year; may be general in coverage, limited to one subject, or restricted to one geographical area (ex. *Britannica Book of the Year*)

***Figure 8.1.** Types of reference sources.*

Selecting a Reference Source

Determine the Type of Reference Source

The first step in selecting an appropriate reference source is to determine those sources which will be most useful. It is helpful to start the search by analyzing the question to determine what sort of information is needed. Figure 8.2 illustrates several types of sources that might be used for the topic discrimination of working women.

TOPIC: DISCRIMINATION OF WORKING WOMEN		
Needed information		**Appropriate reference sources**
overview article	----------- consult -----------	subject or general encyclopedia
current statistics	----------- consult -----------	statistical handbook, yearbook, almanac, *Statistical Abstract of the United States*
biographical information	----------- consult -----------	biographical index or biographical dictionary, library catalog
contemporary accounts	----------- consult -----------	periodical indexes, Internet, online databases
definition of legal terms	----------- consult -----------	dictionary, legal dictionary

Figure 8.2. *Sample reference sources for a selected topic.*

Determine the Subject Area (Discipline)

The next step in selecting appropriate reference sources for a topic is to determine the subject category. It is often necessary to broaden the topic into one of the disciplines or larger concepts. For example, to find an encyclopedia article specifically about types of sex discrimination against women, you would have greater results using the broader category of discrimination, or even women. Most subjects are grouped into broad subject areas such as the following: (See Figure 8.3.)

HUMANITIES	SOCIAL SCIENCES	SCIENCE
Architecture	Anthropology	Agriculture
Art	Business	Biology
Classical Studies	Criminal Justice	Chemistry
History	Economics	Computer Science
Journalism	Education	Engineering
Literature	Geography	Environment
Music	History	Health
Philosophy	Law	Mathematics
Poetry	Management	Medicine
Religion	Political Science	Petroleum
	Psychology	Physics
	Social Work	
	Sociology	

Figure 8.3. *Selected subjects within disciplines.*

For example, there are indexes, abstracts, and reference works in all three major subject disciplines. To select the most appropriate sources, first you must determine how the topic will be approached. In developing a research statement, it is extremely helpful to determine the focus of your topic. For example, how would you plan to treat the topic of women and discrimination?

Approach	**Discipline**
1. women and employment	*Social Sciences*
2. the way that discrimination is reflected in literature written by women	*Humanities*
3. the ability of women to handle the same physical jobs as men	*Science*

Finding Reference Sources

Once the topic for research has been analyzed and the appropriate subject areas selected, the next step is to locate the information. There are several strategies to use in locating reference sources.

1. use the library catalog;

2. browse the reference shelves;

3. consult a guide to reference books;

4. explore the Internet;

5. consult a reference librarian.

Library Catalog

Consult the library catalog when the title of a reference source is known, but not its location, or to find titles of works when one knows only the subject. If the topic is not found in the catalog, it may be because it is too specific or it may be that the topic is not used as a subject in the catalog.

The *Library of Congress Subject Headings (LCSH)* (See Figure 6.8) suggests related terms, narrow terms, and broader terms to be used in locating topics in the library catalog. In finding reference sources, it is often necessary to broaden the topic.

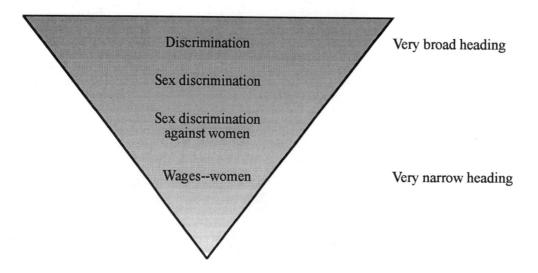

The terms "use" and "used for" in the *LCSH* indicate the proper terminology to be used in locating a subject heading. Reference books are listed in the library catalog by subject and then by the type of reference book. The examples below illustrate various subdivisions of a subject.

> HISTORY--BIBLIOGRAPHY
> HISTORY--DICTIONARIES
> HISTORY--DIRECTORIES
> HISTORY--HANDBOOKS, MANUALS, ETC.
> HISTORY--INDEXES
> HISTORY--YEARBOOKS

Many of the types of reference sources listed in Figure 8.1 can be located by using a keyword approach. For example:

k= history and dictionaries	k= women and biographies
k= science and bibliographies	k= bible and concordance

Browse the Reference Shelves

Class numbers may be found in the library catalog or sometimes in the *LCSH*. For example, to locate reference works on the topic of women, one could browse the reference stacks under the general class number range for women. Relevant works such as *Statistical Handbook on Women in America* (Ref HQ1420.T34 1991), and *Handbook of American Women's History* (Ref HQ 1410.H36 1990) were found. Both works provided charts and financial background information on women's work throughout history.

Some reference departments keep frequently used materials on *ready reference* shelves or on special index tables, making it necessary to browse in several different areas.

Consult a Guide to Reference Sources

The guides list reference sources by subject and often include subdivisions by type such as encyclopedias, handbooks, manuals, etc. Listed below are some of the more useful guides:

American Reference Books Annual. Englewood, CO: Libraries Unlimited, 1970-.
   Lists both general and subject reference books. Comprehensive review of each work with author/title index and subject index.

Ryan, Joe. *First Stop: The Master Index to Subject Encyclopedias.* Phoenix: Oryx, 1989.
   Subject and keyword indexes allow easy searching for a broad range of topics. Includes encyclopedias, dictionaries, handbooks, and yearbooks.

Balay, Robert, ed. *Guide to Reference Books.* 11th ed. Chicago: American Library Association, 1996.
   A comprehensive, annotated work which includes broad subject headings with further subdivisions according to type of source. Includes specific subject headings, and/or geographical location. Index incorporates author, title, subject, editors, compilers, and sponsoring bodies.

Walford, Albert J., ed. *Guide to Reference Material.* 5th ed. 3 vols. London: Library Association, 1989-1991.
   Three volumes, each devoted to a different discipline: science and technology; social and historical sciences, philosophy and religion; generalia, language and literature, and the arts. Each entry is annotated. Includes author/title index and a subject index in each volume.

Consult the Reference Sources on the Internet

Electronic sources are becoming more and important components of the library's reference collection. Most CD-ROMs, online services, and networked systems are located in the reference area. Many traditional reference sources such as Bartlett's *Familiar Quotations, Webster's Dictionary, Roget's Thesaurus,* and the *800 Number Directory,* are readily available on the Internet. Stock market prices, subject bibliographies, directories for e-mail addresses, instructions on resume writing and current employment opportunities, current legislation, both at the state and federal level, can all be retrieved quickly from remote access. Today's library staff is well versed in the access and use of search engines such as Yahoo, Lycos, WebCrawler or others to help the patrons find what they need, regardless of the format. Two relevant sources for the topic of women and discrimination in employment include "Women's Contract With America," available at: http://worcester.lm.com/women/contract.html, and "Salary Gap Narrows for All, Women," available at: http://detnews.com/menu/stories/32277.htm.

Ask the Reference Librarian for Assistance

Reference librarians are information specialists who are trained to analyze patrons' research needs and assist them in locating different sources of information. Reference staff can also provide guidance in developing search strategies.

Evaluating Reference Sources

A final step in the search for appropriate reference materials is to evaluate the sources. The researcher will ordinarily select the particular reference work which meets his/her information needs.

■ What is being asked?

■ What reference source contains the answers to that question?

Once the researcher finds a source that supplies the information, it is essential that he/she exercise some critical judgment regarding the work.

■ Is the information accurate? Is it up-to-date? Is the information clearly presented?

It is difficult for users to determine the worth of a particular reference source because they are dealing primarily with unknowns. However, the following guidelines are useful in evaluating sources:

■ *Authority.* Was the article written by an expert in the field? A signed article is usually an indication of reliable information. Information about authors can usually be found in the reference book itself; but if this is not the case, biographical information can be found elsewhere, such as in biographical dictionaries and biographical indexes. (See Chapter 10.) The library catalog will indicate other works by the same author.

■ *Completeness of information.* Are all aspects of the subject covered or have obvious facts been omitted? These questions may be difficult for the novice researcher to answer, but comparing information in one source with that in another may reveal additional details.

■ *Accuracy.* Is the information correct, or are there obvious errors in the information? Again, it may be necessary to sample several sources to determine if there are inconsistencies in reporting such things as times, dates, places, etc. Statistical information is vulnerable to such inaccuracies, and one might do well to verify statistical information in more than one source whenever this is possible.

■ *Currency.* Is the information up-to-date or have discoveries been made or events taken place since the copyright date of the work? To determine currency of information found in a reference book, one might check journal articles on the same topic to see if there have been new events or developments.

■ *Objective or biased treatment.* Do facts support the author's viewpoint or is a biased viewpoint being presented? Knowing something about the author's background, training, and other works is useful in determining possible bias. Often this information can be obtained from biographical dictionaries and indexes. The periodical indexes and abstracts might be checked to see if the author has written biased literature or if there has been controversy surrounding his/her publications.

■ *Publisher.* Is the publisher well known in the field? When many of the reference sources on a subject are published by the same commercial publisher, professional association, or university press, it can usually be assumed that the materials are authoritative.

■ *Documentation.* Are the sources used in the research listed? For some reference works, primary, or original, sources are preferred. In others, secondary sources are acceptable. For example, books of statistics are usually compiled from primary sources; encyclopedia articles, on the other hand, are usually based on secondary sources. In either case, it is important that the author give the source of the information, either in notes or in a bibliography listing the sources. Sometimes bibliographies also include other sources in addition to those which the author used in the research.

■ *Illustrations.* Does the reference source contain pictures, drawings, maps, statistical tables, etc. which would enhance its usefulness? The use of illustrations not only makes a work more interesting, but often makes a significant contribution to the understanding of the materials being presented.

Selected Reference Sources by Type

Almanacs and Yearbooks

Almanacs

Information Please Almanac, Atlas and Yearbook. New York: Simon and Schuster, 1947-.
   A one-volume work arranged into broad subject areas such as astronomy, economics and business, nutrition and health, religion, science, etc. Articles include both discussion and statistical material. Some signed articles on important issues of the period. Maps and some pictures are included. Topical arrangement with a subject index.

Whitaker, Joseph, ed. *An Almanack*. London: Whitaker, 1868-.
> British counterpart of *The World Almanac*. A compilation of excerpts from news stories, statistical information, and events of the preceding year. While Great Britain and Europe are highlighted, the United States is also covered.

The World Almanac and Book of Facts. New York: World Almanac, 1868-.
> Covers a wide variety of subjects. An excellent source for statistics. Features a chronology of events that took place during the preceding year. Contains biographical information on U.S. Presidents. Includes a few maps and some pictures. Index located at the front of the book.

Yearbooks

Americana Annual: an Encyclopedia of Events. New York: Encyclopedia Americana, 1923-.
> A supplement to the encyclopedia. Long signed articles discuss the year's political, economic, scientific and cultural developments. Includes a list of significant monthly events. Extensive biographical material on people in the news and of major figures who have died during the year. Available on CD-ROM.

Britannica Book of the Year. Chicago: Encyclopaedia Britannica, 1938-.
> Annual supplement to the encyclopedia. Includes several feature articles on newsworthy events. The "Year in Review" section covers the major events of the year as well as biographical information on people in the news. A separate section entitled "Britannica World Data" provides up-to-date statistical information on all countries of the world. Articles are signed and a list of contributors is provided.

Europa Year Book. 30th ed. 2 vols. 1989-. London: Europa Publications, 1926-.
> The new edition represents a change of title from previous volumes subtitled *A World Survey*. Provides information on the organization and activities of the United Nations and other international organizations. Chapters on the major countries of the world discuss such things as government, economic affairs, social welfare, education, and recent history.

Statesmen's Year Book: Statistical and Historical Annual of the States of the World. New York: St. Martin's, 1864-.
> Handy reference source for information on various countries of the world. Gives brief history, statistical information, area and population, climate, constitution and government, and natural resources. For the United States, the information is not only for the whole country, but also for each state.

Statistical Abstract of the United States. Washington: GPO, 1879-.
> Issued annually by the U.S. Bureau of the Census. Consists of a compilation of social, political, and economic statistics gathered from both private and government sources. Most tables give comparative information from prior years. Many of the statistics are from primary sources; all information is documented. Available on CD-ROM.

Atlases, Gazetteers, and Guidebooks

Atlases

Goode, J. Paul. *Goode's World Atlas*. Chicago: Rand McNally, 1993.
> Easy-to-use volume arranged in four major divisions: (1) world thematic maps dealing with the world's climate, raw material distribution, landform, languages, and religions; (2) regional maps which cover the political and topographical features of the continents and the countries within those continents; (3) plate tectonics and ocean floor maps; and (4) maps covering the major cities of the world. Comprehensive index.

Rand McNally and Company. *The New Cosmopolitan World Atlas*. Chicago: Rand McNally, 1992.
> Good discussions with aerial photographs of geologic phenomena such as earthquake zones, volcanoes, glaciers, and floods. Has a section of thematic maps on such subjects as population, religion, languages, agriculture, energy production and consumption, and climate. A new addition to this work includes special cartographic maps and world political tables by country.

Rand McNally Commercial Atlas and Marketing Guide. Chicago: Rand McNally, 1876-.
Contains business and commercial data. Useful for information on transportation, communication, economic conditions, and population. State and national maps are included along with maps of some American and Canadian cities. International in scope, but emphasis is on the United States.

Shepherd, William R. *Historical Atlas.* 9th ed. rev. New York: Barnes & Noble, 1980.
Collection of chronologically arranged maps of the world dating from approximately 3000 BC to the 20th century. Includes plans of Rome (350 AD) and Athens (420 BC). Contains both political and physical maps.

The Times Atlas of the World. New York: Times Books, 1985.
Contains physical and political maps of the world. Includes star charts, discussions of the solar system, and descriptions of the space flights. Comprehensive index of place names and their locations.

The Times Atlas of World History. 4th ed. Maplewood, NJ: Hammond, 1993.
Consists of political and cultural maps beginning with the origin of humankind through the 1980s. Includes chronological charts of geographic regions depicting the major political and cultural events from 9000 BC. Divided into sections: early man, first civilizations, Eurasia, divided regions, emerging West, European dominance, and global civilization.

Gazetteers

Canby, Courtlandt. *Encyclopedia of Historic Places.* 2 vols. New York: Facts on File, 1984.
Lists in alphabetical order names of places of historical significance such as battle sites, archaeological sites, shrines, cities, towns, and countries. Gives geographic location and historical significance. Cross references from former names to present ones. Some illustrations.

Munro, David. *Chambers World Gazetteer: An A-Z of Geographical Information.* 5th ed. Edinburgh: Chambers, 1988.
Alphabetical list of countries, towns, cities, and areas with descriptions of each. Helpful preface notes with specimen entry. Some maps and measurement conversion charts.

Webster's New Geographical Dictionary. Springfield, MA: Merriam, 1988.
Alphabetically arranged list of place names with locations and pronunciations. Information for each state of the U.S. includes list of counties, products manufactured, natural resources, etc.; other countries of the world have similar listings under the country's name. Some maps.

Guidebooks

Baedeker Guidebooks. Englewood Cliffs, NJ: Prentice-Hall, 1828-.
One of the oldest series of guidebooks still being published. Provides information about individual countries, groups of countries, and cities. Gives the history of the area, places to see, places to stay, and restaurants. Many pictures and maps.

Fodor's Travel Guides. New York: McKay, 1936-.
Volumes cover various regions and cities of the United States, Europe, Asia, South America, and the Caribbean. Offers suggestions for transportation to and from an area and places of interest to visit. Discusses local customs and history. Maps of cities and lists of lodging places and restaurants. Well illustrated. Frequently revised.

McLanathan, Richard B. K. *World Art in American Museums.* Garden City, NJ: Doubleday, 1983.
Guide to art collections in museums in the U.S. and Canada. Arranged in three parts: an alphabetical list of museums arranged by state and province; arrangement by artistic period; an alphabetical list of artists with biographical notes and a list of the locations of their works. Some pictures and maps.

Mobil Travel Guide. 8 vols. New York: Prentice-Hall, 1990.
> Each volume covers a different area of the United States and Canada. Contains regional road maps, information on local accommodations, restaurants, places to see, and local events. Some city maps. Each volume is arranged by state and then alphabetically by city and town names.

Bibliographies

Books in Print. New York: Bowker, 1948-.
> Lists books currently available from publishers. Contains separate author, title, subject, and publisher lists. Also available on CD-ROM as BIP Plus.

Cumulative Book Index. New York: Wilson, 1933-.
> Author, title, and subject listing of books published in the English language throughout the world. Bibliographic information along with standard numbers useful for ordering books.

Paperbound Books in Print. New York: Bowker, 1955-.
> Lists over 200,000 titles of paper bound books by author, title, and subject. Full bibliographic information. Entries include the standard numbers used for ordering and the American Bookseller's Association subject classification number. Semiannual.

Concordances

New American Standard Exhaustive Concordance of the Bible. Nashville: Holman, 1981.
> Lists words and phrases found in the *New American Standard Bible;* gives the book, chapter, verse, and reference number to the words listed in the Hebrew/Aramaic and Greek dictionaries found in the back of the book.

Dictionaries

Unabridged

The Random House Dictionary of the English Language. 2nd ed. New York: Random House, 1987.
> Up-to-date, easy to read dictionary with good illustrations. Supplement includes French, Spanish, Italian, and German dictionaries, a style manual, and a world atlas. Names of people are included.

Webster's Third New International Dictionary of the English Language. Springfield, MA: Merriam, 1986.
> Comprehensive dictionary containing all the principal words used in the English language. Provides pronunciations as well as definitions. A separate pronunciation guide is found in the front.

Abridged

The American Heritage Dictionary. 2nd College ed. Boston: Houghton Mifflin, 1985.
> Dictionary designed for "American English." Definitions often accompanied by illustrations. Contains several essays on the use of language. Features a separate style manual, list of abbreviations, geographic entries, and biographical entries.

Merriam-Webster's Collegiate Dictionary. 10th ed. Springfield, MA: Merriam, 1993.
> Chronological within definitions. In some cases quotations are used to clarify the meanings of words. Contains a guide to pronunciation and explanatory notes. Lists of abbreviations, chemical symbols, foreign words and phrases, personal names, geographical names, colleges and universities, and a style manual are found in the back of the book.

Historical Dictionaries

Historical dictionaries place emphasis on the historical perspectives of words and phrases. These often contain useful information about words not found in the traditional dictionary.

Oxford English Dictionary. 2nd ed. 20 vols. New York: Oxford University Press, 1989.
Comprehensive record of the words used in the English language from the twelfth century to contemporary times. Quotations demonstrate how words were used during different time periods. Excellent source for quotations using words in a particular context. Also available on CD-ROM.

Specialized Dictionaries

In addition to the traditional dictionaries, there are a great number of specialized dictionaries which approach the study of words from a different perspective. For example, a thesaurus groups synonyms together.

Chapman, Robert L. *New Dictionary of American Slang.* New York: Harper and Row, 1986.
Extensive list of American slang terms with definitions, parts of speech, examples, and, in some cases, the date of origin. Good introductory essay on slang.

Partridge, Eric. *Dictionary of Slang and Unconventional English.* 8th ed. London: Kegan Paul, 1984.
Emphasis is on British slang although some American terms are included. Where possible, date and place of origin are given. Multiple meanings are included when applicable.

Roget, Peter Mark. *Roget's Thesaurus of English Words and Phrases.* London: Longman, 1987.
Classified list of terms in the English language with synonyms indicating different possible meanings and usage of the word. Includes index of words in the main body of the work. Does not define words but indicates their meanings through their usage. Available on the Internet.

Subject Dictionaries

Subject dictionaries are devoted primarily to a subject field and give the terminology most useful in that field. Many of these dictionaries are updated frequently to keep current with changing terminology and new developments.

Black, Henry Campbell. *Black's Law Dictionary.* 6th ed. St. Paul: West, 1990.
Comprehensive dictionary defining terms used in law and related subjects. Good cross references. Pronunciation guide arranged alphabetically.

Dorland's Illustrated Medical Dictionary. 27th ed. Philadelphia: Saunders, 1987.
Defines medical terms giving pronunciations, alternate definitions, if any, and origin of the word. Numerous plates showing detailed drawings of parts of the human body.

Foreign Language Dictionaries

Foreign language dictionaries can be found for virtually every written language. They may be written entirely in the language covered, or they may be English-foreign language.

Collins-Robert French-English, English-French Dictionary. 2nd ed. Glasgow: Collins, 1987.
Emphasizes contemporary rather than classical terms in both languages. "Style labels" indicate when a term may have stylistic complexities, e.g., local idioms that cannot be literally translated. Includes phrases as well as single words.

Collins German-English, English-German Dictionary. 2nd ed. London: Harper Collins, 1991.
Emphasis on contemporary everyday language, but includes older terms and technical language. Entries are listed in specific context.

Falla, P. S., ed. *The Oxford English-Russian Dictionary.* New York: Oxford, 1984.
Wheeler, Marcus. *The Oxford Russian-English Dictionary.* 2nd ed. New York: Oxford, 1984.
These two volumes can be used together to alternate between the two languages.

Directories

United States Congress. Official Congressional Directory. Washington: GPO, 1809-.
   Published for each session of Congress. Contains names, addresses, committee assignments, and biographical sketches of members of Congress. Also includes names and addresses of top officials in all government agencies, international organizations, diplomatic missions, and the press corps. Contains maps of each Congressional district.

Encyclopedia of Associations. Detroit: Gale, 1956-.
   Multi-volume directory of active organizations in the United States and Canada. Has a separate volume for international organizations. Arranged by broad subject areas with separate organization name, executive name, keyword, and geographic indexes. Available on CD-ROM.

Thomas' Register of American Manufacturers. New York: Thomas Publishing, 1905/06-.
   Multi-volume lists of products and services available from American companies. Includes product and brand name indexes, company profiles, and a file of company catalogs. Available online, through *Thomas' Register CD-ROM,* and as *Thomas' Register Database.*

The World of Learning. London: Europa, 1947-.
   Directory of research organizations, libraries and archives, colleges and universities, learned societies, museums, and art galleries found throughout the world. Arranged alphabetically by country. Includes names, addresses and some annotations.

Encyclopedias

General

Encyclopedia Americana. 30 vols. Danbury, CT: Grolier. 1990.
   The first encyclopedia published in the United States. It covers the arts and humanities as well as scientific development. Signed articles by experts in the field. Unique feature is the "century'" articles which discuss the outstanding events and trends of various time periods. Long articles contain a table of contents for easy reference. Supplemented by *Americana Annual.* Available on CD-ROM.

The Grolier Multimedia Encyclopedia. Database. Danbury, Conn.: Grolier, c1995-.
   First of the CD-ROM encyclopedias. Full text of the printed *Academic American Encyclopedia.* Enhanced 1995 edition includes additional audiovisual effects. Text is available online.

The New Encyclopaedia Britannica. 30 vols. Chicago: Encyclopaedia Britannica, 1990.
   Consists of three parts with a two-volume index. Volume 30, the *Propaedia* is an "Outline of Knowledge," which serves as a topical approach to the articles in volumes 1-12, the *Micropaedia,* and in volumes 13-29, the *Macropaedia.* The twelve-volume *Micropaedia* contains brief entries with cross references to the longer articles in the *Macropaedia.* The *Macropaedia* volumes contain long comprehensive articles complete with bibliographies. Articles are signed with initials which can be identified by referring to Volume 30. Supplemented by *Britannica Book of the Year. Britannica CD-ROM* includes full text of the print encyclopedia and a dictionary and thesaurus.

World Book Encyclopedia. 22 vols. Chicago: World Book, 1995.
   Designed for elementary through high school students, but because of its extremely wide coverage, it is excellent for general reference. Major articles provide subject headings for related articles, an outline of the subject, and review questions. Numerous diagrams and pictures, good cross references, and signed articles. Updated by *World Book Yearbook.*

Subject Encyclopedias

Encyclopedia of Bioethics. Rev. ed. New York: Simon & Schuster, 1995.
   Lengthy signed articles with good cross references and bibliographies. Covers the ethical concerns with human problems such as abortion, aging, human experimentation, population policies, reproductive technologies, etc.

Encyclopedia of Psychology. 2nd ed. New York: Wiley, 1994.
   Alphabetically arranged by specific topics. Some articles signed and have short bibliographies.

International Encyclopedia of the Social Sciences. 19 vols.(in progress). New York: Macmillan, 1968-91.
   Long scholarly articles with bibliographies covering all aspects of the social sciences from anthropology to statistics. Treats narrow subjects within the broad subjects. Good cross references. The *Biographical Supplement* contains a classified subject list to the alphabetically arranged biographies.

McGraw-Hill Encyclopedia of Science and Technology. 7th ed. 20 vols. New York: McGraw-Hill, 1992.
   Covers all aspects of science and technology. Scholarly, yet non-technical articles, most of which are signed. Illustrations, bibliographies, and cross references. Volume 20 contains topical and analytical indexes and a section on scientific notation. Kept up-to-date by *McGraw-Hill Yearbook of Science and Technology*.

Handbooks and Manuals

Handbooks

Benét's Reader's Encyclopedia. 3rd ed. New York: Harper & Row, 1987.
   Primarily concerned with literature but useful for identifying movements and important people in art and music. Contains references to literary characters and plot summaries. International in scope, but emphasis is on American and British works.

Gibaldi, Joseph. *MLA Handbook for Writers of Research Papers*. 4th ed. New York: Modern Language Association of America, 1995.
   An authoritative manual which explains the mechanics of preparing, organizing, and writing research papers using the methods and forms prescribed by the Modern Language Association. Contains examples for documenting both print and non-print materials such as films, computer software, recordings, etc.

Robert's Rules of Order. New York: Berkley Books, 1993.
   Guide to standard parliamentary procedure used by organizations to conduct business meetings. Introduction explains the history and development of parliamentary rules; a center section codifies procedures for conducting meetings. Other chapters explain the duties of organization officers, committee members, and board members. An index is included.

Manuals

United States Government Manual. Washington: GPO, 1935-.
   Official guide to the organization of the United States Government. Lists all of the government agencies, both official and semi-official, along with the names, addresses, and phone numbers of their top personnel. Contains a copy of the U.S. Constitution, a list of abbreviations useful for identifying government agencies, an index of names, and an agency/subject index.

Selected Reference Sources by Subject

Agriculture
Agricultural Statistics. 1963-.
Farm Chemicals Handbook. 1990.
Handbook of Engineering in Agriculture. 3 vols. 1988.
Yearbook of Agriculture. 1894 -.

Anthropology
Dictionary of Human Geography. 3rd ed. 1993.
Encyclopedia of Human Evolution and Prehistory. 1988.
A Hundred Years of Anthropology. 1974.

Archaeology
Atlas of Archaeology. 1982.
Cambridge Encyclopedia of Archaeology. 1980.
Dictionary of Terms and Techniques in Archaeology. 1980.
Larousse Encyclopedia of Archaeology. 1983.

Architecture
Encyclopedia of Architecture: Design, Engineering, and Construction. 2 vols. 1989.
A History of Western Architecture. 1986.

Art & Interior Design
Art Across America. 1990.
Encyclopedia of World Art. 1959-1987.
Gardner's Art Through the Ages. 9th ed. 1990.
The Oxford Dictionary of Art. 1994.

Astronomy
Cambridge Atlas of Astronomy. 1994.
Encyclopedia of Astronomy and Astrophysics. 1992.
International Encyclopedia of Astronomy. 1987.

Biology
Cambridge Encyclopedia of Life Sciences. 1985.
Fishes of the World. 1994.

Botany
A Dictionary of Botany. 1984.
A Dictionary of Plant Pathology. 1989.

Business & Economics
Accountant's Handbook. 7th ed. 1991.
American Advertising: A Reference Guide. 1988.
Data Sources for Business and Market Analysis. 4th ed. 1994.
Dictionary of Accounting Terms. 1995.
Dow Jones-Irwin Business and Investment Almanac. 1982-1990.
Encyclopedia of Business Information Sources. 11th ed. 1996.

Chemistry & Physics
Beilstein's Handbook of Organic Chemistry. 5th ed. 1991.
CRC Handbook of Chemistry and Physics. 1995-1996.
Concise Dictionary of Physics. 1990.
Handbook of Industrial Robotics. 1992.

Criminal Justice
The Encyclopedia of Child Abuse. 1989.
The Encyclopedia of Criminology. 1995.
The Encyclopedia of Psychoactive Drugs. 25 vols. 1985-1991.
Handbook on Crime and Delinquency Prevention. 1987.
The Police Dictionary and Encyclopedia. 1988.

Education
American Educators Encyclopedia. 1991.
Education Yearbook. 1972/73 -.
Encyclopedia of Careers and Vocational Guidance. 3 vols. 9th ed. 1993.
Encyclopedia of Educational Research. 4 vols. 1992.
International Encyclopedia of Education. 1994.
Mental Measurements Yearbook. 1941-.

Engineering Technology
Civil Engineers Reference Book. 1994.
Electrical Engineering Handbook. 1993.
Handbook of Industrial Engineering. 2nd ed. 1992.
Metals Handbook. 10th ed. 1990.
SAE Handbook. 1994.

Environment & Ecology
Encyclopedia of Climatology. 1987.
The Weather Almanac. 6th ed. 1992.

Ethnology
Atlas of World Cultures. 1990.
Handbook of North American Indians. 1984-.
Negro Almanac: A Reference Work of the African-American. 6th ed. 1993.

Genealogy
A Dictionary of Heraldry. 1995.
A Dictionary of Surnames. 1989.
Source: A Guidebook of American Genealogy. 1984.

Geography
Cities of the World. 4 vols. 4th ed. 1993.
Cambridge Encyclopedia of Africa. 1981.
Dictionary of Human Geography. 1994.
Harper Atlas of World History. 1993.
Worldmark Encyclopedia of the States. 3rd ed. 1995.

Geology
Dictionary of Geology. 6th ed. 1986.
International Petroleum Encyclopedia. 1994.
McGraw-Hill Encyclopedia of the Geological Sciences. 2nd ed. 1988.

History: The Americas
Annals of America. 21 vols. 1976 - 1987.
Dictionary of Indian Tribes of the Americas. 4 vols. 1980.
Dictionary of Mexican American History. 1981.
Documents of American History. 10th ed. 1988.
International Library of Afro-American Life and History. 10 vols. 1978.

History: The World
Africa South of the Sahara. 25th ed. 1996.
The Annual Register: A Record of World Events. 1788 -.
Dictionary of the Middle Ages. 13 vols. 1989.
Encyclopedia of the Holocaust. 4 vols. 1990. Supp. 1995.
Great Soviet Encyclopedia. 31 vols. 3rd ed. 1982.

Journalism
Communication Yearbook. 1977-.
Editorials on File. 1970-.
Facts on File: A Weekly World News Digest with Cumulative Index. 1940-.
The Gallup Poll: Public Opinion. 1935-.
Keesing's Record of World Events. 1931-.
What They Said: A Yearbook of Spoken Opinion. 1969-.

Language & Literature
Black American Writers, Past and Present. 2 vols. 1975.
Cambridge Encyclopedia of Language. 1991.
Cambridge Guide Literature in English. 2nd ed.1994.
Columbia Dictionary of Modern European Literature. 2nd ed. 1980.
Columbia Literary History of the United States. 1988.
Contemporary Literary Criticism. 8 vols. 1973-.
Familiar Quotations (Bartlett's). 1994.
Harbrace College Handbook. 12th ed. 1993.
Harvard Concordance to Shakespeare. 1973.
Oxford Companion to English Literature. Rev. ed. 1995.
Webster's Dictionary of English Usage. 1994.

Mathematics
CRC Handbook of Mathematical Science. 1962-.
Encyclopedic Dictionary of Mathematics. 4 vols. 1986.

Medicine
Anatomy of the Human Body. 1985.
Cyclopedia of Medicine, Surgery, Specialties. 15 vols. 1964-.
Merck Manual of Diagnosis and Therapy. 1899-.
Physician's Desk Reference Book. 1947-.
Stedman's Medical Dictionary. 26th ed. 1995.

Motion Pictures, Radio & Television
International Television and Video Almanac. 1956-.
Magill's Cinema Annual. 1981-.
Radio's Golden Years: The Encyclopedia of Radio Programs, 1930-1960.

Music
The Encyclopedia of Folk, Country, and Western Music. 1983.
New Grove Dictionary of American Music. 4 vols. 1986.
New Grove Dictionary of Jazz. 2 vols. 1988.
Norton/Grove Concise Encyclopedia of Music. 1988.

Mythology, Folklore, Parapsychology
The Arthurian Encyclopedia. 1986.
Dictionary of Mysticism and the Occult. 1985.
Folklore of American Holidays. 1991.
Man, Myth, and Magic. 21 vols. 1994.

Philosophy

Dictionary of Philosophy. 1992.
Dictionary of the History of Ideas. 5 vols. 1980.
Encyclopedia of Philosophy. 8 vols. in 4. 1972.
World Philosophy: Essay-reviews of 225 Major Works. 5 vols. 1982.

Political Science

Almanac of American Politics. 1972-.
Countries of the World and Their Leaders Yearbook. 1980-.
County Year Book. 1975-.
Demographic Yearbook. 1949-.
Politics in America. 1982-.

Psychology

American Handbook of Psychiatry. 8 vols. 2nd ed. 1974-1986.
Encyclopedia of Phobias, Fears, and Anxieties. 1989.
Handbook of Developmental Psychology. 1982.
Oxford Companion to the Mind. 1987.

Religion

Encyclopedia of Judaism. 1989.
Encyclopedia of Religion. 15 vols. 1987.
New Catholic Encyclopedia. 18 vols. 1967-1989.

Science—General

Britannica Yearbook of Science and the Future. 1968-.
Dictionary of the History of Science. 1985.
Van Nostrand's Scientific Encyclopedia. 8th ed. 1995.

Sociology & Social Work

Encyclopedia of Aging. 1987.
Encyclopedia of Social Work. 1995.
International Encyclopedia of Sociology. 1985.
Sourcebook on Pornography. 1989.

Statistics

Demographic Yearbook. 1949-.
The World in Figures. 1987.

Theater

Best Plays and the Yearbook of Drama in America. 1894/99-.
The Drama Dictionary. 1988.
Cambridge Guide to World Theatre. 1989.
Historical Encyclopedia of Costume. 1988.

Women's Studies

Women: A Bibliography (Ballou) 1986.
Women of Achievement. 1981.
The Women's Annual, the Year in Review. 1980-.
Women's Studies Encyclopedia. 1989.

Zoology

Encyclopedia of the Animal World. 11 vols. 1980.
Grzimek's Animal Life Encyclopedia. 13 vols. 1972-1975.
Grzimek's Encyclopedia of Mammals. 5 vols., 1990.
The New Larousse Encyclopedia of Animal Life. Rev. ed. 1980.

Instructor: _____   **Name:** _____

Course/Section: _____   **Date:** _____

Review Questions for Chapter Eight

1. Give three characteristics of reference sources.

   a.

   b.

   c.

2. How are reference sources used in research?

3. Name and define three different types of reference sources.

   a.

   b.

   c.

4. What types of reference source would you use for an overview of a topic?

5. Explain the difference between *direct* and *indirect* reference sources.

6. Which discipline would you look under to find information on each of the following?

      <u>Topic</u>   <u>Discipline</u>

    a. medicine

    b. religion

    c. political science

    d. agriculture

    e. education

    f. music

7. Name five possible strategies you might consider in locating reference sources.

    a.

    b.

    c.

    d.

    e.

8. Why is it important to determine the date of the reference source being used in research?

9. Why is it important to look for signed articles in a reference book?

10. Why are bibliographies useful additions to articles found in reference sources?

11. Why is it important to have cross references in a reference source?

12. When looking for reference books in the library catalog, what form subdivisions in the subject heading would be useful?

Instructor: _____   **Name:** _____

Course/Section: _____   **Date:** _____

Types of Reference Sources Exercise

Various kinds of information may be obtained from many different reference sources. Name the type of reference source or sources in which you would probably find the following information. A source may be used more than once and may include non-book sources discussed in earlier chapters. (See Figure 8.1)

EXAMPLE: Meaning and pronunciation   **Dictionary**

1. Brief, miscellaneous facts about Russia.   _____

2. A list of sources about one author.   _____

3. A published list of sources on political science.   _____

4. Broad survey of atomic energy.   _____

5. Recent map of Bosnia.   _____

6. Brief description of the Mississippi River.   _____

7. A brief survey of art history.   _____

8. A short description of the current economy in Peru.   _____

9. Illustrations of famous works of art.   _____

10. Materials published by the American Sociological Association.   _____

11. Events or trends of the last year.   _____

12. List of manufacturers of air conditioners.   _____

13. The 1990 population of Alaska.   _____

14. The latitude and longitude of the Alps.   _____

15. How to conduct an experiment in physics.   _____

16. Short discussion of the function of the U.S. Department of the Interior.   _____

17. Addresses of U.S. Government officials.   _____

18. Location of words used in Shakespeare's plays.   _____

19. Diagram of an engine of a 1984 Ford.   _____

20. Definitions of terms in anthropology.   _____

21. A brief survey of education. _____

22. The capital of North Dakota. _____

23. Brief, miscellaneous facts about Haiti. _____

24. Your congressman's phone number in Washington. _____

25. A list of articles published by a biology professor. _____

26. A book covering all aspects of engineering. _____

27. Major happenings in the field of science last year. _____

28. Location of the word "marriage" in the Bible. _____

29. Major events at the United Nations last year. _____

30. The correct spelling of a medical term. _____

31. A current picture of a famous actor. _____

32. A book illustrating how to change oil in your car. _____

33. A list of newspaper articles on a particular topic. _____

34. Pictures of the U.S. flag throughout history. _____

35. The number of currently employed males in your state. _____

36. The medical procedure involved in a laser surgery. _____

37. A quotation from a poem when you only know the first line. _____

38. The exact dates of the Korean War. _____

39. Detailed description of hiking trails in England. _____

40. The correct spelling of the highest mountain in Tanzania. _____

Instructor: _____   **Name:** _____

Course/Section: _____   **Date:** _____

Locating Reference Books Exercise

Locate two different reference books which contain information on a topic. <u>DO NOT</u> use an abstract, index, or bibliography. Give the information listed below for each book:

TOPIC: _____

Since reference books often are not listed under specific subject headings, what broad subject heading would be appropriate for your topic?

First reference book

1. Method used to locate book:

2. If you used the online catalog, write the exact command you used.

3. Call number and location:

4. Author (or) editor of the book:

5. Title of the book:

6. Date of publication:

7. Single or multi-volume:

8. What is the arrangement of the book (alphabetical, topical, chronological)?

9. What subjects are covered in the book?

10. Give the title of an article on your topic, if applicable.

11. Author of article (if any):

12. Volume number (if applicable) and inclusive pages of article:

Second reference book

1. Method used to locate book:

2. If you used the online catalog, write the exact command used.

3. Call number and location:

4. Author (or) editor of the book:

5. Title of the book:

6. Date of publication:

7. Single or multi-volume:

8. What is the arrangement of the book (alphabetical, topical, chronological)?

9. What subjects are covered in the book?

10. Give the title of an article on your topic, if applicable.

11. Author of article (if any):

12. Volume number (if applicable) and inclusive pages of article:

Instructor: _____   **Name:** _____

Course/Section: _____   **Date:** _____

Evaluating Reference Books Exercise

Select a topic of your choice. Locate information on the topic in each of the types of reference sources listed below and give the requested information about each.

*TOPIC:*_____

1a. *Abridged dictionary*
Title and date:

1b. *Unabridged dictionary*
Title and date:

2. Compare the two sources. How is the information similar? How does it differ?

3. Write a bibliographic citation for each of the sources used. (Use the examples in Chapter 14.)

4a. *General encyclopedia*
   Title and date:

4b. *Subject encyclopedia*
   Title and date:

5. Compare the two sources. How is the information similar? How does it differ?

6. Write a bibliographic citation for each of the sources used. (Use the examples in Chapter 14.)

7. *Subject or general bibliography*
   Title and date:

8. Arrangement (alphabetically, topically, chronologically):

9. Number of references in bibliography:

10. Bibliographic citation: (Use the examples in Chapter 14.)

11. *Handbook or manual*
   Title and date:

12. Write a brief summary of the information located.

13. Bibliographic citation: (Use the examples in Chapter 14.)

Using a state or a city as a topic, look up information in each of the types of reference sources listed below and give the requested information about each.

14. TOPIC: _____

   a. *Almanac*
      Title and date of almanac:

      Population:

   b. *Yearbook*
      Title and date:

      Population:

15. Compare the two sources. How is the information similar? How does it differ?

16. Use the bibliographic citations in **Chapter 14 and write a correct citation for each of the sources used.**

_____

Using a country as a topic, look up information in each of the types of reference sources listed below and give the requested information about each.

17. TOPIC: _____

    a. *Atlas*
        title and date:

        Population:

    b. *Gazetteer*
        Title and date:

        Population:

18. Compare the two sources. How is the information similar? How does it differ?

19. Use the bibliographic citations in **Chapter 14 and write a correct citation for each of the sources used.**

PERIODICAL LITERATURE

A PREVIEW

Just as one may think of the library catalog as an index to its holdings, a large variety of indexes serve the same purpose for the contents of individual periodical titles. Effective and critical use of the library often depends on a mastery of these access tools for finding information in newspapers, magazines and journals. It is the goal of this chapter to demystify this subject by describing and analyzing the major types of indexes and their use.

KEY TERMS AND CONCEPTS

Periodical
Serial
Citation
Newspaper
Magazine
Journal
Index
Abstract
Online Service
Internet
Citation Indexes
CD-ROM
Database

INTRODUCTION

Serials are publications that are issued on a continuing basis at regularly stated intervals. They include periodicals, newspapers, annuals and yearbooks, and the proceedings, transactions, memoirs, etc. of societies and associations. Chapter 8 discussed annuals and yearbooks; this chapter will discuss periodicals (magazines and journals) and newspapers.

Importance of Periodical Literature

Periodical literature is valuable as a research medium for several reasons: information appearing in periodicals constitutes the bulk of published information; there are thousands of periodicals published regularly, each containing an abundance of articles on different topics; and the material found in newspapers, magazines, and journals is the most recent printed information one can find. By locating an article written shortly after an event occurred, whether it be in the 19th century, the 1930s, or the 1990's, the library user will find contemporary opinion which reflects what people thought of the event at the time it occurred.

Periodical literature reflects the constantly evolving nature of information. No matter when an event occurred, it is constantly being reexamined and new revelations brought forward. It is also possible to find comparative information for different periods. Sometimes periodical literature is the only information available—the topic may be too faddish ever to appear in a book. The findings of researchers and scholars are published in professional journals which supplement other types of literature in a particular field, such as medicine or education.

Types of Periodical Literature

There are two basic types of periodical literature: *popular* and *scholarly:*

Popular

- *Magazines* are designed to appeal to a broad segment of the population. They are characterized by relatively short articles written in non-technical language, usually by staff writers. The style of writing is easy to understand and concise. The articles are especially useful for information on current events or the contemporary treatment of a topic. Magazines are published weekly or monthly.

- *Newspapers* provide short articles written in non-technical language. Newspaper articles are a *primary* source of information because they provide a first-hand account of an event. They are useful both for current and historical perspectives on a topic. Newspapers are usually published daily or weekly.

Scholarly

- *Journals* are intended for a more limited readership. The articles are written by scholars or experts in a field. The vocabulary is often technical, and the style of writing is more complex than that found in popular magazines. They provide research articles on specific topics, and may include charts and graphs. Journal articles include extensive bibliographies. They are usually published monthly, quarterly, or annually.

How to Find Periodical Literature

The library catalog lists the cataloged works contained in the library and gives location information, but does not include individual articles in periodicals. The following types of library resources are useful in finding articles in newspapers, magazines, and journals.

Printed Indexes

Citations to articles in newspapers, magazines and journals must first be identified through an *index,* a guide that lists articles by subject and tells where they may be found. Although indexes to periodical literature have existed since the middle of the nineteenth century, the number of indexes to periodical literature has increased considerably over the past few years. A basic knowledge of indexes available is necessary in order to take advantage of the wealth of information.

The scope of indexes are: 1) *general* - these index articles in popular magazines or newspapers and include many subjects; and 2) *subject* - these index scholarly articles in journals and cover either several related subjects or one specific subject area.

Most of the paper versions of periodical indexes are published monthly with an annual cumulation in which all of the articles included throughout the year are arranged in one alphabet. A section in the front of each index usually lists alphabetically all the periodical titles indexed and gives the abbreviations used in the entries. There is also a "Key to the Abbreviations" used in the entries.

Printed Abstracts

An *abstract* is a type of index which gives the location of the literature cited and includes a summary of each item. Abstracts are important reference sources because the summary will tell users whether or not the literature is appropriate for their needs. Although the summaries in abstracts vary in length, there is usually sufficient information to determine the main ideas presented in the original work.

Electronic Indexes and Abstracts (Databases)

Although many indexes and abstracts continue to be published in printed form, indexes in electronic format have become the norm. The information which is included in the index or abstract is either on CD-ROM or online. That information, called a *database,* can then be searched more quickly and more efficiently than the paper indexes. Basic search techniques for electronic searching are discussed in Chapter 4.

Selecting an Index/Abstract

Finding periodical information is a multiple-step operation, as shown in the illustration below. The first step is to determine a topic and decide which keywords might be used to find articles about the topic. The next step is to determine whether popular or scholarly publications would be most relevant to the topic and then locate the appropriate index(es). To locate articles in popular magazines, the user may select one of the general indexes listed in this chapter. The subject indexes and abstracts will lead to more scholarly and technical information. Many of these indexes are listed in this chapter. Subject indexes are also listed in guides to literature. Abstracts and indexes may be located in the library catalog as a form subdivision following the subject. For example:

COMPUTERS--INDEXES
COMPUTERS--ABSTRACTS

The steps involved in selecting appropriate indexes for magazine and journal articles are shown below.

	SELECTING APPROPRIATE INDEXES
Step 1:	**Decide on a topic.** What keywords would you use to find articles about your topic?
Step 2:	Decide if the information you need will be found in **popular magazines** or in **scholarly journals.**
Step 3:	Select an **appropriate index** for your subject. Explore the various printed indexes, electronic databases, and online services available at your library. A selection of indexes and abstracts is listed below.

Humanities	**Science**	**Social Sciences**

America: History & Life
Historical Abstracts
Humanities Index
MLA International
  Bibliography
Music Index
Art Index
Arts & Humanities Citation
  Index
	Agricola
	Biological Abstracts
	Biological & Agricultural
	  Index
	General Science Index
	Science Citation Index
	ACM Guide to Computing
	Engineering Index
		ABI/Inform
		Education Index
		ERIC
		PsycLit
		Social Sciences Index
		Social Sciences Citation
		  Index
		PAIS International

	LEXIS/NEXIS, a full-text database, can be used for both popular and scholarly full-text articles in newspapers, magazines, and journals. VISTA can be useful for full-text articles or abstracts of magazine and newspaper articles. It also includes ABI/INFORM, a business database.
Step 4:	Interpret the citation correctly. Identify the full title of the magazine or journal, the volume, issue, pages, and date for the articles you select.
Step 5:	Copy, download, or print the citations you need.
Step 6:	Check the library catalog to see if the library has the magazine or journal title you need. Review the holdings record for the title to see where the library houses the particular issue you need.

The reference librarian can also advise on the proper index to use. It is a good idea in doing a thorough search of the literature to use both general and subject indexes and abstracts.

Using Indexes/Abstracts

General/Popular Indexes

Readers' Guide to Periodical Literature

Use of the various indexes is relatively simple; most contain the same basic information. If the researcher understands the arrangement of one, it is possible to use almost any of the other indexes, including those on CD-ROM. The following explanation of the print version of *Readers' Guide to Periodical Literature* is provided to illustrate a typical index to periodicals.

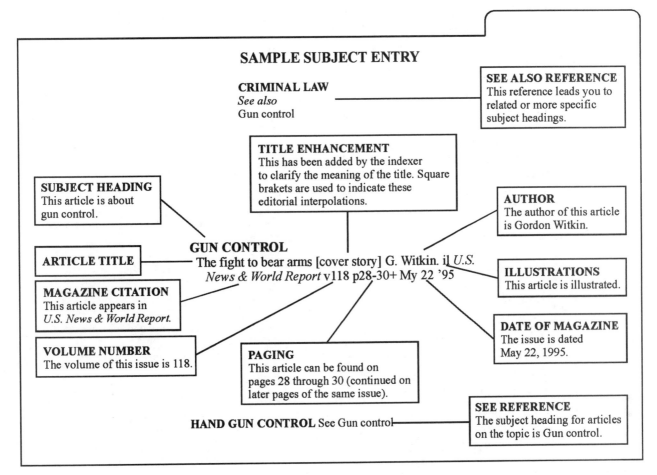

SAMPLE SUBJECT ENTRY

CRIMINAL LAW
See also
Gun control

SEE ALSO REFERENCE
This reference leads you to related or more specific subject headings.

TITLE ENHANCEMENT
This has been added by the indexer to clarify the meaning of the title. Square brakets are used to indicate these editorial interpolations.

SUBJECT HEADING
This article is about gun control.

AUTHOR
The author of this article is Gordon Witkin.

GUN CONTROL

ARTICLE TITLE
The fight to bear arms [cover story] G. Witkin. il *U.S. News & World Report* v118 p28-30+ My 22 '95

ILLUSTRATIONS
This article is illustrated.

MAGAZINE CITATION
This article appears in *U.S. News & World Report*.

DATE OF MAGAZINE
The issue is dated May 22, 1995.

VOLUME NUMBER
The volume of this issue is 118.

PAGING
This article can be found on pages 28 through 30 (continued on later pages of the same issue).

HAND GUN CONTROL See Gun control

SEE REFERENCE
The subject heading for articles on the topic is Gun control.

***Figure 9.1** Sample subject entry from* Readers' Guide to Perodical Literature

Readers' Guide to Periodical Literature also indexes articles by and about individuals. A sample name entry is shown below in Figure 9.2.

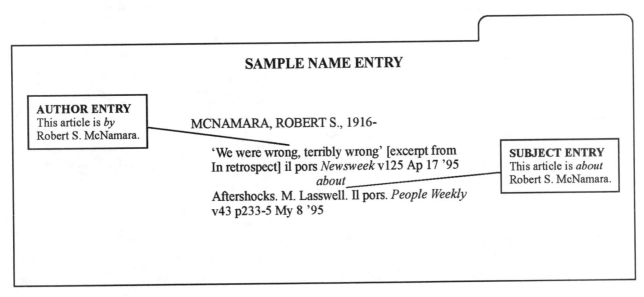

SAMPLE NAME ENTRY

AUTHOR ENTRY
This article is *by* Robert S. McNamara.

MCNAMARA, ROBERT S., 1916-

'We were wrong, terribly wrong' [excerpt from In retrospect] il pors *Newsweek* v125 Ap 17 '95
about

SUBJECT ENTRY
This article is *about* Robert S. McNamara.

Aftershocks. M. Lasswell. Il pors. *People Weekly* v43 p233-5 My 8 '95

***Figure 9.2** Sample name entry from* Readers' Guide to Perodical Literature

Each issue of *Readers' Guide* is divided into several important sections. These are: (1) a list of the periodicals indexed (Figure 9.3); (2) a list of other abbreviations used in the index (Figure 9.4); (3) the main body of the index consisting of subject and author entries (Figure 9.5); and (4) a listing of book reviews by authors with citations. (Book reviews will be discussed in Chapter 11.) Articles are listed alphabetically by subject and author.

PERIODICALS INDEXED

All data as of latest issue received

*50 Plus. $15. m (ISSN 0163-2027) 50 Plus, 99 Garden St., Marion, OH 43302
   Name changed to New Choices for the Best Years with December 1988

A

Ad Astra. $30. m (ISSN 1041-102X) National Space Society, 922 Pennsylvania Ave., S.E., Washington, DC 20003-2140
   Continuation of: Space World
Aging. $5. q (ISSN 0002-0966) Superintendent of Documents, U.S. Government Printing Office, Washington, DC 20402
America. $28. w (except first Saturday of the year, and alternate Saturdays in Jl and Ag) (ISSN 0002-7049) America Press Inc., 106 W. 56th St., New York, NY 10019
American Artist. $24. m (ISSN 0002-7375) American Artist, 1 Color Court, Marion, OH 43305
American Craft. $40. bi-m (ISSN 0194-8008) Membership Dept., American Craft Council, P.O. Box 1308-CL, Fort Lee, NJ 07024
American Film. $20. m (except bi-m Ja/F, Jl/Ag) (ISSN 0361-4751) Membership Services, American Film, P.O. Box 2046, Marion, OH 43305
American Health. $14.95. m (except F, Ag) (ISSN 0730-7004) American Health: Fitness of Body and Mind, P.O. Box 3015, Harlan, IA 51537
*American Heritage. $24. 8 times a yr (ISSN 0002-8738) American Heritage Subscription Dept., Forbes Building, 60 Fifth Ave., New York, NY 10011
American History Illustrated. $20. bi-m (ISSN 0002-8770) American History Illustrated, Box 8200, Harrisburg, PA 17105
The American Scholar. $19. q (ISSN 0003-0937) The American Scholar, Editorial and Circulation Offices, 1811 Q St., N.W., Washington, DC 20009
The American Spectator. $30. m (ISSN 0148-8414) American Spectator, P.O. Box 10448, Arlington, VA 22210
American Visions. $18. bi-m (ISSN 0884-9390) American Visions, P.O. Box 53129, Boulder, CO 80322-3129
Americana. $14.97. bi-m (ISSN 0090-9114) Americana Subscription Office, 205 W. Center St., Marion, OH 43302
Américas. $42. bi-m (ISSN 0379-0940) Américas, Journals Div., CUA Press, 303 Administration Bldg., Catholic University of America, Washington, DC 20064
Antiques. $38. m (ISSN 0161-9284) The Magazine Antiques, Old Mill Rd., P.O. Box 1975, Marion, OH 43306
Antiques & Collecting Hobbies. $22. m (ISSN 0884-6294) Antiques & Collecting Hobbies, Circulation Dept., 1006 S. Michigan Ave., Chicago, IL 60605
Architectural Digest. $39.95. m (ISSN 0003-8520) Architectural Digest, P.O. Box 10040, Des Moines, IA 50350
Architectural Record. $42.50. m (semi-m Ap, S) (ISSN 0003-858X) Architectural Record, P.O. Box 2025, Mahopac, NY 10541
Art in America. $39.95. m (ISSN 0004-3214) Art in America, 542 Pacific Ave., Marion, OH 43306
Art News. $32.95. m (q Je-Ag) (ISSN 0004-3273) Art News, Subscription Service, P.O. Box 969, Farmingdale, NY 11737
Astronomy. $24. m (ISSN 0091-6358) Astronomy, 21027 Crossroads Circle, P.O. Box 1612, Waukesha, WI 53187

B

*Better Homes and Gardens. $14.97. m (ISSN 0006-0151) Better Homes and Gardens, P.O. Box 4536, Des Moines, IA 50336
Bicycling. $15.97. 10 times a yr (ISSN 0006-2073) Rodale Press, Inc., 33 E. Minor St., Emmaus, PA 18049
BioScience. $96.50. m (bi-m Jl, Ag) (ISSN 0006-3568) BioScience Circulation, AIBS, 730 11th St. N.W., Washington, DC 20001-4584
Black Enterprise. $15. m (ISSN 0006-4165) Black Enterprise, Circulation Service Center, P.O. Box 3009, Harlan, IA 51537-3009
The Bulletin of the Atomic Scientists. $30. m (except F, Ag) (ISSN 0096-3402) Bulletin of the Atomic Scientists, Circulation Dept., 6042 S. Kimbark Ave., Chicago, IL 60637
Business Week. $39.95. w (except 1 issue in Ja) (ISSN 0007-7135) Business Week, P.O. Box 430, Hightstown, NJ 08520
Byte. $29.95. m (except 2 issues in O) (ISSN 0360-5280) Byte Subscriber Service, P.O. Box 551, Hightstown, NJ 08520

C

Car and Driver. $16.98. m (ISSN 0008-6002) Car and Driver, P.O. Box 2770, Boulder, CO 80302
The Center Magazine. $25. bi-m (ISSN 0008-9125) Center Magazine, Box 4068, Santa Barbara, CA 93103
   Continued by: New Perspectives Quarterly
Change. $40. bi-m (ISSN 0009-1383) Heldref Publications, 4000 Albemarle St., N.W., Washington, DC 20016
*Changing Times. $18. m (ISSN 0009-143X) Changing Times, The Kiplinger Magazine, Editors Park, MD 20782
Channels (New York, N.Y.: 1986). $65. m (bi-m Jl/Ag) (ISSN 0895-643X) Channels, Subscription Service Dept., P.O. Box 6438, Duluth, MN 55806
Children Today. $7.50. bi-m (ISSN 0361-4336) Superintendent of Documents, U.S. Government Printing Office, Washington, DC 20402
The Christian Century. $28. w (occasional bi-w issues) (ISSN 0009-5281) Christian Century, Subscription Service Dept., 5615 W. Cermak Rd., Cicero, IL 60650
Christianity Today. $24.95. semi-m (m Ja, My, Je, Jl, Ag, D) (ISSN 0009-5753) Christianity Today Subscription Services, 465 Gundersen Dr., Carol Stream, IL 60188
Commentary. $39. m (ISSN 0010-2601) American Jewish Committee, 165 E. 56th St., New York, NY 10022
Common Cause Magazine. $20. bi-m (ISSN 0271-9592) Common Cause Membership Dept., 2030 M St., N.W., Washington, DC 20036
Commonweal. $32. bi-w (m Christmas-New Year's and Jl, Ag) (ISSN 0010-3330) Commonweal Foundation, 15 Dutch St., New York, NY 10038
Compute!. $19.94. m (ISSN 0194-357X) Compute! Publications, Inc., P.O. Box 3245, Harlan, IA 51537
Congressional Digest. $28. m (bi-m Je-Jl, Ag-S) (ISSN 0010-5899) Congressional Digest Corp., 3231 P St., N.W., Washington, DC 20007
The Conservationist. $5. bi-m (ISSN 0010-650X) Conservationist Circulation Office, P.O. Box 1500, Latham, NY 12110
Conservative Digest. $18. bi-m (ISSN 0146-0978) Conservative Digest, P.O. Box 84905, Phoenix, AZ 85071

Figure 9.3 *Selected "Periodicals indexed" from* Reader's Guide to Periodical Literature. *(Copyright 1990 by the H. W. Wilson Company. Material reproduced by permission of the publisher.)*

ABBREVIATIONS

+	continued on later pages of same issue	Ltd	Limited
Ag	August	m	monthly
ann	annual	Mr	March
Ap	April	My	May
Assn	Association	N	November
Aut	Autumn	no	number
Ave	Avenue		
		O	October
bi-m	bimonthly		
bi-w	biweekly	p	page
bibl	bibliography	por	portrait
bibl f	bibliographical footnotes	pt	part
bldg	building		
		q	quarterly
Co	Company		
cont	continued	rev	revised
Corp	Corporation		
		S	September
D	December	semi-m	semimonthly
Dept	Department	Spr	Spring
		Sr	Senior
ed	edited, edition, editor	St	Street
		Summ	Summer
F	February	supp	supplement
f	footnotes		
		tr	translated, translation, translator
il	illustration,-s		
Inc	Incorporated	v	volume
introd	introduction, introductory		
		w	weekly
Ja	January	Wint	Winter
Je	June		
Jl	July	yr	year
Jr	Junior		
jt auth	joint author		

Figure 9.4 *"Abbreviations" used in entries in* Reader's Guide to Periodical Literature. *(Copyright 1990 by the H. W. Wilson Company. Material reproduced by permission of the publisher.)*

In an author entry, the author's full name appears first in heavy print on a line by itself. The author entries contain the same information as the subject entries except that the author's name is not repeated after the title. The December, 1995 issue of *Readers' Guide* lists several articles under the topic "women."

WOLVES—*cont.*
Wolves, moose, and tree rings on Isle Royale. B. E. McLaren and R. O. Peterson. bibl f il *Science* v266 p1555-8 D 2 '94

Control
Wolves: shoot first, investigate second [wolf shot dead after being released into River of No Return Wilderness] *Newsweek* v125 p60 Mr 27 '95

Photographs and photography
In the company of wolves. J. Brandenburg. il *National Wildlife* v33 p4-11 D '94/Ja '95
Pro profiles [R. McIntyre] K. McGee. il *Petersen's Photographic Magazine* v23 p46 N '94
WOMAN *See* Women

WOMAN SUFFRAGE
Canada
A battle not yet won. R. J. Taylor. il *Canada and the World Backgrounder* v60 no4 p4-7 '95

SUBJECT
HEADING   WOMEN

See also ——— CROSS REFERENCES
Alcohol and women
Beauty, Personal
Black women
Computers and women
Cuban American women
Drugs and women
Eskimos—Women
Farm women
Feminism
Heroes and heroines
Hispanic American women
Jewish women
Lebanese American women
Married women
Muslim women
Sex differences
Single women
Young women
1994 in review: the good news. K. Golden and G. Kirshenbaum. il *Ms.* v5 p46-53 Ja/F '95
Wonder women. il *Gentlemen's Quarterly* v65 p152-3 F '95

TITLE OF ARTICLE

Anatomy and physiology
See also
Breast
Menstruation
The great shape debate [fat and diseases] D. Points. il *Mademoiselle* v100 p77 Je '94
High heelhell [women's shoes] R. Berg. il *Vogue* v185 p224-5 F '95

MAGAZINE

Attitudes
Are there harder times ahead? [views of Albert Sidlinger] J. Schor. il *Working Woman* v20 p22 Mr '95
In our January/February 1994 issue, we asked: does women's equality depend on what we do about pornography? [survey results] J. Furio. il *Ms.* v5 p24-8 Ja/F '95

Clothing and dress
See Clothing and dress
Conferences
See also
World Conference on Women
Crimes against
See also
Abused women
Rape
Self defense for women
Sex crimes
Mosadi [worldwide mistreatment of women] R. J. Taylor. il *Canada and the World Backgrounder* v60 no4 p29-31 '95
Women and crime: do your fears fit the facts? D. Christiano. il *Glamour* v92 p134 S '94

Diseases
See also
AIDS (Disease) and women
Anorexia nervosa
Breast—Cancer
Bulimia
Menstruation—Disorders
Osteoporosis
Premenstrual syndrome
Sexually transmitted diseases
Hormonal havoc [effects on women's oral health] L. B. McGrath. il *American Health* v14 p23 Ja/F '95
Science by quota [NIH guidelines mandating inclusion of women and minorities in clinical research] S. Satel. *The New Republic* v212 p14+ F 27 '95

Too tired too often? Surprising new culprits. K. Feiden. il *McCall's* v121 p42+ S '94

Economic conditions
See also
Wages and salaries
Buoying women investors. P. J. Black. il *Business Week* p126-7 F 27 '95
The feminization of poverty. L. E. Taylor. il *Canada and the World Backgrounder* v60 no2 p16-18 '94
Mind over money [study by National Center for Women and Retirement Research; cover story] C. Willis. il *Working Woman* v20 p30-4+ F '95
Stop living paycheck to paycheck. C. E. Cohen. il *Working Woman* v20 p40-3+ Ja '95
What's your money personality? [quiz] C. L. Hayes. *Working Woman* v20 p35-7 F '95

Education
See also
Archer School for Girls (Los Angeles, Calif.)
Brearley School (New York, N.Y.)
Coeducation
Sex discrimination in education
Boys + girls together. M. Sajbel. il *Los Angeles* v40 p88-94+ Mr '95
Keep culture from keeping girls out of science. S. Tobias. *The Education Digest* v60 p19-20 S '94
Math challenged? [women tend not to excel in math] L. E. Taylor. il *Canada and the World Backgrounder* v60 no4 p20-1 '95
Riveters to rocket scientists: exploring the gender gap in quantitative fields [hard sciences] il *Change* v26 p41-4 N/D '94
The smarter sex? [academic performance of girls surpasses boys in British schools] L. Grant. il *World Press Review* v42 p45 Ja '95

Employment
See also
Black women—Employment
Married women—Employment   VOLUME PAGES
Mothers—Employment   DATE
Single mothers—Employment
Women—Occupations
1994 Hall of Shame [individuals, companies and organizations that hindered working women; cover story] il *Working Woman* v19 p28-31 D '94   ILLUSTRATED
The divorce backlash [judgments against working women] L. Mansnerus. il *Working Woman* v20 p40-5+ F '95
Joining the old boys' club [Canada] L. E. Taylor. il *Canada and the World Backgrounder* v60 no4 p12-13+ '95
Pregnant—and now without a job [discrimination] M. Lord. il *U.S. News & World Report* v118 p66 Ja 23 '95
What about women? [affirmative action] B. Cohn and others. il *Newsweek* v125 p22-5 Mr 27 '95
Women: where they stand in today's Los Angeles [study by the Los Angeles Women's Foundation] N. P. Jacoby. il *Los Angeles* v39 p74-84 Jl '94
Women working a third shift. H. Hartmann. il *Working Woman* v19 p16 D '94

History
Present since the creation [Alumnae Advisory Center] A. G. King. *American Heritage* v45 p24-6 D '94

Equal rights
See also
Sex discrimination
Woman suffrage
Women—Employment
Culture and women's rights: time to choose. L. D. Howell. *USA Today (Periodical)* v123 p53 Ja '95
Empowering women [discussion of December 1994 article] G. H. Brundtland. il *Environment* v37 p2-3+ Ja/F '95
Empowering women: an essential objective [International Conference on Population and Development] il *UN Chronicle* v31 p47 S '94
In our January/February 1994 issue, we asked: does women's equality depend on what we do about pornography? [survey results] J. Furio. il *Ms.* v5 p24-8 Ja/F '95
Invest in our future, invest in women. J. D. Hair. il *International Wildlife* v25 p26 Ja/F '95
The U.N. & women [World Conference on Women] M. Tax. *The Nation* v260 p405 Mr 27 '95
Women empowered: the earth's last hope [interview with N. Sadik] L. Conners. *New Perspectives Quarterly* v11 p13-15 Fall '94
Women, politics, and global management. L. C. Chen and others. bibl f il *Environment* v37 p4-9+ Ja/F '95

Figure 9.5 Sample page, Reader's Guide, *December, 1995, p. 758*

Under the subject heading, "women," a subheading of "employment" is found. The first article listed after the see also reference begins with the title, rather than an author. When no author is given, entries begin with the first word of the title, omitting the articles *a, an*, and *the* as the first word. Additional notes for illustrations, portraits, bibliographies and other material may be included in the entry.

Newspaper Indexes

Newspapers are a good source for information on local, state, national, and international levels. Periodical indexes give the library user references to many different publications, but the newspaper index usually accesses only one newspaper. The exceptions to this are *DataTimes* and *NewsBank*. Newspaper indexes generally have subject entries and do not give the exact title of an article; instead, they give a brief description of the article.

A sample page from *The New York Times Index* (Figure 9.6) on the topic of women is typical of the format of most newspaper indexes. In the November, 1995, issue, the index lists several additional subject headings for articles on "women." An article dealing with "Affirmative Action" and women will be found in the November 20 issue of *The New York Times*. The description gives additional information: the length of the article, the section, page, and column where the article may be found.

Since newspaper indexes usually cover only one newspaper, the year and title of the newspaper is located only on the front cover of the index, rather than listed in each individual citation. One must be careful to record the exact year and title of the newspaper index as part of the note-taking process.

Once an article is selected, the newspaper title must be searched in the online catalog to determine whether the library subscribes to the publication. The holdings record must be checked to determine the exact location of this issue. Figures 9.7-9.9 indicate that the November 20, 1995, issue of *The New York Times* are on microfilm.

The New York Times
INDEX
Master-Key to the News Since 1851

November 16-30, 1995

The presidents of three Balkan states, joined by United States Secretary of State Warren Christopher (right), initial an agreement to end four years of terror and bloodletting in Bosnia, ceremony at Wright-Patterson Air Force Base, Dayton, Ohio.

WOLF, MATT. See also ——— CROSS REFERENCE
Theater, N 26
WOLFE, GEORGE C. See also
Theater—Bring in Da Noise, Bring in Da Funk
(Revue), N 16,26
WOLFF, FRANCIS. See also
Books and Literature—Blue Note Years, The (Book),
N 19
WOLIN, WENDY SUE. See also
Murders and Attempted Murders, N 30
WOLRAICH, MARK L (DR). See also
Hyperactivity, N 22
WOLTERS KLUWER NV. See also
CCH Inc, N 28
WOMEN. See also ———————— SUBJECT HEADING
Abortion
Affirmative Action, N 20
Archeology and Anthropology, N 21
Basketball, N 19
Boxing, N 19
Colleges and Universities, N 16,17,20
Gambling, N 26
Hunting and Trapping, N 24
Jews, N 21
Labor, N 23,26
Millionaires and Billionaires, N 19
Motion Pictures—American President, the (Movie),
N 29
Motion Pictures—Toy Story (Movie), N 29
Philanthropy, N 26
Police, N 19
Pregnancy and Obstetrics
Restaurants, N 16
Roman Catholic Church, N 19,21,25,26
Sex Crimes, N 26
Stocks and Bonds, N 19
Tennis, N 20
United States Armament and Defense, N 19,22
Virginia Military Institute, N 20,27
Westchester County (NY), N 19
    Natalie Angier comment on revived use of word
'gal,' after years of dangling in feminist lexical limbo;

photo (S), N 19,IV,2:1
    Frank Rich Op-Ed column says two new movies,
The American President and Toy Story, suggest all is
not well as far as American family is concerned; says
American President reflects uneasiness about women
in power, such as Hillary Clinton, while Toy Story
reinforces with a vengeance pre-eminent role of
women in home (M), N 29,A,23:1
WOMEN'S PHILANTHROPIC COUNCIL. See also
Philanthropy, N 26
WOOD AND WOOD PRODUCTS
    Metropolitan Lumber draws people in construction to
11th Avenue between 45th and 46th Streets; photo
(M), N 26,XIII-CY,9:1
WOOL AND WOOLEN GOODS. See also
Apparel

DESCRIPTION
OF
ARTICLE

LENGTH
DATE
SECTION
COLUMN, PAGE

ADVERTISING AGE (MAGAZINE)
    Advertising Age dismisses editor Steve Yahn (S).
N 29,D,4:2
AEG AG
    German rail and engineering company AEG AG
says that it will split off its power transmission and
industrial automation units on Jan 1; says rest of
company will be reorganized to form holding company
(S), N 29,D,3:1
AEROMEXICO. See also
Airlines and Airplanes, N 29
AERONAUTICS. See also
Aerospace Industries and Sciences
Airlines and Airplanes
Balloons
Helicopters
**AEROSPACE INDUSTRIES AND SCIENCES. See
also**
Airlines and Airplanes
Space
AETNA LIFE & CASUALTY CO. See also
Aetna Life & Casualty Co, N 30
    Aetna Life & Casualty Co to sell its property and
liability insurance business to Travelers Group Inc for
$4 billion in cash and concentrate on health care and
life insurance; Travelers plans to merge Aetna
business with its own property and liability insurance
units, cutting $300 million of costs and some 3,300
jobs; Travelers chief executive Sanford I Weill says
merged units, which will form new company and later
sell stock to public, will run initially under both
names; table; graphs (M), N 30,D,1:5
AFFIRMATIVE ACTION. See also
Labor, N 26
    Drive to outlaw California's affirmative action
programs runs into serious financial and political
difficulties, and similar efforts nationwide have also
lost momentum; push to kill programs outright has
failed to stir much definitive legislative action or to
draw large amounts of money and manpower needed
to conduct petition drives; legislators, at strong
combined insistence of civil rights and women's
organizations, are increasingly assuming different
approach, calling for elimination of fixed race and sex
quotas and goals, but urging retention of outreach
programs (M), N 20,A,1:1
AFGHANISTAN. See also
Egypt, N 23
AFIFI, MOHAMMAD. See also
Murders and Attempted Murders, N 16
AFRICA. See also
Animals, N 29
Archeology and Anthropology, N 16
Electronic Information Systems, N 17
Photography, N 24
    Only 12 of Africa's 54 countries are linked to
Internet and list does not include Ivory Coast,
although by African standards it has well-developed
telephone network; this seen seen as a major obstacle
to continent's economic development (M), N 17,A,5:1
AFRICAN-AMERICANS. Use Blacks
AFRICAN NATIONAL CONGRESS. See also
South Africa, N 27
AGASSI, ANDRE. See also
Tennis, N 19,29
AGE, CHRONOLOGICAL. See also
Computer and Video Games, N 24
Heart, N 21
Police, N 28
AGED. See also
Age, Chronological
Blood Pressure, N 28
Exercise, N 30
Heart, N 21
Housing, N 17,19
Jews, N 19
Medicare
Medicine and Health, N 28
Nursing Homes
Pensions and Retirement Plans
Robberies and Thefts, N 19
Stocks and Bonds, N 18
Travel and Vacations, N 26
    Southington, Conn, police force is undertaking 2-day
sensitivity course that offers insights on dealing with
problems that face elderly (M), N 26,XIII-CN,1:1
    Residents of luxury cooperative that was once Police
Headquarters protest New York City's plan to locate
Project Open Door, Chinatown's largest senior center,
in the basement of the building; building fell into into
city's hands after its developers defaulted on real-
estate taxes; photos (M), N 26,XIII-CY,6:3

p.20   p.3

***Figure 9.6** Sample page from* The New York Times Index, *November 16-30, 1995.*

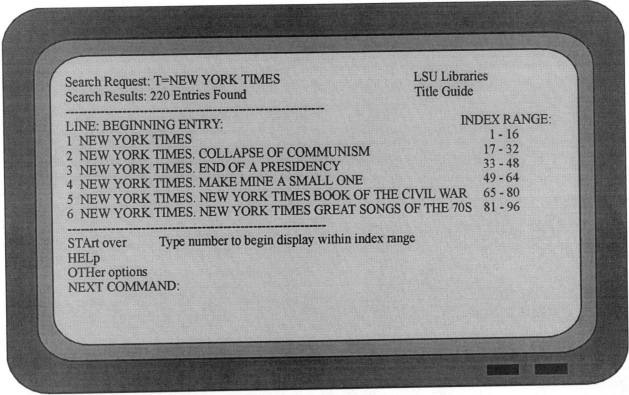

Figure 9.7 OPAC search request for periodical title, Title Guide screen.

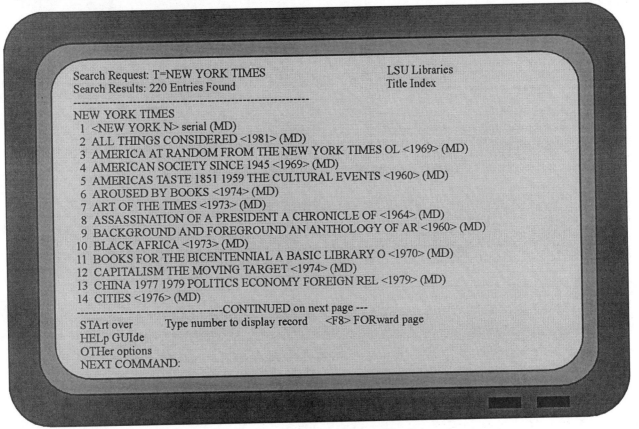

Figure 9.8 OPAC Title Index. Shows search request for periodical title.

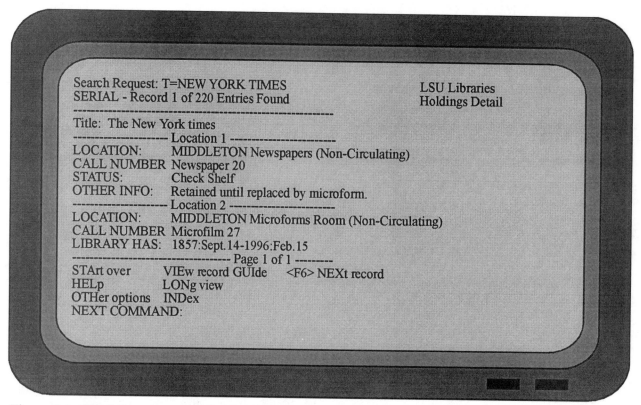

Figure 9.9 OPAC Search request, holdings screen.

Online Databases

LEXIS/NEXIS is a full-text database containing laws, regulations, court cases, law reviews, magazines, newspapers, journals, wire services, newsletters, company reports, transcripts of selected radio and television shows, and medical information. It includes over 7 million records and is an invaluable source of the most current news events. Full text of articles can be printed or downloaded. Academic libraries have special education subscriptions which restrict the use of the database to students for use in connection with course assignments. An illustration of the main menu of libraries and "NEWS" files is shown in Figure 9.10.

How to Search Lexis/Nexis

PLANNING THE SEARCH

1. Formulate the Search Statement
    Define a topic and choose relevant terms

    Consider all synonyms and variations. Standard plurals of terms are automatically searched. Lexis/Nexis is very literal and will search for words/terms exactly as they appear in the full texts of articles, laws or court cases. Identify words your ideal document would contain. Use commonly used terms.
- Simplify terms by truncating them

    ! Finds all possible words that could be made by adding letters to the root word (EXAMPLE: transport! finds transportation, transporting, transported, etc.)

    * Holds one space for a character anywhere in the word.
    (EXAMPLE: wom*n finds woman and women)

LEXIS/NEXIS

What it is: a full text database
online telephone connection

LEXIS: 120+ files in general law, directories, and specialized services; 7 million+ records

NEXIS: over 700 news sources (newspapers, magazines, wire service reports, transcripts of selected radio and TV shows)

Access and retrieval:
1. select a LIBRARY
2. select a FILE
3. enter a search
4. determine format of information: CITE, KWIC, FULL, SEGMENT

LIBRARIES -- PAGE 1 of 3

Please ENTER the NAME (only one) of the library you want to search.
- For more information about a library, ENTER its page (PG) number.
- To see a list of additional libraries, press the NEXT PAGE key.

NAME	PG	NAME	PG	NAME	PG	NAME	PG	NAME	PG	DNAME	PG
--- Types ---						--- Topics ---				---Int'l---	
General			Public	BUSFIN	2	Intellect		Medical		ASIAPC	4
-News-		- Legal -	Records	CMPCOM	2	Property		GENMED	14	DUTCH	4
NEWS	1	CODES	6 DOCKET	5 ENERGY	9	COPYRT	8	MEDLNE	14	CANADA	19
REGNWS	1	LAWREV	11 INCORP	5 ENTERT	2	PATENT	12			EUROPE	4
TOPNWS	1	LEGNEW	1 LEXPAT	5 ENVIRN	9	TRDMRK	13	Political		GERMAN	4
		MEGA	6 LIENS	5 INSURE	10			CMPGN	3	MDEAFR	4
		MODEL	11 VERDCT	5 MARKET	1	-Legal-		EXEC	3	NSAMER	4
				PEOPLE	2	BANKNG	7	LEGIS	3	WORLD	4
				SPORTS	2	FEDSEC	10			TXTLNE	18
Financial				TRANS	13	GENFED	6	--Tax--			
ACCTG	2					LABOR	11	FEDTAX	10	Assists	
COMPNY	2					PUBCON	12	STTAX	12	EASY	14
NAARS	2		Reference			STATES	6			GUIDE	14
		BUSREF	2							PRACT	14
		LEXREF	11							TERMS	14
										CATLOG	14

Please ENTER, separated by commas, the NAMES of the files you want to search.
You may select as many files as you want, including files that do not appear below, but you must enter them all at one time. To see a description of a file, ENTER its page (PG) number.

FILES - PAGE 1 of 79 (NEXT PAGE for additional files)

NAME	PG	DESCRIP	NAME	PG	DESCRIP	NAME	PG	DESCRIP
			------ THE NEWS LIBRARY ------					
--- Full-Text Group Files ---			---Full-Text By Type ---			--- Full-Text By Region ---		
CURNWS	1	Last 2 years	MAGS	3	Magazines	--- Papers & Wires ---		
ARCNWS	1	Beyond 2 years	MAJPAP	3	Major Papers	NON-US	1	English Non-US
ALLNWS	1	All News Files	NWLTRS	3	Newsletters	US	1	US News
			PAPERS	3	Newspapers	--- US Sources ---		
			SCRIPT	3	Transcripts	MWEST	3	Midwest
--- Group File Exclusions ---			WIRES	3	Wires	NEAST	3	Northeast
ALLABS	4	All Abstracts	------Hot Files------			SEAST	3	Sotheast
NONENG	1	Non-English News	HOTTOP	2	Hot Topics *	WEST	3	West
TXTNWS	1	Textline News *				-------- Assists --------		
TODAY	1	Today's News *				GUIDE	2	Descriptions *
						LNTHS	2	L-N Index Ths *

Files marked * may not be combined.
Press Alt-H for Help or SQ to End Session or Alt-Q to Quit Software.

***Figure 9.10** LEXIS/NEXIS Overview.*

-Connectors

> AND Finds documents containing both search terms.
> (EXAMPLE: unions and unemployment)
> OR Finds all documents containing either search term.
> (EXAMPLE: doctor or physician)
> W/n Finds documents containing words or phrases within words of each other.
> (EXAMPLE: homeless w/5 shelter)

-Date limiting

> date aft (after) a certain date
> (EXAMPLE: baseball and date aft 6/1989)
> date bef (before) a certain date
> (EXAMPLE: baseball and date bef 1990)
> date is (equals) a certain date
> (EXAMPLE: baseball and date is 10/17/93)
> You can enter dates using any of the following formats:
>> April 15, 1994
>> Apr 15, 1994
>> 4/15/94
>> 4-15-94

-Segment Searching

> You may limit your search to specific parts of a document. To see what segments are available in a given file, press <shift><F10> or <.se>. To search for terms within the syllabus of a court case, type: syllabus (abortion and minor). For reports on a company, type: company (Sony). For news stories on a particular topic, type: head(Simpson and wife). For news stories on a particular person, type: person(Helmut w/3 Kohl).

2. Choose a Library and File

> Consult Lexis/Nexis Library Contents and Alphabetical List. (See Figure 9.10)

DOING THE SEARCH

1. Logging on and entering the search

-Select Lexis/Nexis from the menu.

> Press <enter>. You will be asked to identify your search. It is not necessary; just press <enter>.

-Type selected library.

> This is a six-letter code, not a number. Press <enter>.

-Type selected file name

> Press <enter>.

-Type your search statement.

> Press <enter>.

-Choose a format

> Selected formats include:
> KWIC <F5> or <.kw>
> To view highlighted search terms with a small block of text on either side.
> CITE <F7> or <.ci>
> To see bibliographic citations of documents retrieved.
> FULL <F6> or <.fu>
> To view entire document.

2. To move within a document or from document to document.

> Use the following function keys or dot commands:
>
> | | | |
> |---|---|---|
> | Next page | F1 | .np |
> | Previous page | F2 | .pp |

Next document	F3	.nd
Previous document	F4	.pd

-To modify a search:

Type <m>, press <enter>, and type a connector and another term.
(EXAMPLE: and date aft 12/93)

3. To Print or Download

To see how long a document is, type <p> and press <enter>.

-You can only print individual screens.

For each screen, press <shift><print screen>.

-To download use session record.

After enabling session record, everything you view will be saved. To turn on, press <alt><F2>. Name your file to the appropriate disk drive (e.g.: a: drive). RC will be displayed in the bottom right hand corner of your terminal screen. Press <alt><F2> to turn off session record.

4. Changing Libraries or Files or Starting a New Search

Use the following function keys or dot commands:

Change File	F9	.cf
Change Library	F10	.cl
New Search	F8	.ns

SIGNING OFF

Press <alt><F9> or <alt q> or <.so>. You will be asked if you want to save your search. Type <n>, press <enter>.

(NOTE: The instructions above are for computers equipped with dial-in modems. Lexis/Nexis is also available on the Internet. On the Internet there will be a menu that replaces the function keys. In this case just move the mouse to the proper box on the menu and click to execute the command.)

The LEXIS/NEXIS instructions were prepared by Penny Beile, Reference Librarian, Louisiana State University Libraries.

Figures 9.11-9.13 show the results in LEXIS/NEXIS of a search for the terms: "women and equal pay." The search was in the CURNWS Library and the MAGS file.

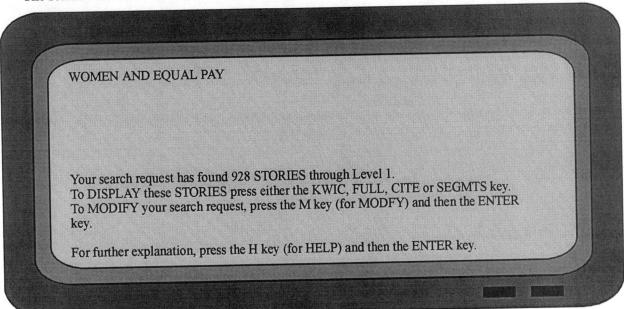

Figure 9.11 LEXIS/NEXIS. Initial search for women and equal pay.

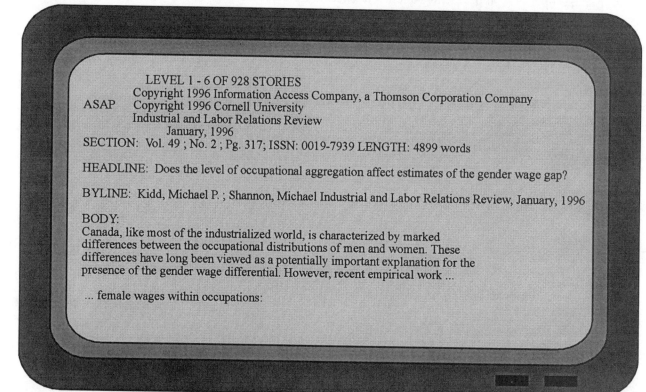

Figure 9.12. *LEXIS/NEXIS, CITE Format for Women and Equal Pay search.*

LEVEL 1 - 6 OF 928 STORIES
Copyright 1996 Information Access Company, a Thomson Corporation Company
ASAP   Copyright 1996 Cornell University
Industrial and Labor Relations Review
January, 1996
SECTION: Vol. 49 ; No. 2 ; Pg. 317; ISSN: 0019-7939 LENGTH: 4899 words

HEADLINE: Does the level of occupational aggregation affect estimates of the gender wage gap?

BYLINE: Kidd, Michael P. ; Shannon, Michael Industrial and Labor Relations Review, January, 1996

BODY:
Canada, like most of the industrialized world, is characterized by marked
differences between the occupational distributions of men and women. These
differences have long been viewed as a potentially important explanation for the
presence of the gender wage differential. However, recent empirical work ...

... female wages within occupations:

Figure 9.13 *LEXIS/NEXIS, KWIC Format. Citation for no. 6 in Figure 9.12.*

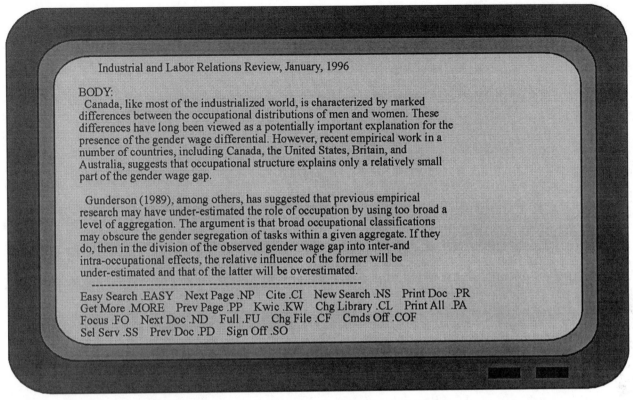

Figure 9.14 LEXIS/NEXIS, FULL TEXT citation for no. 6 in Figure 9.12.*

Subject/Scholarly Indexes

Scholarly information may be found in subject indexes and abstracts in both print and electronic formats. These may cover broad subject areas such as humanities, social sciences, or science; or they may cover more specific subject areas such as art, education, political science, and biology. Print versions of most subject indexes are searched similar to *Readers' Guide*. The steps outlined below are procedures to be followed when using a periodical database in an integrated (online catalog and periodical databases) system.

Finding Periodical Articles Using an Integrated Online Catalog/Periodical Database

Louisiana Online University Information System (LOUIS) provides access to periodical indexes along with the online catalogs of other libraries. Access to the indexes is restricted to LOUIS members. To use the indexes:

- from the main menu select INDEX (Figure 9.15);

- from the list of available indexes, select an appropriate database and type in the abbreviation of the selected database, e.g. *Social Sciences Index, SOCI,* (Figure 9.16);

- search by author, title, subject or keyword in the same manner as you would search the online catalog; for example: k=women and wages (Figure 9.17);

- when the results of your search appear, select a line number to view the complete citation (Figure 9.18);

- if the periodical is held by the library, a message indicating this will appear at the bottom of the screen;

- type **hol** to see if the library owns the specific issue needed and to get the call number and the location (Figure 9.19).

---

* Reprinted with permission of LEXIS-NEXIS, a division of Reed Elsevier, Inc. LEXIS® and NEXIS® are registered trademarks of Reed Elsevier Properties, Inc.

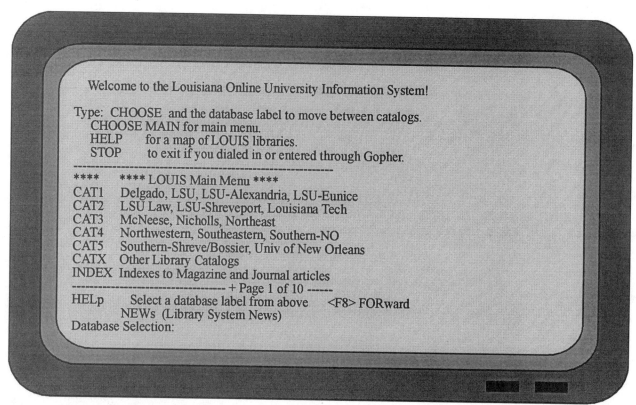

Welcome to the Louisiana Online University Information System!

Type: CHOOSE and the database label to move between catalogs.
    CHOOSE MAIN for main menu.
    HELP   for a map of LOUIS libraries.
    STOP   to exit if you dialed in or entered through Gopher.

****   **** LOUIS Main Menu ****
CAT1   Delgado, LSU, LSU-Alexandria, LSU-Eunice
CAT2   LSU Law, LSU-Shreveport, Louisiana Tech
CAT3   McNeese, Nicholls, Northeast
CAT4   Northwestern, Southeastern, Southern-NO
CAT5   Southern-Shreve/Bossier, Univ of New Orleans
CATX   Other Library Catalogs
INDEX Indexes to Magazine and Journal articles
---------------------------------- + Page 1 of 10 ------
HELp   Select a database label from above   <F8> FORward
              NEWs (Library System News)
Database Selection:

Figure 9.15 Main screen, state network system, LOUIS.

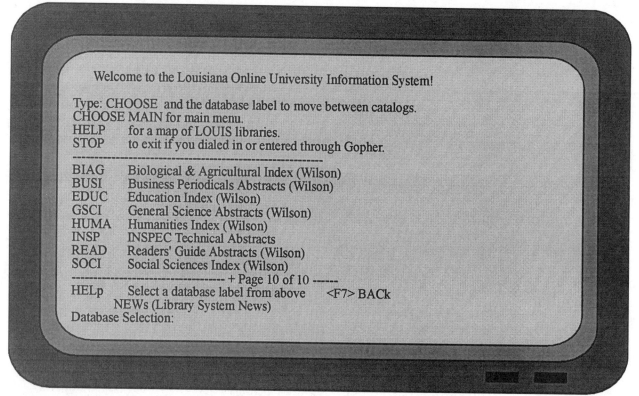

Welcome to the Louisiana Online University Information System!

Type: CHOOSE and the database label to move between catalogs.
CHOOSE MAIN for main menu.
HELP   for a map of LOUIS libraries.
STOP   to exit if you dialed in or entered through Gopher.

BIAG   Biological & Agricultural Index (Wilson)
BUSI   Business Periodicals Abstracts (Wilson)
EDUC   Education Index (Wilson)
GSCI   General Science Abstracts (Wilson)
HUMA   Humanities Index (Wilson)
INSP   INSPEC Technical Abstracts
READ   Readers' Guide Abstracts (Wilson)
SOCI   Social Sciences Index (Wilson)
---------------------------------- + Page 10 of 10 ------
HELp   Select a database label from above   <F7> BACk
              NEWs (Library System News)
Database Selection:

Figure 9.16 INDEX Screen from LOUIS.

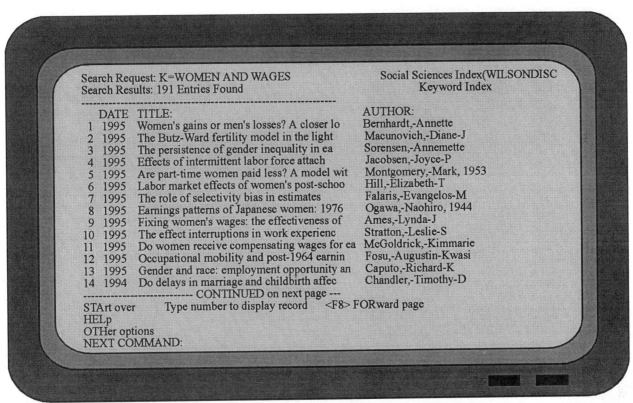

Figure 9.17 *Keyword search for women and wages in Social Sciences Index database.*

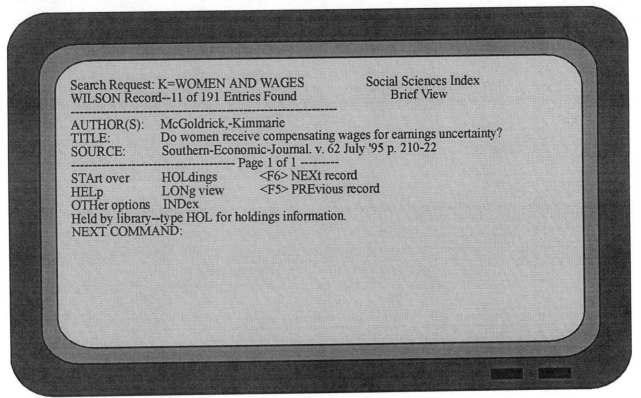

Figure 9.18 *Periodical Title Record, Social Sciences Index Database.*

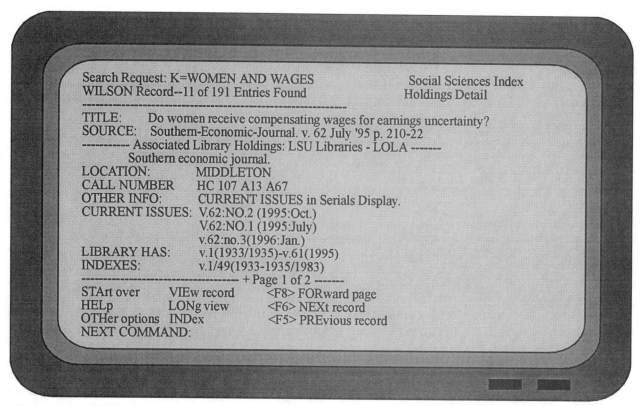

Search Request: K=WOMEN AND WAGES   Social Sciences Index
WILSON Record--11 of 191 Entries Found   Holdings Detail

TITLE: Do women receive compensating wages for earnings uncertainty?
SOURCE: Southern-Economic-Journal. v. 62 July '95 p. 210-22
----------- Associated Library Holdings: LSU Libraries - LOLA -------
          Southern economic journal.
LOCATION: MIDDLETON
CALL NUMBER   HC 107 A13 A67
OTHER INFO: CURRENT ISSUES in Serials Display.
CURRENT ISSUES: V.62:NO.2 (1995:Oct.)
                  V.62:NO.1 (1995:July)
                  v.62:no.3(1996:Jan.)
LIBRARY HAS: v.1(1933/1935)-v.61(1995)
INDEXES: v.1/49(1933-1935/1983)
------------------------------- + Page 1 of 2 -------
STArt over   VIEw record   <F8> FORward page
HELp   LONg view   <F6> NEXt record
OTHer options   INDex   <F5> PREvious record
NEXT COMMAND:

Figure 9.19 *LSU holdings record for entry.* *

Finding Periodical Articles Using a CD-ROM Database

Many indexes and abstracts are also available in CD-ROM format and are searched in the same manner as *Social Sciences Index* in the online example discussed above. Figure 9.20 shows an abstract retrieved from a search on the topic "wage differential" in *ABI/Inform*, a CD-ROM database.

CD-ROM databases usually display a labeled screen much like the OPAC record. The title, author, and journal citation can easily be interpreted in Figure 9.20. To retrieve the article in your library, the following steps are necessary:

■ conduct a title search for the periodical in the online catalog (Figure 9.21);

■ select the appropriate entry (look for a place of publication followed by the word "serial") and press Enter to get the serial record (Figure 9.22);

■ type **hol** to see if the library owns the specific issue needed and to determine the location (Figure 9.23).

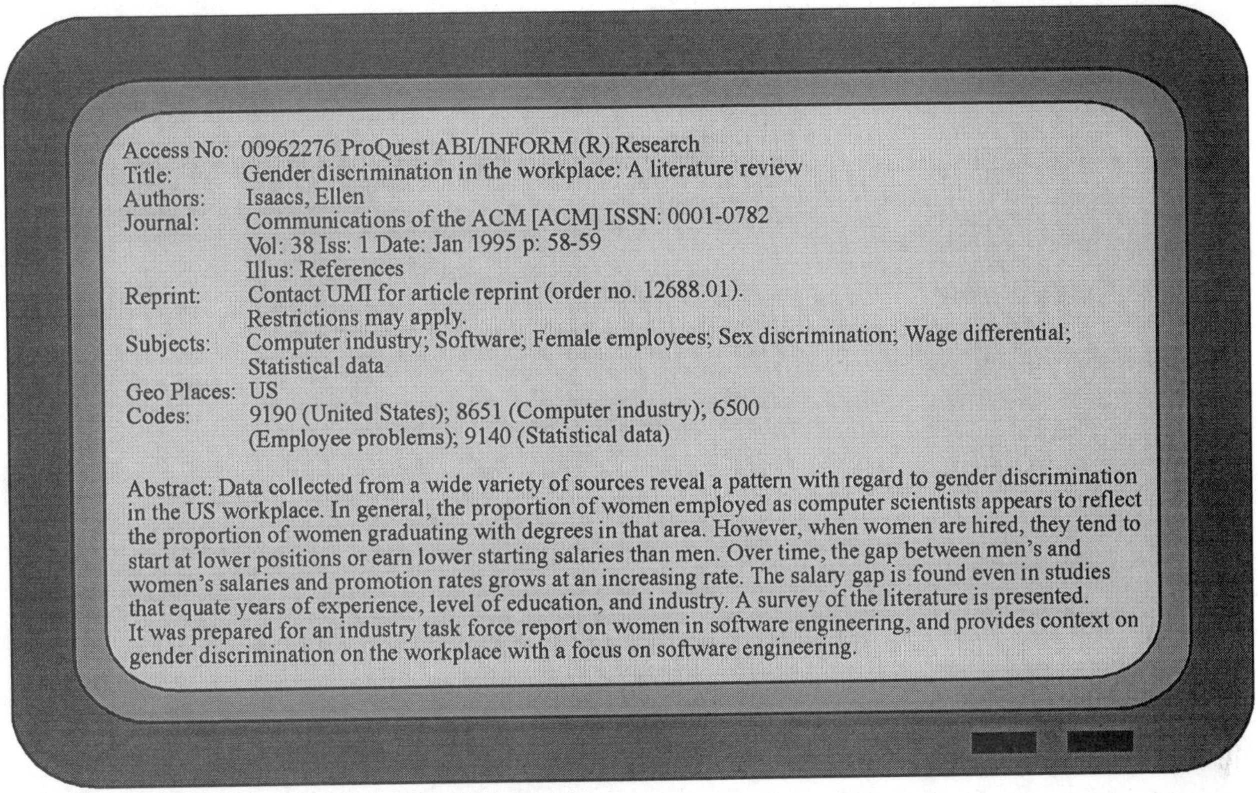

Access No: 00962276 ProQuest ABI/INFORM (R) Research
Title: Gender discrimination in the workplace: A literature review
Authors: Isaacs, Ellen
Journal: Communications of the ACM [ACM] ISSN: 0001-0782
Vol: 38 Iss: 1 Date: Jan 1995 p: 58-59
Illus: References
Reprint: Contact UMI for article reprint (order no. 12688.01).
Restrictions may apply.
Subjects: Computer industry; Software; Female employees; Sex discrimination; Wage differential;
Statistical data
Geo Places: US
Codes: 9190 (United States); 8651 (Computer industry); 6500
(Employee problems); 9140 (Statistical data)

Abstract: Data collected from a wide variety of sources reveal a pattern with regard to gender discrimination in the US workplace. In general, the proportion of women employed as computer scientists appears to reflect the proportion of women graduating with degrees in that area. However, when women are hired, they tend to start at lower positions or earn lower starting salaries than men. Over time, the gap between men's and women's salaries and promotion rates grows at an increasing rate. The salary gap is found even in studies that equate years of experience, level of education, and industry. A survey of the literature is presented. It was prepared for an industry task force report on women in software engineering, and provides context on gender discrimination on the workplace with a focus on software engineering.

Figure 9.20 Sample abstract from ABI/Inform.*

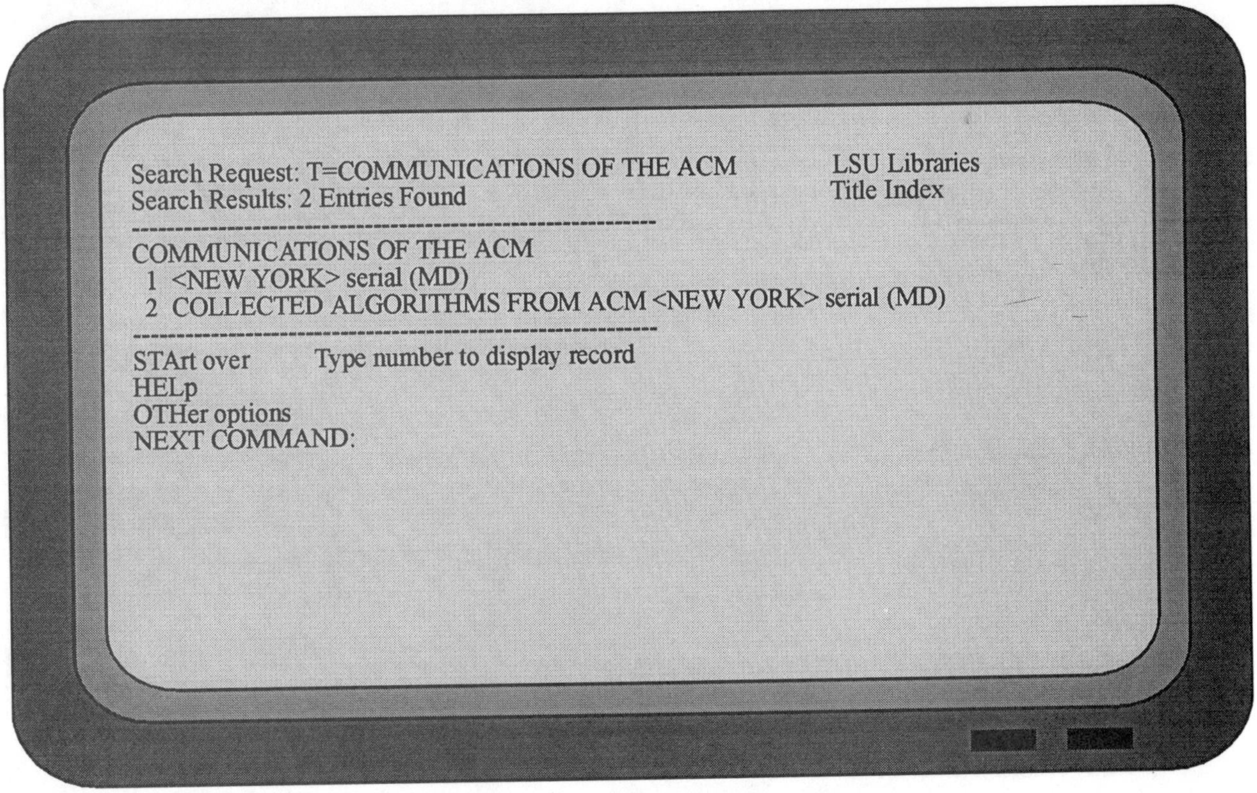

Search Request: T=COMMUNICATIONS OF THE ACM   LSU Libraries
Search Results: 2 Entries Found   Title Index

COMMUNICATIONS OF THE ACM
  1 <NEW YORK> serial (MD)
  2 COLLECTED ALGORITHMS FROM ACM <NEW YORK> serial (MD)

STArt over   Type number to display record
HELp
OTHer options
NEXT COMMAND:

Figure 9.21 OPAC periodical title search.

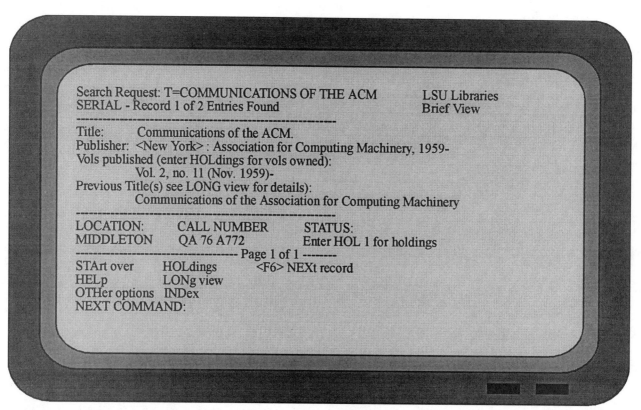

Figure 9.22 *OPAC periodical holdings detail.*

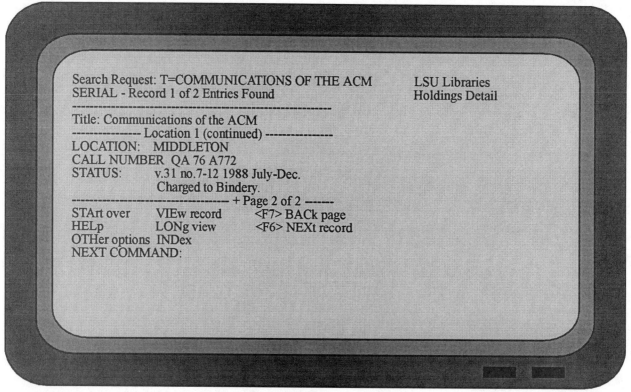

Figure 9.23 *OPAC periodical holdings detail, continued.*

CARL Database

CARL UnCover is both an index to scholarly journals and a *document delivery* service. That is, individuals or libraries can arrange to have articles faxed or mailed directly to them, usually within 24 hours of the request. Access to the UnCover database is free; document delivery is not. The CARL UnCover database is an index to the tables of contents of over 17,000 unique journals. It covers all subject areas, but concentrates heavily on the sciences and social sciences. CARL UnCover is available on the Internet.

HOW TO SEARCH CARL UNCOVER

Logging on
1) Telnet to this resource and log in as a guest of the system (that is, without a "profile").
   href=telnet://database.carl.org
2) Connect to CARL. Type 5 and press Enter when asked to identify your terminal. (Your terminal type is VT100.)
3) Type 1 (one) and press Enter to select UnCover.
4) Press Enter several times until the "Welcome to UnCover" screen appears. (You do not need to have or create a profile to search UnCover.)

How to Search UnCover
Uncover may be searched in any of three ways:
To use UnCover, enter: W for WORD or TOPIC search
                        N for AUTHOR search
                        B to BROWSE by journal title
Follow the commands at the bottom of each screen for searching.
For additional help while logged into UnCover: Type h2 and press Enter.
You may use Boolean and logical connectors:
 AND, OR, AND NOT, BUT NOT (For help with Boolean searching type **?b.**
Use date qualifiers to limit a search by date:
          //Wsolar energy [>1990]
          //Wpoetry [=1989]
          //Bdimensions [1992-1993]

To Exit: Press Enter until the option "Type S to try your search in another database" appears.
Type s> and press Enter to stop using UnCover.
Type //exit at the WELCOME TO THE CARL CORPORATION menu.
Type //exit again, if necessary, until disconnected from CARL.
Close the telnet window, if necessary.

Printed Abstracts

A printed abstract uses a two-step process to find citations to scholarly articles. First, a subject index similar to that in *Readers' Guide* is used to find an appropriate subject heading. A brief description is listed under the subject heading, with an *abstract number* or *accession number* to locate the abstract of the individual article.

- Using the subject index, look under the subject heading (Figure 9.24).

- Select an appropriate article, e.g. abstract number.

- Turn to the abstract section and look for the abstract number (Figure 9.25).

- To retrieve the article, conduct a search for the journal title in the library catalog and follow the steps as outlined above for retrieving the *ABI/Inform* article.

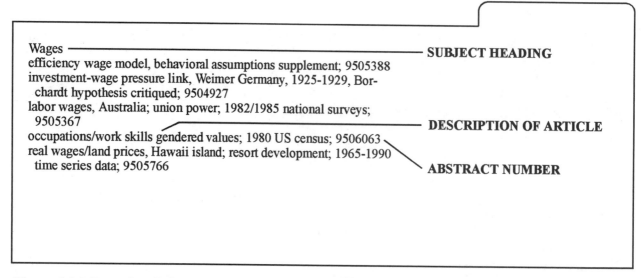

Wages ——————————————————————— **SUBJECT HEADING**
efficiency wage model, behavioral assumptions supplement; 9505388
investment-wage pressure link, Weimer Germany, 1925-1929, Bor-
   chardt hypothesis critiqued; 9504927
labor wages, Australia; union power; 1982/1985 national surveys;
   9505367 ———————————————————————— **DESCRIPTION OF ARTICLE**
occupations/work skills gendered values; 1980 US census; 9506063
real wages/land prices, Hawaii island; resort development; 1965-1990
   time series data; 9505766 ————————————————— **ABSTRACT NUMBER**

Figure 9.24   Entry from Subject Index, Sociological Abstracts, volume 43, number 3, June, 1995, p. 1709.

Using the abstract number for the desired article, (9506063), you would then turn to the main entry section of *Sociological Abstracts* and find the abstract, as shown below in Figure 9.26.

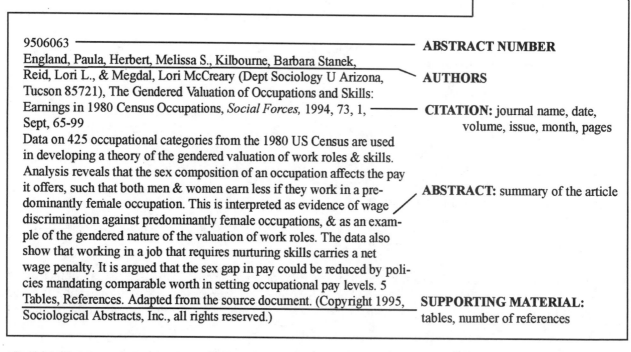

9506063 ——————————————————————— **ABSTRACT NUMBER**
England, Paula, Herbert, Melissa S., Kilbourne, Barbara Stanek,
Reid, Lori L., & Megdal, Lori McCreary (Dept Sociology U Arizona, —— **AUTHORS**
Tucson 85721), The Gendered Valuation of Occupations and Skills:
Earnings in 1980 Census Occupations, *Social Forces*, 1994, 73, 1, ——— **CITATION:** journal name, date,
Sept, 65-99   volume, issue, month, pages
Data on 425 occupational categories from the 1980 US Census are used
in developing a theory of the gendered valuation of work roles & skills.
Analysis reveals that the sex composition of an occupation affects the pay
it offers, such that both men & women earn less if they work in a pre-
dominantly female occupation. This is interpreted as evidence of wage   —— **ABSTRACT:** summary of the article
discrimination against predominantly female occupations, & as an exam-
ple of the gendered nature of the valuation of work roles. The data also
show that working in a job that requires nurturing skills carries a net
wage penalty. It is argued that the sex gap in pay could be reduced by policies mandating comparable worth in setting occupational pay levels. 5
Tables, References. Adapted from the source document. (Copyright 1995, —— **SUPPORTING MATERIAL:**
Sociological Abstracts, Inc., all rights reserved.)   tables, number of references

Figure 9.25   Main entry section, Sociological Abstracts, volume 43, number 3, June, 1995.

Although the summaries in some abstracting services may be quite lengthy, they should not be used in lieu of the article itself. It is important to locate the article to get the complete information. The citation in the bibliography should cite the article, not the abstract.

———————————

Citation Indexes

Citation indexes list the works that are cited by authors in writing books, articles, theses and dissertations, conference proceedings, and the like. Citation indexes are useful in tracking all the literature related to a particular topic and for following cited references of a particular author or title. Although citation indexes are intended to list works cited, they usually include subject indexes. The author index, called a *Source Index,* lists the original author's work and the sources which he/she cited. The major citation indexes are: *Arts and Humanities Citation Index, Social Sciences Citation Index*, and *Science Citation Index.*

A sample entry for the subject women is shown below from the *Social Sciences Citation Index, Permuterm Subject Index.* (Figure 9.26.)

```
WOMEN

VULNERABLE    OZOWA M N
WAGES         MCGOLDRICK K
WAITING       MILLER D A
```

Figure 9.26 *Subject entries from* Permuterm Subject Index, Social Sciences Citation Index, *May to August, 1995, p. 5073.*

An article *on "women and wages"* by K. McGoldrick is listed in the index. You would then use the *Source Index* of *Social Sciences Citation Index* to locate the full citation for McGoldrick's article, as shown below in Figure 9.27.

```
MCGOLDRICK K ─────────────────────────────── AUTHOR
DO WOMEN RECEIVE COMPENSATING WAGES FOR EARNINGS─── TITLE OF ARTICLE
UNCERTAINTY?
S ECON J      62(1):210-222        95    12R  RH033 ──── CITATION: journal name;
UNIV RICHMOND, RICHMOND, VA 23173, USA                    volume and issue;
BELLANTE D    81    IND LABOR RELATI    APR    408        pages;
CLARK D       88    SO EC J             JAN    701        number of references
FEINBERG R    81    SO EC J             JUL    156        used in this article;
              81    APPLIED EC          JUN    257        purchasing information
JOHNSON W     77    DISTRIB EC WELL            379
KING A        74    IND LABOR RELATI    JUL    586
LEIGH J P     83    Q REV ECON BUS      MAY     54
LEVHARI       74    AM EC REV           DEC    950
ORAZEM P      86    REV EC STATSTIC     MAY    265
SIOW A        84    ECOMETRICA          MAY    631
SIOW A        90    INT EC REV          FEB    195
```

Figure 9.27 *Complete citation for the article listed in Figure 9.26. Entry from* Source Index, Social Sciences Citation Index, *May to August, 1995, p. 3230.*

A sample display for interpreting citations in this work is located in the front of the index, as shown in Figure 9.28.

Source Index

To locate a full description of a source item, look up the first author. Under a given name, publications of primary authorship are described first. Items of secondary authorship follow, cross-referenced to the first author by a SEE reference.

Sample Display

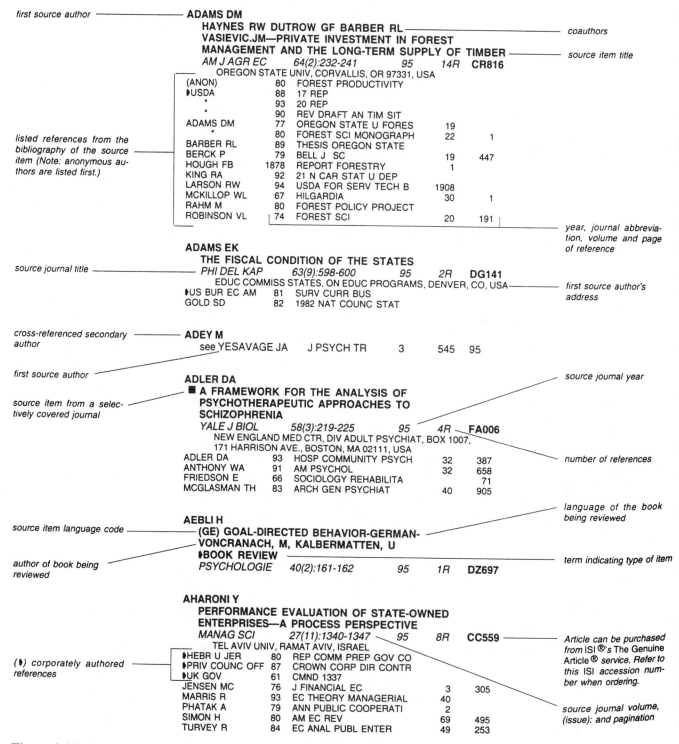

Figure 9.28 Sample Display, Source Index, Social Sciences Citation Index.

Selected Periodical Indexes

General/Popular

Magazines

InfoTrac. Los Altos, CA: Information Access, 1985-.
>   Provides access to three databases—*Infotrac, Government Publications Index,* and *LegalTrac*. Includes citations to over half a million articles from more than 1,000 popular magazines and business and professional journals published since January 1982. The index to United States Government documents provides access to about a quarter million documents published since 1979. Available online and on CD-ROM.

The Magazine Index. Los Altos, CA: Information Access, 1976-.
>   Arranged alphabetically by author and subject. Includes news reports, editorials on major issues, product evaluations, biographies, short stories, poetry, recipes and reviews. On microfilm. Available online and on CD-ROM.

LEXIS/NEXIS. Dayton:Reed Elsevier.
>   Full-text database for legal, business, and current issues, including U.S. Supreme Court decisions, lower court cases, and a host of other databases in the legal field. Covers most large city newspapers and some international newspapers, television news transcripts, news releases, company reports, and some bibliographic citation databases, including *ABI/Inform* and *Medline*. Dates of coverage varies. Available online.

Poole's Index to Periodical Literature 1802-1897. 7 vols. Boston: Houghton, 1882-1908.
>   A subject index covering American and English magazines published in the 1800s. Entries do not include the date of articles. Alphabetical list of periodicals with chronological number which leads the reader to the date.

Readers' Guide to Periodical Literature Index/Abstracts. New York: H. W. Wilson, 1900-.
>   The most widely used and well known of all the periodical indexes. Indexes 240 popular and general interest magazines and *The New York Times*. Dates from 1900. Covers news and current events, business, fine arts, sports, fashion, health, politics, education, science, photography, religion and foreign affairs. Includes biographies, obituaries, recipes, and editorials. (Available online and on CD-ROM with abstracts cover 1990 to the present; index, from 1983.)

Newspapers

DataTimes. Oklahoma City: DataTimes, 1985-.
>   Online newspaper database accessing several leading newspapers and newswires, including the *Washington Post,* the *Dallas Morning News*, the *San Francisco Chronicle* and others. Available online.

Index to the *Christian Science Monitor International Daily Newspaper*. Boston: Christian Science Monitor, 1960-.
>   Titles of articles listed under subject with day, month, section, page and column noted. Available online.

New York Times Index. New York: New York Times Co., 1913-.
>   Earlier series covers the years 1851-1912.
>   Subject index to *The New York Times* newspaper. Published twice monthly with annual cumulations. Available online.

NewsBank Index. New Canaan, CT: Newsbank, Inc., 1982-.
>   Microfiche collection covering current events and issues from newspapers in over 100 cities. Topics are arranged alphabetically by name and subject. To find the correct *NewsBank* microfiche file, use the year, microfiche category, and microfiche number cited in the index. Available on CD-ROM.

The Times Index (London). Reading, England: Newspaper Archive Development, 1957-.

> Provides author and subject index to the daily *Times*, the *Sunday Times*, the *Times Literary Supplement*, the *Times Educational Supplement*, and the *Times Higher Education Supplement*. Available online.

Wall Street Journal Index. New York: Dow Jones, 1959-.

> Emphasizes financial news from the newspaper. Includes *Barron's Index*, a subject and corporate index to *Barron's Business and Financial Weekly*. Available online.

The Washington Post Newspaper Index. Ann Arbor, MI: UMI, 1978-.

> Useful for coverage of news from the nation's capital. Available online.

Subject/Scholarly

Broad Subject

Humanities Index. New York: H. W. Wilson, 1974-.

> Author and subject index to articles in more than 345 English language periodicals in the humanities: archaeology, classical studies, folklore, history, language and literature, theology, and related subjects. Available online and on CD-ROM.

Social Sciences Index. New York: H. W. Wilson, 1974-.

> Author and subject index for articles in more than 350 periodicals. Includes anthropology, area studies, economics, environmental science, geography, law and criminology, medical science, political science, psychology, public administration, sociology, and related subjects. Available online and on CD-ROM.

General Science Index. New York: H. W. Wilson, 1978-.

> A cumulative subject/author index to 109 English language science periodicals. Includes astronomy, atmospheric science, biology, botany, chemistry, earth science, environment and conservation, food and nutrition, genetics, mathematics, medicine and health, microbiology, oceanography, physics, physiology, psychology, and zoology. Available online and on CD-ROM.

Agriculture

Agricola. Beltsville, MD; U.S. National Agricultural Library. 1972-.

> Most records include agricultural literature in both journal articles and book chapters. International coverage includes some monographs, series, microforms, audio-visuals, maps, and other types of materials. Available online and on CD-ROM.

Biological Abstracts. Philadelphia, PA: BIOSIS. 1989-.

> Bibliographic database containing citations with abstracts to the world's biological and biomedical literature. Updated quarterly. Available online and on CD-ROM.

Biological and Agricultural Index. New York: H. W. Wilson, 1964-. (Continues *Agricultural Index.* 1916-1964.)

> A cumulative subject index to 226 English language periodicals in the fields of biology, agriculture, and related sciences. Available online and on CD-ROM.

Art and Humanities

American History & Life. Santa Barbara, CA: CLIO Press. 1964-.

> Scholarly material in American history and culture. Indexes journal articles, books, book chapters, films, videos, microforms, and dissertations. Citations and abstracts. Available on CD-ROM.

Art Index. New York: H. W. Wilson, 1933-.

> Includes citations to articles on painting, sculpture, architecture, ceramics, graphic arts, landscape architecture, archaeology, and other related subjects. Available online and on CD-ROM. *Art Abstracts* on CD-ROM also available with coverage since 1993.

Arts and Humanities Citation Index. Philadelphia: Institute for Scientific Information, 1976-.
    Accesses about 6,900 journals in literature, poetry, plays, short stories, music, film, radio, dance, theater, etc. Available online and on CD-ROM.

Historical Abstracts. Santa Barbara, CA: CLIO Press. 1971-.
    Research in world history but not American. Two sections: Modern History 1450-1914, and Twentieth Century 1914 to the present. Citations from journals, books, dissertations, and audio-visual materials. Available online and on CD-ROM.

MLA International Bibliography. New York: Modern Language Association of America. 1981-.
    Scholarly research in over 3,000 journals and series; covers relevant monographs, working papers, proceedings, bibliographies and other formats. Available online and on CD-ROM.

Business

ABI/Inform. Ann Arbor, MI: UMI, 1984-. CD-ROM.
    Indexes over 800 business and trade journals. Citations and abstracts to articles in all business-related topics, economics, and managerial science. Allows keyword searching and several print options. Also available online.

Business Index. Los Altos, CA: Information Access, 1979-.
    Provides a cumulative author/subject index on microfilm to over 800 business periodicals, including articles in the *Wall Street Journal, Barron's*, and the financial section of *The New York Times*. Also covers articles relating to business appearing in over 1,100 general and legal periodicals. Available online and on CD-ROM.

Business Periodicals Index. New York: H. W. Wilson, 1958-. Continues *Industrial Arts Index*. 1913-1957.
    Citations to articles on advertising, banking and finance, marketing, accounting, labor and management, insurance, and general business. Good source for information about an industry and about individual companies. Available online and on CD-ROM.

Education

CIJE, Current Index to Journals in Education. Phoenix: Oryx, 1969-.
    Provides citations and abstracts to articles in over 700 major educational and education-related journals. Included in *ERIC* CD-ROM.

Education Index. New York: H. W. Wilson, 1929-.
    Subject index to educational literature including 339 periodicals, pamphlets, reports, and books. Includes counseling and personnel service, teaching methods and curriculum, special education and rehabilitation, educational research. Available online and on CD-ROM.

ERIC. Rockville, MD: U.S. Department of Education, Office of Educational Research and Improvement, 1966-. CD-ROM.
    Contains a combination of the *Resources in Education* (RIE) file of ERIC document citations and the *Current Index to Journals in Education* (CIJE) journal article citations from over 750 professional journals. Includes all aspects of education. Also available online.

Public Affairs

PAIS International. New York: Public Affairs Information Service, 1915-. (Previous title *PAIS Bulletin*.)
    Citations to articles on international affairs, public administration, political science, history, economics, finance, and sociology. Both U.S. and U.N. government documents are included, as well as books, pamphlets, society publications, and periodicals. Published twice monthly; cumulates annually. Available online and on CD-ROM.

Science and Technology

Applied Science and Technology Index. New York: H. W. Wilson, 1958-. Continues *Industrial Arts Index*. 1913-1957.

Citations to articles in the fields of aeronautics, automation, construction, electricity, engineering, and related subjects. Available online and on CD-ROM.

Biological Abstracts (Described under Agriculture.)

Biological and Agricultural Index. (Described under Agriculture.)

Chemical Abstracts. Columbus, OH: American Chemical Society. 1907-.

Contains literature related to chemistry appearing in books, reports, annotated documents, and about 14,000 journals and conferences. Available online and on CD-ROM.

Engineering Index. Baltimore: Engineering Index, Inc., 1984-.

Contains abstracts of literature published in engineering journals, technical reports, monographs, and conference proceedings. Issued monthly and cumulated annually. Annual volumes are divided into subject volumes and an author index volume. Available online and on CD-ROM as COMPENDEX.

GEOREF. Alexandria, VA: American Geological Institute. 1990-.

Comprehensive coverage of more than 4,500 international journals, books, proceedings, dissertations, and maps in geology and geography. Covers 1785- (North American), 1967- (Worldwide). Available online and on CD-ROM.

Inspec. Stevage, Herts., England: Institution of Electrical Engineers. 1993-.

Indexes scientific and technical literature in electrical engineering, electronics, communications, control engineering, computers and computing, and information technology. Covers 1969-. Available online and on CD-ROM.

MathSci Disc. Providence, RI: American Mathematical Society. CD-ROM.

Includes information relating to mathematics, statistics, physics, and computer science. Covers 1973-. Also available online.

Medline. Bethesda, MD: U.S. National Library of Medicine.

Designed primarily for the medical professional, but is also useful to lay persons interested in medical-related topics. Covers 1966-. Available online and on CD-ROM.

SCI, Science Citation Index. Philadelphia: Institute for Scientific Information, 1965-.

Bimonthly with calendar year cumulations. Published in three sections:

Source Index	- lists all journals indexed with abbreviations used in the entries. Use to locate authors.
Permuterm Subject	- has the full information on the article (title of article, name of journal, volume, issue number, pages, and date).
Citation Index	- used to locate authors' names cited in other publications.

Available online and on CD-ROM.

Social Sciences

NCJRS Documents Database. National Institute of Justice/National Criminal Justice Reference Service. CD-ROM.

Contains references to periodical articles, research reports, books and unpublished materials from private sources as well as from local, state, and national governments. Covers 1972-. Also available online.

PsycInfo. Washington, D.C.: American Psychological Association. CD-ROM.

Comprehensive, international coverage of the psychological literature. Indexes 1300 journals, technical reports, dissertations, and books. *PsycLit* is a separate index with the same type coverage, but not as comprehensive as *PsycInfo*. Covers 1967-. Also available online.

Psychological Abstracts. Arlington, VA: American Psychological Association, 1927-.
 Abstracts of journal articles, monographs, and reports on psychology and related studies arranged by major classification groups. Includes author and subject index. Issued monthly. Available online and on CD-ROM. CD-ROM versions are called *PsycLit* and *PsycInfo*.

Sociological Abstracts. New York: Sociological Abstracts, 1952-.
 International in scope; covers articles from journals concerned with sociology. CD-ROM version called *SocioFile*. Also available online.

SSCI, Social Sciences Citation Index. Philadelphia: Institute for Scientific Information, 1966-.
 Indexes most recent significant journal literature in social, behavioral, and related sciences. Organized like *SCI*.

Instructor: _____   Name: _____

Course/Section: _____   Date: _____

Review Questions for Chapter Nine

1. Give three reasons why periodical materials are important sources for research.

2. List three different kinds of indexes discussed in this chapter.

3. What is the difference in scope between a magazine or journal index and a newspaper index?

4. How does an abstract differ from an index?

5. What is the purpose of a citation index?

6. Name two electronic indexes which could be useful in searching for popular articles.

7. Explain the difference between a popular and a scholarly index.

8. List three broad subject indexes.

9. How does one locate periodical articles in the library after the information has been found in an index?

Instructor: _____　**Name:** _____

Course/Section: _____　**Date:** _____

Readers' Guide Exercise

Answer the following questions based upon the entries taken from *Readers' Guide to Periodical Literature*, Figure 9.5.

1. What subject heading would you use to locate additional information on women and employment?

2. Who wrote the article on women suffrage?

3. Is the first article about women's employment illustrated? Justify your answer.

4. In which magazines can you locate some articles on equal rights for women?

5. What subject heading would you look under for articles on women and crime?

6. Which magazines contain articles on women's attitudes?

7. What does the p4-9+ mean in the last article in the right column?

8. Who wrote the article on women's history?

9. What do you consult in your library to locate call numbers or titles of magazines?

10. List the steps you would need to take to retrieve one of these articles.

Instructor: _____   Name: _____

Course/Section: _____   Date: _____

Periodical Index Exercise

Locate two different periodical indexes or abstracts which have references to articles on your topic. Give the following information:

First periodical index or abstract

1. Method used to find the index:

2. Entry used in library catalog to locate information (if applicable):

3. Call number of index or abstract (if applicable):

4. Title of index or abstract:

5. What are the subjects covered in the index or abstract?

6. How is the index arranged? (Alphabetically or by broad topics?) (Applies only to print indexes.)

7. Subject heading(s) or keywords used in index for an article on your topic:

8. Citation to the article as it appeared in the index or abstract:

   Author: Title of the magazine or journal:

   Title of the article:

   volume / issue: pages of article: date:

9. Full title of periodical:

10. Is the issue cited above in your library? If so, where is it located?

11. Call number and location of the issue you need:

12. Bibliographic citation for the article: (Use the examples in Chapter 14.)

Second periodical index

1. Method used to find the index or abstract:

2. Entry used in library catalog to locate information (if applicable):

3. Call number of index or abstract (if applicable):

4. Title of index or abstract:

5. What are the subjects covered in the index or abstract?

6. How is the index or abstract arranged? (Alphabetically or by broad topics?) (Applies only to print indexes.)

7. Subject heading(s) or keywords used in index or abstract for an article on your topic:

8. Citation to the article as it appeared in the index or abstract:

   Author: Title of the magazine or journal:

   Title of the article:

   Volume / issue: pages of article: date:

9. Full title of the periodical:

10. Is the issue cited above in your library? If so, where is it located?

10. Call number and location of the issue you need:

12. Bibliographic citation for the article: (Use the examples in Chapter 14.)

Instructor: _____   Name: _____

Course/Section: _____   Date: _____

Abstract Identification

1. Identify the parts of this entry from the printed entry from *Sociological Abstracts*. Write the correct number next to the entry.

9505360   **2**   **3**   **4**
1   **Levine, Phillip B. & Zimmerman, David J.** (Wellesley Coll, MA 02181). **A comparison of the Sex-Type of Occupational Aspirations and Subsequent Achievement,** UM *Work and Occupations*, 1995, 22, 1, Feb, 73-84.
                                                            5   **6**   **7**   **6**   **8**
        Explores the connection between the sex-type of a girl's occupational aspirations & that of her achieved occupation, replicating previous work by Jerry Jacobs (see SA 35:5/87R9890) & building on it by using more recent data & an alternative methodology. Two cohorts of data (1968 & 1979) from the National Longitudinal Surveys are employed to
9   estimate transition probability matrices between the sex-types of aspired & achieved occupations. Then, multivariate models of the probability of entering a traditional (ie, female-dominated or nontraditional (ie, male-dominated) occupation are estimated. Findings indicate that Jacobs actually overestimated the relationship between aspirations & achievement, & that this relationship has, in some ways, grown weaker over time. 2 Tables, 18 References. Adapted
10   from the source document. (Copyright 1995, Sociological Abstracts, Inc., all rights reserved.)

a.	date of publication	_____
b.	abstract (summary) of the article	_____
c.	title of the journal (publication)	_____
d.	author of article	_____
e.	title of the article	_____
f.	supplementary material provided in article	_____
g.	volume and issue number of journal	_____
h.	abstract (accession) number	_____
i.	author's affiliation	_____
j.	page in journal where article appears	_____

2. Is this a popular or a scholarly work? Give three reasons to justify your answer.

3. Write the correct bibliographic citation for this article. (Use examples in Chapter 14.)

Instructor: _____   **Name:** _____

Course/Section: _____   **Date:** _____

Newspaper Exercise

Newspapers are valuable for current information. They provide a chronological listing of articles on an event and can be very useful in gathering background for issues or in scanning current events.

Use a copy of *The New York Times Index* or another newspaper index in your library to find articles on a topic you select.

1. Topic selected:

2. Subject heading(s) used (if different from original topic):

Follow the example from Figure 9.6 and write the retrieval information for two articles you find on your topic. (Remember to copy the name of the newspaper and the year from the cover.)

1. **First article:**

   month: day: year:

   section: column: page(s):

2. **Second article:**

   month: day: year:

   section: column: page(s):

3. Locate one of these articles in your library. How did you find the call number and location for your issue?

4. Read one of the articles you found and give a brief summary of the article.

5. Use the bibliographic citation examples in Chapter 14 to write the correct bibliographic citation for this article.

6. Locate the headlines of a major newspaper published on the day you were born. Name at least two other important events of that day.

Instructor: _____   **Name:** _____

Course/Section: _____   **Date:** _____

Current Events Exercise

Use printed indexes, an electronic database, and the Internet to find two current articles on a topic of your choice. You may select either one newspaper and two magazine articles, or a combination of one of these and an Internet site.

1. What source did you select? (Give the name of the index or database.)

2. What command or subject heading(s) did you use in the source?

<u>If you selected a printed source:</u>

3. Give the citations for two articles:

4. If you selected a newspaper or magazine article, give the call numbers and locations here.

<u>If you select a Web site on the Internet:</u>

5. Describe the process you used to find this article. (Review search engines in Chapter 7.)

6. Print out the page or write the correct title of the work here. Write the appropriate URL here. (HTTP://)

BIOGRAPHICAL SOURCES

A PREVIEW

In one way or another, the research process has a human dimension. Are any individuals important to the topic? Is it important to know something about the author? Information about the lives of individuals can be found in biographical sources. This chapter's objective is to survey the library's biographical resources and to help the user access appropriate information.

KEY TERMS AND CONCEPTS

Biography
Biographical Index
Biographical Dictionary

INTRODUCTION

A biography is a written history of a person's life and accomplishments. Questions dealing with biographical information are among the most frequently asked in a library. People want to know about the lives of other people, both the famous and the not-so-famous. Popular literature is rich with sources which satisfy that need. Biography makes for wonderful reading, but more than that, it is an important source in the research process. Research on most subjects can be approached through the lives of individuals who have shaped developments in the field. For example, to learn about the development of the polio vaccine, one must read about Jonas Salk.

Biographical information is so important to the contribution of knowledge that it can be found in almost all reference sources, including dictionaries, almanacs, and encyclopedias. There are numerous books written about people's lives; information about individuals appear in the daily newspapers and in magazines and journals. In addition, there are dictionaries which are devoted exclusively to presenting facts about the lives of individuals. The Internet is a rich source of biographical information. It contains Home Pages of fan clubs, authors, and many individuals—some well known, many not so well known.

Finding Biographical Sources

The search strategy for finding biographical information depends on the question being asked and the extent of information needed. Below are some steps (not necessarily in order) to assist in finding biographical information:

- use a specialized biographical index such as *Biography Index;*

- look in the appropriate biographical dictionary;

- consult the library catalog to see if the library owns a book by or about the individual;

- try a reference book such as a general or subject encyclopedia;

- check the general and/or appropriate subject indexes and abstracts to locate articles by or about the individual;

- look for information in a newspaper index;

- search the Internet;

- ask a reference librarian for help.

It is not difficult to find biographical information on noteworthy persons. Articles about famous persons appear in a number of sources, including encyclopedias and dictionaries. It is the not-so-famous which cause problems. In order to select the appropriate source without having to go through all the steps listed above, the researcher needs to determine certain basic information about the person, such as nationality, profession, and whether the person is living or not.

Using Biographical Sources

The two main types of biographical sources are *biographical indexes* and *biographical dictionaries*.

Biographical Indexes

The first type of source available for locating biographical information is through the use of an index devoted exclusively to biographical information. *Biographical indexes* are indirect sources of information; that is, they do not contain information about people; rather they provide references to sources which do. They index the biographical literature which appears in books, periodicals, newspapers and reference sources.

Biographical indexes may be general in coverage, or they may cover a particular subject. For example, *Biography and Genealogy Master Index* covers persons of all professions, occupations, nationalities, and time periods. *Performing Arts Biography Master Index* provides references to articles about people who are outstanding in the theater arts. The coverage of some biographical indexes is limited to certain types of literature. *People in History* indexes only history journals and dissertations, while *Biography Index* is very broad in scope and indexes both periodicals and books. Figures 10.1 and 10.2 compare the excerpts from *Biography and Genealogy Master Index* in both print and CD-ROM formats. Figure 10.1 illustrates an entry found in the print version of *Biography and Genealogy Master Index* for Claudia Goldin, author of *Understanding the Gender Gap.*

Goldin, Barbara Diamond 1946-
  Int Au&W93
Goldin, Claudia Dale 1946- WhoAm95,
  WhoAmW 95
Goldin, Daniel S 1940- AmMWSc95,
  BioIn18,-19,WhoAm95,WhoWor95

IntAu&W = International Authors and Writers
            Who's Who
WhoAm = Who's Who in America
WhoAmW = Who's Who of American Women
AmMWSc = American Men & Women of Science
WhoWor = Who's Who in the World

Figure 10.1 Entries from Biography and Genealogy Master Index, *1996.*

Using the "Key to Source Codes" provided at the front of the index, it can be determined that biographical information on this author will be found in two sources: *Who's Who in America*, 1995 and *Who's Who of American Women*, 1995 edition.

Goldin, Claudia Dale
1946-

American Economic Association, Directory of Members, 1974. Edited by
  Rendigs Fels. Published as Volume 64, Number 5 (October, 1974) of The
  American Economic Review.

American Men & Women of Science. A biographical directory of today's
  Leaders in physical, biological, and related sciences. 13th edition,
  Social & Behavioral Sciences. One volume. New York: R.R. Bowker Co.,
  1978.

Who's Who in America. 48th edition, 1994. New Providence, NJ: Marquis
  Who's Who, 1993.

Figure 10.2 Sample entry from Biography and Master Genealogy Index, (BMGI), *CD-ROM.*

Other biographical indexes include citations to articles about individuals, including obituaries. These indexes are searched in the same manner as the general periodical indexes—alphabetically, using the individual's name as the subject. The figures (10.3-10.6) represent sample pages taken from *Biography Index* and are typical of the format of this type of biographical index.

Biography Index

FEBRUARY 1990

A

Abbey, Edward, 1927-1989, author
Obituary
Natl Parks por 63:42 My/Je '89
Sierra 74:100-1 My/Je '89
Abbot, Willis John, 1863-1934, author and journalist
Biographical dictionary of American journalism; edited
by Joseph P. McKerns. Greenwood Press 1989 p1-3
bibl
Abbott, Jim, baseball player
Brofman, R. One for the Angels. il pors *Life* 12:118+
Je '89
Abbott, Lyman, 1835-1922, clergyman
Biographical dictionary of American journalism; edited
by Joseph P. McKerns. Greenwood Press 1989 p3-4
bibl
Abbott, Robert S., 1868-1940, journalist
Biographical dictionary of American journalism; edited
by Joseph P. McKerns. Greenwood Press 1989 p4-6
bibl
Abdul-Jabbar, Kareem, 1947-, basketball player
Kareem Abdul-Jabbar: what will he do after basketball?
il pors *Jet* 76:46-8+ Je 26 '89
Lyons, D. C. Kareem's last hurrah. il pors *Ebony* 44:102+
My '89
Renaud, L. A fitting farewell. por *Macleans* 102:51 My
22 '89
Abel, Elie, Canadian journalist and educator
Biographical dictionary of American journalism; edited
by Joseph P. McKerns. Greenwood Press 1989 p6-7
bibl
Abernathy, Ralph D., clergyman and civil rights leader
Abernathy, Ralph D. And the walls came tumbling down;
an autobiography. Harper & Row 1989 638p il
A fight among Dr. King's faithful. por *Newsweek* 114:31
O 23 '89
Hampton, H. Dr. King's best friend. por *N Y Times
Book Rev* p3 O 29 '89
Tattletale memoir. por *Time* 134:42 O 23 '89
Able, David, handicapped child
Grant, M. When the spirit takes wing. il pors *People
Wkly* 31:50-5 My 15 '89
Abraham, F. Murray, actor
Copelin, D. "F" is for Farid: an interview with F. Murray
Abraham. pors *Cineaste* 17 no1:[supp] 14-16 '89
Abraham, Gerald, 1904-1988, English musicologist
Obituary
19th Century Music 12:188-9 Fall '88
Abu Nidal, Palestinian revolutionary
Brand, D. Finis for the master terrorist? por *Time* 134:69
D 11 '89
Abu Suud, Khaled, Kuwaiti government official
Master of the money game. por *Fortune* 120:184+ Jl
31 '89
Acevedo Díaz, Eduardo, 1851-1921, Uruguayan author
Ruffinelli, Jorge. Eduardo Acevedo Díaz. (In Latin Ameri-
can writers. Scribner 1989 p299-303) bibl
**Achitoff, Louis, d. 1989, aviation expert and government
employee**
Obituary
N Y Times p44 N 26 '89
Achucarro, Joaquin, 1932-, Spanish pianist
Elder, D. Joaquin Achucarro: the spirit and passion
of Spain. il por *Clavier* 28:10-13 My/Je '89
Ackerley, J. R. (Joe Randolph), 1896-1967, English author
Jenkyns, R. Dog days. *New Repub* 201:31-4 D 18 '89
Lurie, A. Love with the perfect dog. por *N Y Times
Book Rev* p12 N 12 '89
Parker, Peter. Ackerley; the life of J.R. Ackerley. Farrar,
Straus & Giroux 1989 465p il
Ackerley, Joe Randolph *See* Ackerley, J. R. (Joe Randolph),
1896-1967
Ackerman, Arthur F., 1903-1989, pediatrician
Obituary
N Y Times pD-17 Ag 25 '89

**Acosta, Joseph de, 1540-1600, Spanish missionary and
historian**
Arocena, Luis A. Father Joseph de Acosta. (In Latin
American writers. Scribner 1989 p47-51) bibl
**Adams, Abigail, 1744-1818, wife of John Adams and mother
of John Quincy Adams**
Gelles, E. B. Gossip: an eighteenth-century case. *J Soc
Hist* 22:667-83 Summ '89
Juvenile literature
Lindsay, Rae. The presidents' first ladies. Watts 1989
p29-37 bibl il pors
**Adams, Abigail, d. 1813, daughter of John and Abigail
Adams**
Gelles, E. B. Gossip: an eighteenth-century case. *J Soc
Hist* 22:667-83 Summ '89
Adams, Ansel, 1902-1984, photographer
Biographical dictionary of American journalism; edited
by Joseph P. McKerns. Greenwood Press 1989 p7-8
bibl
Adams, Brooks, 1848-1927, historian
Auchincloss, Louis. The Vanderbilt era; profiles of a
gilded age. Scribner 1989 p163-74 il pors
**Adams, Charles Francis, 1835-1915, lawyer, railroad execu-
tive and historian**
Auchincloss, Louis. The Vanderbilt era; profiles of a
gilded age. Scribner 1989 p163-74 il pors
Adams, Franklin P. (Franklin Pierce), 1881-1960, humorist
Biographical dictionary of American journalism; edited
by Joseph P. McKerns. Greenwood Press 1989 p8-10
bibl
Adams, Gerry, Irish political leader
Fletcher, B. Interview with Sinn Fein President Gerry
Adams. *Mon Rev* 41:16-26 My '89
Adams, Henry, 1838-1918, historian
Auchincloss, Louis. The Vanderbilt era; profiles of a
gilded age. Scribner 1989 p163-74 il pors
Brogan, H. Faithful to his class. *N Y Times Book Rev*
p22 N 19 '89
Delbanco, A. The seer of Lafayette Square. por *New
Repub* 201:32-8 O 16 '89
Samuels, Ernest. Henry Adams. Belknap Press 1989 504p
bibl
Adams, John, 1735-1826, president
Gelles, E. B. Gossip: an eighteenth-century case. *J Soc
Hist* 22:667-83 Summ '89
Juvenile literature
Dwyer, Frank. John Adams. Chelsea House 1989 109p
bibl il
**Adams, John F. (John Franklin), 1919-1989, professor
of insurance**
Obituary
Natl Underwrit (Life Health Financ Serv Ed) 93:5
Mr 20 '89
Adams, Julius J., d. 1989, newspaper editor
Obituary
N Y Times Biogr Serv 20:741 Ag '89
Adams, Louisa Catherine, 1775-1852, president's wife
Juvenile literature
Lindsay, Rae. The presidents' first ladies. Watts 1989
p56-61 bibl il pors
Adams, Ralph E., d. 1989, seaman
Obituary
N Y Times Biogr Serv 20:402 My '89
Adams, Samuel, 1722-1803, statesman
Biographical dictionary of American journalism; edited
by Joseph P. McKerns. Greenwood Press 1989 p10-11
bibl
Pencak, W. Samuel Adams and Shays's Rebellion. *N
Engl Q* 62:63-74 Mr '89
Adams, Samuel Hopkins, 1871-1958, author and journalist
Adams, Samuel Hopkins. Grandfather stories. Syracuse
Univ. Press 1989 312p
Biographical dictionary of American journalism; edited
by Joseph P. McKerns. Greenwood Press 1989 p11-13
bibl
Adams-Ender, Clara, general
Cheers, D. M. Nurse Corps chief. il pors *Ebony* 44:64+
Je '89

Figure 10.3 *Selected reference from* Biography Index. *(Copyright 1990 by the H. W. Wilson Co. Material
reproduced by permission of the publisher.)*

Key to Periodical Abbreviations

19th Century Music — 19th Century Music

A

A + U — A + U
AB Bookman's Wkly — AB Bookman's Weekly
Academe — Academe
Accountancy — Accountancy
Ad Astra — Ad Astra
Advert Age — Advertising Age
AdWeek Mark Week — AdWeek's Marketing Week
Afterimage — Afterimage
Am Antiq — American Antiquity
Am Arch — The American Archivist
Am Art J — The American Art Journal
Am Artist — American Artist
Am Cinematogr — American Cinematographer
Am Craft — American Craft
Am Ethnol — American Ethnologist
Am Film — American Film
Am Health — American Health
Am Herit — American Heritage
Am Hist Illus — American History Illustrated
Am J Agric Econ — American Journal of Agricultural Economics
Am J Archaeol — American Journal of Archaeology
Am J Art Ther — American Journal of Art Therapy
Am J Econ Sociol — The American Journal of Economics and Sociology
Am J Orthopsychiatry — American Journal of Orthopsychiatry
Am J Psychol — The American Journal of Psychology
Am J Public Health — American Journal of Public Health
Am Jew Hist — American Jewish History
Am Libr — American Libraries
Am Music — American Music
Am Music Teach — The American Music Teacher
Am Photogr — American Photographer
Am Psychol — American Psychologist
Am Q — American Quarterly
Am Sch — The American Scholar
Am Visions — American Visions
Am West — American West
America — America
Americana — Americana
Américas — Américas
Annu Rev Biochem — Annual Review of Biochemistry
Annu Rev Plant Physiol Plant Mol Biol — Annual Review of Plant Physiology and Plant Molecular Biology
Antaeus — Antaeus
Antiques — Antiques
Antiques Collect Hobbies — Antiques & Collecting Hobbies
Apollo — Apollo (London, England)
Archaeology — Archaeology
Archit Aujourd'hui — L'Architecture d'Aujourd'hui
Archit Dig — Architectural Digest
Archit Rev — The Architectural Review
Architecture — Architecture
Archivo Esp Arte — Archivo Español de Arte
Art Am — Art in America
Art Antiqu — Art & Antiques
Art Dir — Art Direction
Art News — Art News
Arts Afr Noire — Arts d'Afrique Noire
Arts Rev — Arts Review (London, England)
Asian Aff — Asian Affairs (London, England)
Assoc Manage — Association Management
ASTM Stand News — ASTM Standardization News
Atlantic — The Atlantic
Audio — Audio
Audubon — Audubon
Automot News — Automotive News

B

Barrons — Barron's
Beijing Rev — Beijing Review
Bibliotekar' (U S S R) — Bibliotekar' (Moscow, Soviet Union)

Bicycling — Bicycling
Black Am Lit Forum — Black American Literature Forum
Black Enterp — Black Enterprise
Black Sch — The Black Scholar
Bookbird — Bookbird
Booklist — Booklist
Br J Criminol — The British Journal of Criminology
Br J Photogr — British Journal of Photography
Broadcasting — Broadcasting
Bull Am Meteorol Soc — Bulletin of the American Meteorological Society
Bull Am Sch Orient Res — Bulletin of the American Schools of Oriental Research
Bull At Sci — The Bulletin of the Atomic Scientists
Bull John Rylands Univ Libr Manchester — Bulletin of the John Rylands University Library of Manchester
Bull Med Libr Assoc — Bulletin of the Medical Library Association
Bull Res Humanit — Bulletin of Research in the Humanities
Burlington Mag — The Burlington Magazine
Bus Insur — Business Insurance
Bus Mark — Business Marketing
Bus Week — Business Week

C

Cah Cinema — Cahiers du Cinema
Can Archit — The Canadian Architect
Can Bus — Canadian Business
Can Hist Rev — Canadian Historical Review
Can J Hist — Canadian Journal of History
Car Driv — Car and Driver
Casabella — Casabella
Cathol Biblic Q — The Catholic Biblical Quarterly
Ceram Rev — Ceramic Review
Chain Store Age Exec — Chain Store Age Executive with Shopping Center Age
Change — Change
Changing Times — Changing Times
Channels — Channels (New York, N.Y.: 1986)
Chaucer Rev — The Chaucer Review
Chem Eng News — Chemical & Engineering News
Chem Rev — Chemical Reviews
Chem Week — Chemical Week
Child Today — Children Today
Christ Century — The Christian Century
Christ Crisis — Christianity and Crisis
Christ Today — Christianity Today
Chron Higher Educ — The Chronicle of Higher Education
Cineaste — Cineaste
Civ War Hist — Civil War History
Clarion — The Clarion
Clavier — Clavier
Columbia J Rev — Columbia Journalism Review
Columbia Libr Columns — Columbia Library Columns
Commentary — Commentary
Common Cause Mag — Common Cause Magazine
Commonweal — Commonweal
Commun ACM — Communications of the ACM
Community Jr Coll Libr — Community & Junior College Libraries
Comp Educ — Comparative Education
Comput Decis — Computer Decisions
Congr Q Wkly Rep — Congressional Quarterly Weekly Report
Connoisseur — Connoisseur
Conservationist — The Conservationist
Conservative Dig — Conservative Digest
Contemp Rev — Contemporary Review
Courier — The Courier (Unesco)
Creat Camera — Creative Camera
Ctry J — Country Journal
Curr Biogr — Current Biography
Cycle — Cycle

Figure 10.4 *Selected "Key to Periodical Abbreviations" from* Biography Index. *(Copyright 1990 by the H. W. Wilson Co. Material reproduced by permission of the publisher.)*

Checklist of Composite Books Analyzed

Works of collective biography (starred) are completely analyzed. Other books are analyzed for incidental biographical material only. Works of individual biography and autobiography are not included in this list, but will be found in the main alphabet under the names of the biographees.

† denotes juvenile literature.

A

*Auchincloss, Louis. The Vanderbilt era; profiles of a gilded age. Scribner 1989 214p il pors

B

* Biographical dictionary of American journalism; edited by Joseph P. McKerns. Greenwood Press 1989 820p bibl

C

Cannadine, David. The pleasures of the past. Norton 1989 338p il pors
Cox, Thomas R. The park builders; a history of state parks in the Pacific Northwest. University of Wash. Press 1988 248p bibl il pors maps

D

Dahl, Linda. Stormy weather; the music and lives of a century of jazzwomen. Limelight Eds. 1989 371p bibl il pors
Dictionary of the Russian Revolution; George Jackson, editor-in-chief; Robert Devlin, assistant editor. Greenwood Press 1989 704p bibl maps

G

Gardens and ghettos; the art of Jewish life in Italy; edited by Vivian B. Mann. University of Calif. Press 1989 354p bibl il pors
*Goldberg, Hillel. Between Berlin and Slobodka; Jewish transition figures from Eastern Europe. Ktav 1989 269p bibl
Gutin, Myra G. The president's partner; the first lady in the twentieth century. Greenwood Press 1989 195p bibl il por

H

*Healey, Charles J. Modern spiritual writers; their legacies of prayer. Alba House 1989 203p bibl

J

Jasen, David A. Tin Pan Alley; the composers, the songs, the performers and their times: the golden age of American popular music from 1886 to 1956. Fine, D.I. 1989 312p bibl il pors facsims

K

Kostelanetz, Richard. On innovative music(ian)s. Limelight Eds. 1989 319p

L

* Latin American writers; Carlos A. Solé, editor in chief; Maria Isabel Abreu, associate editor. Scribner 1989 1497p bibl
Lieven, D. C. B. Russia's rulers under the old regime. Yale Univ. Press 1989 407p bibl il pors
*†Lindsay, Rae. The presidents' first ladies. Watts 1989 288p bibl il pors
Lucie-Smith, Edward. Impressionist women. Harmony Bks. 1989 160p bibl il pors

M

*Mayeski, Marie Anne. Women: models of liberation. Sheed & Ward (Kansas City) 1988 240p bibl
*Meyer, Michael R. The Alexander complex; the dreams that drive the great businessmen. Times Bks. 1989 258p
Milton, Joyce. The yellow kids; foreign correspondents in the heyday of yellow journalism. Harper & Row 1989 412p bibl

P

*Perri, Colleen. Entrepreneurial women, Book II. Possibilities Pub. 1989 139p bibl il pors

R

* Reader's digest great biographies, v7; selected and condensed by the editors of Reader's digest. Reader's Digest Assn. 1989 570p il pors maps facsims autogs
* Reader's digest great biographies, v8; selected and condensed by the editors of Reader's digest. Reader's Digest Assn. 1989 605p il pors facsims
Roberts, Chalmers McGeagh. In the shadow of power; the story of the Washington post. Seven Locks Press 1989 539p bibl il
*Russell, Diana E. H. Lives of courage; women for a new South Africa. Basic Bks. 1989 375p bibl pors map

S

Smith, Lucinda. Women who write; from the past and the present to the future. Messner 1989 165p bibl pors

Figure 10.5 *Selected "Checklist of Composite Books Analyzed" from* Biography Index. *(Copyright 1990 by the H. W. Wilson Co. Material reproduced by permission of the publisher.)*

Index to Professions and Occupations

A

Abbesses
Héloïse, 1101-1164
Abbots
Marmion, Columba, 1858-1923
Abolitionists
Anthony, Susan Brownell, 1820-1906
Clay, Cassius Marcellus, 1810-1903
Douglass, Frederick, 1817?-1895
Garrison, William Lloyd, 1805-1879
Grimké, Sarah Moore, 1792-1873
Lovejoy, Elijah Parish, 1802-1837
Lundy, Benjamin, 1789-1839
Swisshelm, Jane Grey Cannon, 1815-1884
Abrasives industry
Farbstein, Burt
Accountants
See also
Auditors
Bookkeepers
Albano, James R., d. 1989
Couse, Philip Edward
Crumbley, D. Larry
Gluckman, Simon, d. 1989
Lowden, Gordon, 1927-
O'Toole, Thomas M.
Primoff, Bertram S., d. 1989
Wittenstein, Arthur, 1926-1989
Acoustic engineers
Cremer, Lothar, 1905-
Hamilton, Mark F.
Actors and actresses
See also
Children as actors
Chorus girls
Comedians
Entertainers
Pantomimists
Performance artists
Abraham, F. Murray
Alda, Alan
Allen, Woody
Alter, Tom
Anders, David
Andrews, Julie
Andrews, Nancy, d. 1989
Applegate, Christina
Arness, James
Arnette, Jeannetta
Ashcroft, Dame Peggy, 1907-
Attenborough, Richard
Aykroyd, Dan
Backus, Jim
Baker, Josephine, 1906-1975
Balaban, Bob
Ball, Lucille, 1911-1989
Banks, Jonathan
Barkin, Ellen
Béart, Emmanuelle
Bergen, Candice
Berle, Milton
Bernsen, Corbin
Bertinelli, Valerie, 1960?-
Birdsall, Jesse
Bisset, Jacqueline
Black, Shirley Temple, 1928-
Blake, Amanda, 1929-1989
Blanc, Mel
Bledsoe, Tempestt
Bond, Raleigh Verne, d. 1989
Bonnaire, Sandrine
Bostwick, Barry
Bowie, David
Bracco, Lorraine

Bragg, Bernard, 1928-
Branagh, Kenneth
Brandauer, Klaus Maria
Brooks, Avery
Brooks, Louise, 1906-1985
Brooks, Mel
Brosnan, Pierce
Brown, Tally, d. 1989
Brynner, Yul, d. 1985
Burke, Delta
Burnett, Carol
Burns, George, 1896-
Burnum Burnum
Burton, Richard, 1925-1984
Busch, Charles
Busey, Gary
Campbell, Mrs. Patrick, 1865-1940
Cannon, Dyan
Cantor, Eddie, 1892-1964
Carmine, Michael, d. 1989
Carney, Art
Carradine, Calista
Cassavetes, John
Chamberlain, Richard
Chaplin, Charlie, 1889-1977
Chapman, Graham
Cher, 1946-
Cherry, Eagle-Eye
Christopher, William
Cohan, George M., 1878-1942
Coleman, Gary
Connery, Sean
Cosby, Bill, 1937-
Coward, Noel
Cox, Courteney
Crosby, Bing, 1904-1977
Crystal, Billy
Culp, Robert
Curtis, Jamie Lee
Damian, Michael
Danson, Ted
Danza, Tony
Davis, Bette, 1908-1989
Davis, Geena
Davis, Sammy, Jr.
Day-Lewis, Daniel
De Santis, Joe, 1909-1989
Dean, James, 1931-1955
DeHaven, Gloria, 1925-
DeLuise, Peter
Dennehy, Brian
Desiderio, Robert
Dey, Susan
Dietrich, Marlene, 1904-
Dolenz, Ami
Doody, Alison
Dors, Diana
Douglas, Michael
Douglas, Suzzanne
Draper, Polly
Dryer, Fred, 1946-
Duffy, Julia
Dunaway, Faye
Eastwood, Clint
Eikenberry, Jill
Estevez, Emilio, 1963-
Evans, Peter, 1950-1989
Farmer, Gary
Fawcett, Farrah
Field, Kate, 1838-1896
Fonda, Bridget
Fonda, Jane, 1937-
Foster, Kimberly
Fox, Michael J.
Franklin, Hugh, d. 1986
French, Victor, d. 1989
Furst, Stephen

Figure 10.6 *Selected "Index to Professions and Occupations" from* Biography Index. *(Copyright 1990 by the H. W. Wilson Co. Material reproduced by permission of the publisher.)*

Biographical Dictionaries

Biographical dictionaries are works which contain limited information about people. They may be published either in a single volume or in multiple volumes. Some are monographs which are published only once, while others are serial publications which are issued on a monthly, quarterly, annual, or biennial basis.

The *Biographical Directory of the American Congress, 1774-1989*, is an example of a single volume monographic work; the *Dictionary of American Biography* is a monograph which is published in multiple volumes. *Who's Who in America* and *Current Biography* are serial publications which are issued biennially and monthly respectively.

A short biography of Claudia Golden, the author used as an example in Figure 10.1, was found in *Who's Who in America*. (See Figure 10.7.) This index is an example of most biographical dictionaries. It is arranged alphabetically by name of the individual.

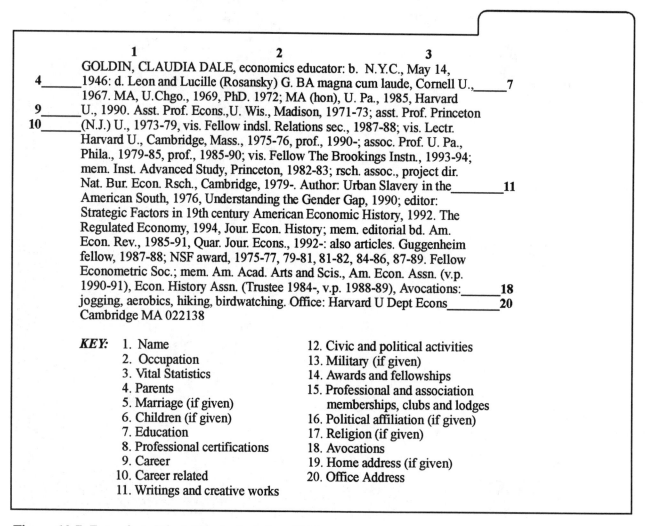

Figure 10.7 is reproduced as the following:

	1	2	3

GOLDIN, CLAUDIA DALE, economics educator: b. N.Y.C., May 14, 1946: d. Leon and Lucille (Rosansky) G. BA magna cum laude, Cornell U., 1967. MA, U.Chgo., 1969, PhD. 1972; MA (hon), U. Pa., 1985, Harvard U., 1990. Asst. Prof. Econs.,U. Wis., Madison, 1971-73; asst. Prof. Princeton (N.J.) U., 1973-79, vis. Fellow indsl. Relations sec., 1987-88; vis. Lectr. Harvard U., Cambridge, Mass., 1975-76, prof., 1990-; assoc. Prof. U. Pa., Phila., 1979-85, prof., 1985-90; vis. Fellow The Brookings Instn., 1993-94; mem. Inst. Advanced Study, Princeton, 1982-83; rsch. assoc., project dir. Nat. Bur. Econ. Rsch., Cambridge, 1979-. Author: Urban Slavery in the American South, 1976, Understanding the Gender Gap, 1990; editor: Strategic Factors in 19th century American Economic History, 1992. The Regulated Economy, 1994, Jour. Econ. History; mem. editorial bd. Am. Econ. Rev., 1985-91, Quar. Jour. Econs., 1992-: also articles. Guggenheim fellow, 1987-88; NSF award, 1975-77, 79-81, 81-82, 84-86, 87-89. Fellow Econometric Soc.; mem. Am. Acad. Arts and Scis., Am. Econ. Assn. (v.p. 1990-91), Econ. History Assn. (Trustee 1984-, v.p. 1988-89), Avocations: jogging, aerobics, hiking, birdwatching. Office: Harvard U Dept Econs Cambridge MA 022138

KEY:

1. Name
2. Occupation
3. Vital Statistics
4. Parents
5. Marriage (if given)
6. Children (if given)
7. Education
8. Professional certifications
9. Career
10. Career related
11. Writings and creative works

12. Civic and political activities
13. Military (if given)
14. Awards and fellowships
15. Professional and association memberships, clubs and lodges
16. Political affiliation (if given)
17. Religion (if given)
18. Avocations
19. Home address (if given)
20. Office Address

Figure 10.7 Entry from Who's Who in America, 1996.

Some biographical dictionaries such as *Twentieth Century Authors* and *Current Biography* contain pictures of the biographee. The length of the entries in biographical dictionaries varies; for example, the entries in the *International Who's Who* consist of a few brief facts about the person, while those in the *Dictionary of National Biography* are long, descriptive, signed articles with bibliographies. *Current Biography* usually provides a picture with a narrative of the individual being discussed. Monthly issues highlight prominent people in the news in a wide variety of occupations, including national and international affairs.

Retrospective biographical dictionaries such as *Webster's New Biographical Dictionary* include only persons who are no longer living; others such as *Contemporary Authors* contain information on persons of the present day. Some biographical dictionaries list both living and non-living persons.

The Library Catalog and Biographical Sources

The library catalog is helpful as a guide to biographical works. Usually, biographies about individuals are listed by the name of the individual with no form subdivision. Use the individual's last name as the subject.
SALK JONAS

Biographical dictionaries are listed under the heading:
BIOGRAPHY--DICTIONARIES
Figure 10.8 illustrates a typical subject search for a specific author (Shakespeare).

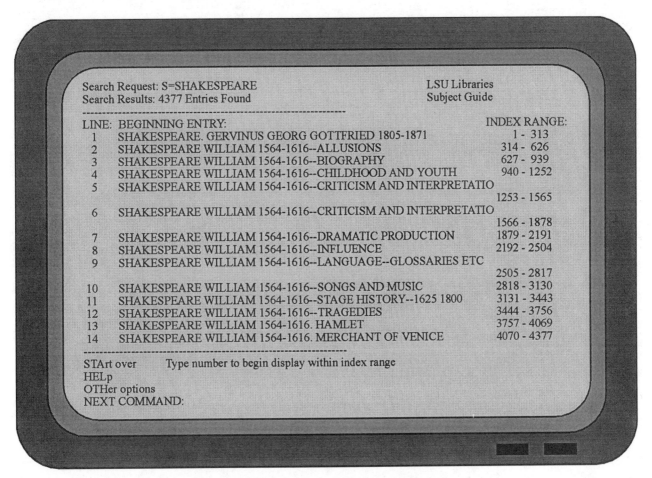

| Search Request: S=SHAKESPEARE | LSU Libraries |
| Search Results: 4377 Entries Found | Subject Guide |

LINE:	BEGINNING ENTRY:	INDEX RANGE:
1	SHAKESPEARE. GERVINUS GEORG GOTTFRIED 1805-1871	1 - 313
2	SHAKESPEARE WILLIAM 1564-1616--ALLUSIONS	314 - 626
3	SHAKESPEARE WILLIAM 1564-1616--BIOGRAPHY	627 - 939
4	SHAKESPEARE WILLIAM 1564-1616--CHILDHOOD AND YOUTH	940 - 1252
5	SHAKESPEARE WILLIAM 1564-1616--CRITICISM AND INTERPRETATIO	1253 - 1565
6	SHAKESPEARE WILLIAM 1564-1616--CRITICISM AND INTERPRETATIO	1566 - 1878
7	SHAKESPEARE WILLIAM 1564-1616--DRAMATIC PRODUCTION	1879 - 2191
8	SHAKESPEARE WILLIAM 1564-1616--INFLUENCE	2192 - 2504
9	SHAKESPEARE WILLIAM 1564-1616--LANGUAGE--GLOSSARIES ETC	2505 - 2817
10	SHAKESPEARE WILLIAM 1564-1616--SONGS AND MUSIC	2818 - 3130
11	SHAKESPEARE WILLIAM 1564-1616--STAGE HISTORY--1625 1800	3131 - 3443
12	SHAKESPEARE WILLIAM 1564-1616--TRAGEDIES	3444 - 3756
13	SHAKESPEARE WILLIAM 1564-1616. HAMLET	3757 - 4069
14	SHAKESPEARE WILLIAM 1564-1616. MERCHANT OF VENICE	4070 - 4377

STArt over   Type number to begin display within index range
HELp
OTHer options
NEXT COMMAND:

Figure 10.8 Subject Guide screen. Results of search s=shakespeare.

Notice that there are several subheadings on the subject guide screen which would be useful in researching a biographical account of Shakespeare's life:

-- BIOGRAPHY
--CHILDHOOD AND YOUTH
--CRITICISM AND INTERPRETATION
--INFLUENCE

Subject biographical dictionaries are entered as a form subdivision:

PSYCHOLOGISTS--BIOGRAPHY

Some biographical dictionaries may be found under the form heading for directories. For example, the entry for *American Men and Women of Science is:*

SCIENTISTS AMERICAN--DIRECTORIES

Figure 10.9 illustrates the results of an OPAC search for general biographical information about women.

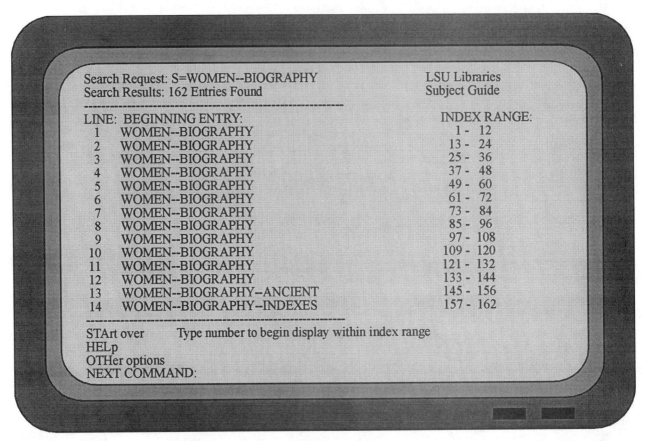

```
Search Request: S=WOMEN--BIOGRAPHY              LSU Libraries
Search Results: 162 Entries Found               Subject Guide
-----------------------------------------------
LINE:  BEGINNING ENTRY:                          INDEX RANGE:
  1    WOMEN--BIOGRAPHY                             1 -  12
  2    WOMEN--BIOGRAPHY                            13 -  24
  3    WOMEN--BIOGRAPHY                            25 -  36
  4    WOMEN--BIOGRAPHY                            37 -  48
  5    WOMEN--BIOGRAPHY                            49 -  60
  6    WOMEN--BIOGRAPHY                            61 -  72
  7    WOMEN--BIOGRAPHY                            73 -  84
  8    WOMEN--BIOGRAPHY                            85 -  96
  9    WOMEN--BIOGRAPHY                            97 - 108
 10    WOMEN--BIOGRAPHY                           109 - 120
 11    WOMEN--BIOGRAPHY                           121 - 132
 12    WOMEN--BIOGRAPHY                           133 - 144
 13    WOMEN--BIOGRAPHY--ANCIENT                  145 - 156
 14    WOMEN--BIOGRAPHY--INDEXES                  157 - 162
-----------------------------------------------
STArt over      Type number to begin display within index range
HELp
OTHer options
NEXT COMMAND:
```

Figure 10.9 OPAC Subject Guide screen for biographies of women.

Additional Sources for Biographical Information

Biographical information may be found in newspaper indexes, in periodicals, and on the Internet. A selected list of biographical reference sources is provided at the end of this chapter.

Selected List of Biographical Indexes

General Biographical Indexes

Author Biographies Master Index. 2 vols. Gale Biographical Index Series # 3. Detroit: Gale, 1984.
Useful source for references to biographical information on authors of all nationalities and all periods. Indexes biographical information in biographical dictionaries, encyclopedias, and directories. Includes information found in bibliographies and criticisms.

Biography and Genealogy Master Index. 2nd ed. 8 vols. Gale Biographical Index Series # 1.
Detroit: Gale, 1980. *Annual Supplement*, 1981-. Also available on CD-ROM.
Name index to biographical dictionaries, subject encyclopedias, literary criticism, and other biographical indexes such as *Biography Index*. Provides names and dates of biography sources. Universal in scope.

Biography Index. New York: H.W. Wilson, 1947-.
Quarterly index to biographical information appearing in books and periodicals. Covers wide range of occupations. Arranged alphabetically, entries include birth and death dates (if available), occupation, and contributions to society. A separate index by occupations is located in the back of the book.

Historical Biographical Dictionaries Master Index. Gale Biographical Index Series # 7. Detroit: Gale, 1980.
Alphabetically arranged index to information on prominent persons now deceased. Indexed sources include biographical dictionaries, encyclopedias, and other reference sources. Coverage is primarily American, but a few non-Americans are also included.

Marquis Who's Who Index to Who's Who Books. Wilmette, IL: Marquis, 1985-.
Annual index to the various Marquis *Who's Who* biographical dictionaries. Each volume lists names of individuals covered in the series during the prior year. If the person is listed in more than one dictionary, the references are given in chronological order. This index eliminates the need to go through all of the Marquis publications to find a particular reference.

Subject Biographical Indexes

Artist Biographies Master Index. Gale Biographical Index Series # 9. Detroit: Gale, 1986.
Provides references to biographical material on artists working in all aspects of art—fine arts, illustration, ceramics, craft, folk art, and architecture. Sources include biographical dictionaries, encyclopedias, directories, and indexes. Both historical and contemporary artists are included.

Business Biography Master Index. Gale Biographical Index Series # 10. Detroit: Gale, 1987.
Lists prominent persons in the field of business. Coverage is primarily contemporary, but includes a few historical figures. Sources include biographical dictionaries, encyclopedias, and directories. Predominately American in scope with a few international figures.

Journalist Biographical Master Index. Gale Biographical Index Series # 4. Detroit: Gale, 1979.
Indexes biographical information for people working in either the print or the broadcast media. Includes historical as well as contemporary journalists. Sources include biographical dictionaries and directories.

People in History: An Index to U.S. and Canadian Biographies in History Journals and Dissertations. 2 vols. Santa Barbara, CA: ABC-CLIO, 1988.
Arranged alphabetically by name of the biographee; each entry includes the author and title of the article, title of the source, and a brief abstract of the article. Volume 2 contains separate author and subject indexes.

People in World History: An Index to Biographies in History Journals and Dissertations Covering All Countries of the World Except Canada and the U.S. 2 vols. Santa Barbara, CA: ABC-CLIO, 1989.

Each entry gives the author and title of the article, the title of the source, subject, and a brief abstract. Entries are arranged alphabetically by the subject of the article. Separate subject and author indexes in the second volume.

Performing Arts Biography Master Index. 2nd ed. Gale Biographical Index Series # 5. Detroit: Gale, 1981.
References to biographical information on persons working in the theatre, films and television, or the concert stage. Sources indexed include biographical dictionaries, subject encyclopedias, and directories.

Twentieth-Century Authors Biographies Master Index. Gale Biographical Index Series # 8. Detroit: Gale, 1984.
Similar to the *Author Biographies Master Index*, but includes only contemporary authors. International in scope. Indexes biographical dictionaries, encyclopedias, criticisms, etc.

Selected List of Biographical Dictionaries

General Biographical Dictionaries

Current Biography. New York: H.W. Wilson, 1940-.
Features people in the news: politicians, sports figures, entertainers, scientists, etc. The articles about the individuals are non-critical but comprehensive. Each article is accompanied by a photograph and a short bibliography. The annual cumulative volume includes a section of obituaries and a multi-year cumulative index.

International Who's Who. London: Europa, 1935-.
Contains information on people from all over the world. Articles are short and unsigned. Includes an obituary section listing those persons who have died since the preceding volume was published. Includes a list of the world's reigning royal families.

Who's Who: An Annual Biographical Dictionary. New York: St. Martin's, 1897-.
Alphabetical listing of outstanding British subjects as well as some prominent international figures. Gives pertinent personal and professional data. Contains list of obituaries and a list of the present royal family.

Who's Who in America. Chicago: Marquis, 1899-.
Published biennially with a supplement issued on the "off year." Lists notable Americans and some international figures. Arrangement is alphabetical with geographic, professional area, retiree, and necrology indexes. Entries are brief and non-critical.

Retrospective Biographical Dictionaries

Dictionary of American Biography. 20 vols. New York: Scribner, 1928-1936. *Supplements* 1-8, 1944-1988.
Published under the auspices of the American Council of Learned Societies, this scholarly and comprehensive work provides biographical information about notable Americans no longer living. Long scholarly signed articles; extensive bibliographies. Includes noteworthy persons from the colonial period to 1970. Supplement eight was published in two volumes and includes specialized indexes to all of the preceding volumes.

Dictionary of National Biography. 22 vols. London: Oxford, 1950. *Supplements* 2-8, 1912-1990.
Originally published in 1895; reprinted at irregular intervals along with supplements. Premier source for historical biographical information on outstanding British subjects. Includes some non-British persons who are important in British history. Long, critical, scholarly signed articles with bibliographies.

Webster's New Biographical Dictionary. Springfield, MA: Merriam, 1988.
This edition contains biographical information on approximately 30,000 notable personages beginning with the year 3100 BC to the twentieth century. Worldwide in scope but most useful for American, British,

and Canadian subjects. Articles are short and include birth and death dates, notable accomplishments, and pronunciations of names.

Who Was Who. 1907-1980. 7 vols. New York: St. Martin's, 1929-1981.

Companion volumes to *Who's Who*; contains reprints of articles about people listed in *Who's Who* who have died since the last compilation. Usually only the death date has been added but occasionally supplemental new material is included. Cumulative index to all seven volumes published in 1981.

Who Was Who in America: Historical Volume 1607-1896. Chicago: Marquis, 1963.

Short biographical sketches of both Americans and non-Americans who were influential in the history of the United States. Contains lists of the names of the early governors, the U.S. presidents and vice-presidents, Supreme Court Justices, and cabinet officers.

Who Was Who in America, with World Notables. 1897-1989. Wilmette, IL: Marquis, 1942-1989.

Compilation of the biographies of people no longer living which originally appeared in *Who's Who in America.* Death dates and, in some cases, other new information have been added. An index to all volumes of *Who Was Who in America 1607-1993* was published in 1993.

Subject Biographical Dictionaries

American Men and Women of Science. New York: Bowker, 1971-.

Multi-volume biographical dictionary listing people who are prominent in the physical and biological sciences. Articles are short and list personal data, accomplishments, and publications. Unsigned and non-critical.

Biographical Directory of the United States Congress, 1774-1989. Washington: GPO, 1989.

Short biographical sketches of the members of Congress beginning with the Continental Congress and continuing through the 100th Congress. Some entries have bibliographies. Contains listings of the executive officers and cabinet members beginning with the administration of George Washington and going through that of Ronald Reagan.

Contemporary Authors. Detroit: Gale, 1962-.

Comprehensive source for biographical as well as bibliographical information on current writers of both fiction and non-fiction. Includes authors who are currently writing for newspapers, magazines, motion pictures, theater, and television. Separate annual cumulative index contains references to all previous volumes as well as other biographical sources published by Gale.

Directory of American Scholars. 8th ed. 4 vols. New York: Bowker, 1982.

Contains profiles of American and Canadian scholars who are actively working in the humanities and the social sciences. Each volume is devoted to a different subject area—Volume I: history; Volume II: English, speech and drama; Volume III: foreign languages, linguistics, and philology; Volume IV: philosophy, religion, and law. Each volume contains a geographic index. In addition, Volume IV has a cumulative index to the scholars listed in all volumes.

Twentieth Century Authors. New York: H.W. Wilson, 1941. *First Supplement,* 1955.

Universal in scope, but limited to authors working in this century. Provides photograph, list of works completed, and a bibliography of sources used to compile the article. Articles are unsigned. Alphabetically arranged by author's name.

World Authors, 1950-1980. New York. H.W. Wilson, 1985.

Continues *Twentieth Century Authors* with a similar arrangement and scope. Set includes three separately issued volumes covering the years 1950-1970, 1970-1975, and 1975-1980.

Selected Biographical Reference Sources

American Women 1935-1940: A Composite Biographical Dictionary. 2 vols. 1981.

Baker's Biographical Dictionary of Musicians. 7th ed. 1984.

Contemporary Designers. 1984.

The Continuum Dictionary of Women's Biography. 1989.

Dictionary of South African Biography. 4 vols. 1968-87.

Directory of the American Psychological Association. 1978-.

The Europa Biographical Dictionary of British Women. 1983.

International Encyclopedia of Women Composers. 2 vols. 1987.

International Who's Who in Music and Musicians' Directory. 1977-.

International Who's Who of the Arab World. 1978/79-.

International Who's Who of Women. 1992-.

Martindale-Hubbell Law Directory. 8 vols. 1931-.

Notable American Women 1607-1950. 3 vols. 1971.

Notable Black American Women. 1990.

Official ABMS Directory of Board Certified Medical Specialists. 1994-.

Reference Encyclopedia of the American Indian. 4th ed. 1986.

Religious Leaders of America. 1991-.

Who's Who Among Black Americans. 5th ed. 1988.

Who's Who in Entertainment. 1988.

Who's Who in Technology. 1995.

Women Anthropologists. 1988.

World Artists, 1950-1980. 1984.

Instructor: _____   Name: _____

Course/Section: _____   Date: _____

Review Questions for Chapter Ten

1. Why are biographies important sources for research?

2. Name four possible steps (other than consulting the reference librarian) which you could take to find information in library sources about the lives of people.

    a.

    b.

    c.

    d.

3. What information about the person is useful in helping to select the appropriate biographical source?

4. What is the difference between a biographical index and a biographical dictionary?

5. What subject heading would be used to find a general biographical dictionary in the library catalog?

6. What subject heading would you use to find a biographical dictionary listing people in psychology?

7. How does a retrospective biographical dictionary such as the *Dictionary of American History* differ from a current one such as *Who's Who in America?*

8. Select a biographical dictionary from among those listed in the chapter that would be appropriate for finding information about each of the following: (Give the title.)

    a.   A popular Spanish musician

    b.   A former national business leader

    c.   A long critical article about Winston Churchill

    d.   Information about a well-known American t.v. news correspondent

    e.   an individual who has contributed to world peace

9. What types of sources are indexed in *Biography Index?*

Instructor: _____   **Name:** _____

Course/Section: _____   **Date:** _____

═══

Biographical Index Exercise

Biographical indexes contain citations to articles about individuals who are outstanding or well known for their accomplishments. Using one of the biographical indexes mentioned in this chapter or one you find in the library catalog, look up information on the life of an individual in whom you are interested or one assigned by your instructor.

Name of Person:

When you have found your reference, note the following information:

1. Title of the biographical index used:

2. Call number of the biographical index used:

3. Identify at least three citations you find for this individual:
   (Make sure you find the full title of the publication.)

4. Look in the library catalog to see whether your library has any of the sources you listed in Question no. 3. Write the call numbers you find for each of these.

5. Locate one of the articles you found. Copy the first page and return it to your instructor with this assignment.

6. Write the correct bibliographic citation for the article you found on this individual.
    (See bibliographic citation examples in Chapter 14.)

Instructor: _____   Name: _____

Course/Section: _____   Date: _____

Biographical Dictionary Exercise

Biographical dictionaries give information on the lives of individuals who are outstanding or well-known for their accomplishments. Using a biographical dictionary, look up information on the life of an individual in whom you are interested or one assigned by your instructor.

Name of person:

When you have found your reference, note the following information:

1. Title of biographical dictionary used:

2. Describe the method used to find this source.

3. Call number of the biographical dictionary used:

4. Identify briefly the individual's:
   a. Place of birth:
   b. Date of birth, and death, if not living:
   c. Occupation or profession:

5. Write a bibliographic entry using the information you have found. (See Chapter 14 for bibliographic citation examples.)

6. Write a short paragraph on the back of this page giving a few facts about the person's accomplishments.

Instructor: _____   **Name:** _____

Course/Section: _____   **Date:** _____

═══

Biographical Dictionary Practice

Find a biography of Thomas Jefferson in the *Biographical Directory of the American Congress, 1774-1989* or another biographical dictionary. Answer the following questions.

1. Was Thomas Jefferson the second President of the United States? If not, which one was he?

2. List three major achievements of Thomas Jefferson.

3. When did he die?

4. Where is he buried?

5. Describe any civic involvements mentioned in the entry.

6. What education did he achieve?

7. What did he study?

8. From which school did he graduate?

Instructor: _____   NAME: _____

Course/Section: _____   DATE: _____

Finding Biographies on the Online Catalog Exercise

1. Use your library's online catalog to find two biographies on any two of the following individuals. Record the titles and call numbers of each work you find.

Malcolm X	John Keats	Frank Lloyd Wright
Simon Bolivar	Genghis Khan	Benjamin Franklin
Ralph Bunche	Jawaharlal Nehru	Cleopatra
Adolf Hitler	Carl Schultz	Joseph Stalin
Sitting Bull	Ho Chi Minh	

2. What commands did you use to find the biographies on your two individuals?

3. Retrieve one biography on one of the individuals above. Write a bibliographic citation to the work that you locate.

4. Briefly describe a few of the major accomplishments of that individual.

LITERATURE IN COLLECTIONS, BOOK REVIEWS, AND LITERARY CRITICISM

A PREVIEW

Have you ever looked for a poem that you learned when you were a child but have not seen in print since? Or a short story that you read several years ago but can't recall where it appeared? Or a review of a book? Or a critique of a novel? The key to finding each of these is using special indexes. These will be discussed in this chapter.

KEY TERMS AND CONCEPTS

Anthologies (Literature in Collections)
Book Reviews
Indexes to Literary Criticism

INTRODUCTION

Just as indexes are used to locate individual articles in magazines, journals, and newspapers, so also must special finding aids be used to locate the types of works listed below:

1. individual poems, stories, essays, plays, and speeches;

2. book reviews;

3. articles or essays which evaluate, judge, describe, analyze or compare an author's literary work.

It is helpful to become familiar with some of the key finding aids for these types of materials.

Indexes to Literature in Collections (Anthologies)

The term *anthology* refers to any collection of varied literary compositions. Anthologies can also include works from a period of history or works devoted to a particular subject or theme. Most anthologies include works of varied authorship, but it is not uncommon to have representative works of one author selected by an editor and collected in an anthology.

The outstanding characteristic of an anthology is the inclusion under one title of many different titles of shorter works. The titles of anthologies which a library owns are listed in the catalog, but titles of the shorter works found in the anthology are not usually included. For example, the title, *Ten Modern Masters: An Anthology of the Short Story*, would be listed in the catalog; the short story, "I'm a Fool," which is included in *Ten Modern Masters*, ordinarily would not be listed.

Essays

Essay and General Literature Index is an index to essays and chapters in collections (anthologies). It is arranged alphabetically by subjects and includes a *List of Books Indexed*, arranged alphabetically by authors. Figure 11.1 is a sample page from the subject index indicating an appropriate essay for the topic of "women and employment."

Note the work listed under the heading "women" and the subheading "employment" by R. L. Coser entitled "Power Lost and Status Gained: A Step in the Direction of Sex Equality." This essay is found in a work entitled *The Nature of Work*, edited by K. Erikson and S. P. Vallas. To retrieve this essay, one would need to conduct a title search in the library catalog under *nature of work*, or an author search under coser r l. The essay will be found on pages 71 through 87.

HEADING   Women—*Continued*

Crime

See Female offenders

Crimes against

See also Rape

MacKinnon, C. A. Crimes of war, crimes of peace. (*In* On human rights; ed. by S. Shute and S. Hurley p83-109)

Morgan, R. A massacre in Montreal. (*In* Morgan, R. The word of a woman p199-205)

Segel, L. Does pornography cause violence? The search for evidence. (*In* Dirty looks: women, pornography, power; ed. by P. C. Gibson and R. Gibson p5-21)

Diseases

See also Gynecology; Women—Health and hygiene

Education

Bee, B. Critical literacy and the politics of gender. (*In* Critical literacy; ed. by C. Lankshear and P. L. McLaren p105-31)

Harris, S. K. Responding to the text(s): women readers and the quest for higher education. (*In* Readers in history; ed. by J. L. Machor p259-82)

Great Britain

Wolff, J. The culture of separate spheres: the role of culture in nineteenth-century public and private life. (*In* Wolff, J. Feminine sentences p12-33)

Ireland

Innes, C. L. 'Groups rather than individuals': women in politics and education. (*In* Innes, C. L. Woman and nation in Irish literature and society, 1880-1935 p110-27)

Middle East

Abadan-Unat, N. The impact of legal and educational reforms on Turkish women. (*In* Women in Middle Eastern history; ed. by N. R. Keddie and B. Baron p177-94)

Berkey, J. P. Women and Islamic education in the Mamluk period. (*In* Women in Middle Eastern history; ed. by N. R. Keddie and B. Baron p143-57)

Education (Higher)

Heilbrun, C. G. The politics of mind: women, tradition, and the university. (*In* Gender in the classroom; ed. by S. L. Gabriel and I. Smithson p28-40)

Kramarae, C., and Treichler, P. A. Power relationships in the classroom. (*In* Gender in the classroom; ed. by S. L. Gabriel and I. Smithson p41-59)

Lee, E. B. Reflections on the education of women. (*In* The Liberal arts in a time of crisis; ed. by B. A. Scott p135-40)

Emancipation

See Women's rights

SUBHEADING   ### Employment

ESSAY—   *See also* Sex discrimination in employment

SOURCE—   Coser, R. L. Power lost and status gained: a step in the direction of sex equality. (*In* The Nature of work; ed. by K. Erikson and S. P. Vallas p71-87)

California

Hossfeld, K. J. "Their logic against them": contradictions in sex, race, and class in Silicon Valley. (*In* Women workers and global restructuring; ed. by K. Ward p149-78)

Developing countries

Tiano, S. Maquiladora women: a new category of workers? (*In* Women workers and global restructuring; ed. by K. Ward p193-223)

Great Britain

Dupree, M. The community perspective in family history: the Potteries during the nineteenth century. (*In* The First modern society; ed. by A. L. Beier, D. Cannadine and J. M. Rosenheim p549-73)

Greece

Hadjicostandi, J. "Façon": women's formal and informal work in the garment industry in Kavala, Greece. (*In* Women workers and global restructuring; ed. by K. Ward p64-81)

Ireland

Pyle, J. L. Export-led development and the underemployment of women: the impact of discriminatory development policy in the Republic of Ireland. (*In* Women workers and global restructuring; ed. by K. Ward p85-112)

Italy

Cammarosano, S. O. Labouring women in northern and central Italy in the nineteenth century. (*In* Society and politics in the age of the Risorgimento; ed. by J. A. Davis and P. Ginsborg p152-83)

Japan

Carney, L. S., and O'Kelly, C. G. Women's work and women's place in the Japanese economic miracle. (*In* Women workers and global restructuring; ed. by K. Ward p113-45)

Java

Wolf, D. L. Linking women's labor with the global economy: factory workers and their families in rural Java. (*In* Women workers and global restructuring; ed. by K. Ward p25-47)

Taiwan

Gallin, R. S. Women and the export industry in Taiwan: the muting of class consciousness. (*In* Women workers and global restructuring; ed. by K. Ward p179-92)

United States

Gabin, N. F. Time out of mind: the UAW's response to female labor laws and mandatory overtime in the 1960s. (*In* Work engendered: toward a new history of American labor; ed. by A. Baron p351-74)

Kessler-Harris, A. Law and a living: the gendered content of "free labor". (*In* Gender, class, race and reform in the Progressive Era; ed. by N. Frankel and N. S. Dye p87-109)

Enfranchisement

See Women—Suffrage

Health and hygiene

See also Clothing and dress

Jacobson, J. L. Improving women's reproductive health. (*In* State of the world, 1992 p83-99)

Figure 11.1 Sample page from Essay and General Literature Index, *1990-1994, p. 1794.*

Individual essays can also be found under the author's name in *Essay and General Literature Index*. Figures 11.2 and 11.3 locate a work co-authored by Claudia Goldin and Stanley L. Engerman.

Goldhurst, William
    Of mice and men; John Steinbeck's parable
of the curse of Cain. (*In* The Short novels
of John Steinbeck: ed. by J. J. Benson
p48-59)
Goldin, Claudia
    (jt. Auth) See Engerman, Stanley L.,
and Goldin, Claudia

Figure 11.2 Excerpt from author index, Essay and General Literature Index, *1990-1994, p. 658.*

Figure 11.3 illustrates the full entry listed under the author Engerman in the same index.

Enger, John Van
    Faith as a concept of order in medieval
Christendom. (*In* Belief in history;
ed. by T. Kselman p19-67)
Engerman, Stanley L., and Goldin, Claudia
    Seasonality in nineteenth-century labor
markets. (*In* American economic development
in historical perspective; ed. by T. Weiss
and D. Schaefer p99-126)

Figure 11.3 Excerpt from author index, Essay and General Literature Index, *1990-1994, p. 495.*

Short Stories

To locate a short story that is in an anthology or a periodical, one should consult *Short Story Index*. It includes both a subject and an author index. Figure 11.4 illustrates an example from the subject "women."

WOMEN
                    See also Black women; Jewish women;
           Muslim women; Single women
Adams, A. Child's play
Adams, A. The end of the world
Adams, A. Molly's dog
Adams, A. Return trips

Figure 11.4 Excerpt from Subject Index, Short Story Index, *1989-1993, p. 960.*

To locate the source where the short story can be found, consult the author index. An example is shown in Figure 11.5.

To retrieve the short story "A Child's Play" by Alice Adams, one would conduct an author search in the library catalog under adams, alice, or a title search under *after you've gone*, the larger work which includes the short story.

Indexes to Book Reviews

Reviews of most new books and of forthcoming books are published in newspapers and magazines. Written by critics and journalists, book reviews provide descriptions and critical evaluations of books. The success or failure of a book's sale frequently depends on the kind of review it receives. Indexes to book reviews are good sources to locate references to reviews of books appearing in periodicals and newspapers. Some of these indexes have excerpts from the reviews, while others only list the sources. References to book reviews can also be located through periodical and newspaper indexes.

Book Review Index provides citations to reviews of published books. Figure 11.6 illustrates references in *Book Review Index* to reviews of Claudia Goldin's work, *Understanding the Gender Gap.*

Note that a review of *Understanding the Gender Gap* is located in *American Historical Review* (AHR) and *Journal of Literary History* (JLH). A list of abbreviations for the journals listed in the entries is provided at the beginning of *Book Review Index.*

The title entry for the book, *Understanding the Gender Gap*, is shown in figure 11.7.

ACTORS—*Continued*
  Besant, Sir W., and Rice, J. The case of Mr. Lucraft
  Bioy Casares, A. Cato
  Bloch, R. Show biz
  Boyd, W. Not yet, Jayette
  Breen, J. L. Starstruck
  Burns, C. Also starring
  Crumley, J. The heavy
  Goldman, E. S. Nelly Fallower's *Streetcar*
  Goldsmith, O. Adventures of a strolling player
  Hagedorn, J. T. Film noir
  Hall, M. M. The pool people
  Lombreglia, R. Jungle video
  Mori, T. Japanese Hamlet
  Nakayama, C. Good afternoon, ladies
  Onetti, J. C. A dream come true
  Palacio Valdés, A. Drama in the flies
  Paul, B. Close, but no cigar
  Runyon, D. Broadway complex
  Saroyan, W. The man with the heart in the highlands
  Schmidt, H. J. The honored guest
  Slesar, H. Starring the defense
  Spencer, D. Our secret's out
  Spencer, S. Credit
  Stoker, B. A criminal star
  Thomas, G. An ample wish
  Urbánek, Z. For dreams that now have ceased
  Villanueva, M. The insult
  Villiers de l'Isle-Adam, A., comte de. The desire to be a man
  Zinnes, H. Wings
The actors company. Finney, E. J.
Actress. Oates, J. C.
ACTRESSES
    See also Motion picture actors and actresses; Theater life
  Aickman, R. The visiting star
  Alcott, L. M. Hope's debut
  Alcott, L. M. La Jeune; or, Actress and woman
  Alcott, L. M. A laugh and a look
  Alcott, L. M. The romance of a bouquet
  Allen, S. The interview
  Brennan, K. Jack
  Carroll, J. The lick of time
  Carter, A. The merchant of shadows
  Cather, W. Coming, Aphrodite!
  Cheever, J. The fourth alarm
  Cliff, M. Screen memory
  Compo, S. The continuity girl
  DePew, A. Rita and Maxine
  Fitzgerald, F. S. Last kiss
  Frame, R. Switchback
  Ganina, M. Stage actress
  Haslam, G. W. Joaquin
  Hébert, A. The first garden
  Ingalls, R. The end of tragedy
  Kinder, R. M. Witches
  Kress, N. With the original cast
  Lewis, S. As P. T.
  Mason, B. A. A new-wave format
  McGahern, J. Peaches
  Minot, S. Île Sèche
  Munro, A. Simon's luck
  Nakayama, C. Star time
  Norman, H. Whatever Lola wants
  Oates, J. C. Actress
  Onetti, J. C. Hell most feared
  Orr, M. The wisdom of Eve
  Palacio Valdés, A. Clotilde's romance
  Poniatowska, E. Park Cinema

  Pritchett, V. S. The chain-smoker
  Salter, J. The cinema
  Tagore, Sir R. Resistance broken
  Tokareva, V. Thou shalt not make . . .
  Turchi, P. Magician
  Uvarova, L. Be still, torments of passion
  Verlaine, M. J. The nude scene
  Vidal, G. Erlinda and Mr. Coffin
  Vivante, A. The last kiss
  Walker, C. Z. The very pineapple
  Wallace, D. F. My appearance
  Whitebird, J. Mrs. Bruja
Acts of contrition. Binstock, R. C.
Acts of kindness. Wagner, M. M.
Acts of mercy. Coleman, J. C.
Actual oil. Steinbach, M.
Ad astra per aspera. Compo, S.
Adam, Christina
  Fires
    Birch Lane Press presents American fiction #3
Adam, one afternoon. Calvino, I.
Adamidou, Irena Ioannidou *See* Ioannidou Adamidou, Irena
Adams, Alice, 1926-   ◄———— AUTHOR
  1940: fall
    Adams, A. After you've gone
    Prize stories, 1990
  After you've gone
    Adams, A. After you've gone
    Legal fictions; ed. by J. Wishingrad
    Prize stories, 1989
  Alaska
    The Oxford book of American short stories; ed. by J. C. Oates
  Alternatives
    American stories II: fiction from the Atlantic monthly
  Beautiful girl
    The Invisible enemy; ed. by M. Dow and J. Regan
  Child's play   ◄—— SHORT STORY
    Adams, A. After you've gone ◄ SOURCE
  Earthquake damage
    The New Yorker v66 p44-9 My 7 '90
    Prize stories, 1991
  The end of the world
    Adams, A. After you've gone
  Favors
    Adams, A. After you've gone
  Fog
    Adams, A. After you've gone
  The islands
    Prize stories, 1993
    The Sophisticated cat; comp. by J. C. Oates and D. Halpern
  The last lovely city
    The Best American short stories, 1992
    The New Yorker v67 p33-9 Mr 11 '91
    Prize stories, 1992
  Lost cat
    Adams, A. After you've gone
    The Company of cats; ed. by M. J. Rosen
  Love and work
    Southwest Review v77 p466-79 Aut '92
  Molly's dog
    The Literary dog; ed. by J. Schinto
  The oasis
    The Rough road home; ed. by R. Gingher
  Ocracoke Island
    Adams, A. After you've gone

Figure 11.5 Author search, Short Story Index.

Fire! The Beginnings of the Labor Movement (Illus. by James Watling)
c BL - v88 - My 1 '92 - p1600 [51-250]
c CCB-B - v45 - Ap '92 - p206 [51-250]
c HB - v68 - Jl '92 - p474 [51-250]
c KR - v60 - My 15 '92 - p677 [51-250]
c LT - v5 - S '92 - p23 [51-250]
c SLJ - v38 - Jl '92 - p73 [51-250]
Just Enough Is Plenty
c Inst - v101 - N '91 - p23
Goldin, Claudia - *Strategic Factors in Nineteenth Century American Economic History*
Choice - v30 - S '92 - p185 [51-250]
Understanding the Gender Gap
AHR - v96 - O '91 - p1271
JEL - v29 - S '91 - p1153
JIH - v22 - Win '92 - p477
JPE - v99 - D '91 - p1332
J Soc H - v25 - Win '91 - p430
Signs - v17 - Aut '91 - p220
Goldin, Grace - *Speak Out for Age*
Bloom Rev - v12 - Mr '92 - p23 [251-500]
Goldin, Ian - *Agricultural Trade Liberalization*
Econ Bks - v18 - Sum '91 - p91
Golding, Sue - *Gramsci's Democratic Theory*
UPBN - v4 - Je '92 - p25 [1-50]
Golding, William - *Lord of the Flies*
y BIC - v20 - O '91 - p26
y BL - v88 - F 15 '92 - p1100 [1-50]
GW - v145 - S 29 '91 - p25
The Paper Men
GW - v145 - S 29 '91 - p25
The Pyramid
GW - v145 - S 29 '91 - p25
Rites of Passage
GW - v145 - S 29 '91 - p25
The Spire
GW - v145 - S 29 '91 - p25
Goldman, Alan H - *Empirical Knowledge*
Phil R - v101 - Ap '92 - p428+ [501+]
Goldman, Albert - *Elvis*
Choice - v29 - Ap '92 - p1192+ [501+]
Ladies and Gentlemen--Lenny Bruce!!
Trib Bks - F 2 '92 - p8
The Lives of John Lennon
Choice - v29 - Ap '92 - p1192+ [501+]
Sound Bites
y BL - v88 - My 15 '92 - p1653 [51-250]
y BL - v88 - My 15 '92 - p1669 [1-50]
BW - v22 - Ag 9 '92 - p6 [251-500]
KR - v60 - Ap 15 '92 - p530 [51-250]
LJ - v117 - My 1 '92 - p83 [51-250]
PW - v239 - Ap 13 '92 - p51 [51-250]
Goldman, Alvin I - *Liaisons: Philosophy Meets the Cognitive and Social Sciences*
Choice - v29 - Jl '92 - p1693 [51-250]
Goldman, Ari L - *The Search for God at Harvard*
CC - v109 - Ja 1 '92 - p19
Ch Today - v35 - N 25 '91 - p35
Comt - v92 - O '91 - p54
NL - v74 - N 4 '91 - p23
NYTBR - v97 - Je 14 '92 - p32 [51-250]
PW - v239 - Ap 20 '92 - p51 [1-50]
TT - v48 - O '91 - p338
Goldman, Benjamin A - *The Truth about Where You Live*
r BL - v88 - F 1 '92 - p1058
r Choice - v29 - My '92 - p1427 [51-250]
r LJ - v117 - Ap 1 '92 - p110+ [51-250]
r New Age - v9 - My '92 - p102 [51-250]
Goldman, Bob - *Death in the Locker Room*
yr BL - v88 - Jl '92 - p1932 [51-250]
Goldman, Francisco - *The Long Night of White Chickens*
BL - v88 - My 15 '92 - p1660 [51-250]
Boston R - v17 - S '92 - p38 [501+]
BW - v22 - Je 7 '92 - p9 [501+]
CSM - v84 - Jl 24 '92 - p14 [501+]
Esq - v117 - Je '92 - p42 [51-250]
KR - v60 - Ap 15 '92 - p484 [51-250]
LATBR - Jl 19 '92 - p3+ [501+]
LJ - v117 - Je 1 '92 - p176 [51-250]
NYTBR - v97 - Ag 16 '92 - p20 [501+]
PW - v239 - Ap 13 '92 - p42+ [51-250]
VV - v37 - Jl 21 '92 - p90+ [501+]
KR - v60 - Ja 15 '92 - p91
LJ - v117 - F 15 '92 - p169
NYTBR - v97 - Jl 12 '92 - p18 [51-250]
Obs - Ag 30 '92 - p51 [51-250]
PW - v239 - F 3 '92 - p74
W&I - v7 - S '92 - p419+ [501+]
Goldman, Judith - *The Early Pictures 1861-1964 (Illus. by James Rosenquist)*
LJ - v117 - Ag '92 - p98 [51-250]
Goldman, Lawrence - *The Blind Victorian*
AHR - v96 - D '91 - p1651
VS - v35 - Aut '91 - p90
Goldman, Marshall I - *What Went Wrong with Perestroika*
BL - v88 - O 15 '91 - p404
BW - v21 - N 10 '91 - p12
Choice - v29 - Mr '92 - p1152 [51-250]
CSM - v83 - N 8 '91 - p14
Econ - v322 - Mr 21 '92 - p97 [501+]
LJ - v116 - O 15 '91 - p102
NYRB - v38 - N 7 '91 - p53
NYTBR - v97 - F 2 '92 - p15
Goldman, Martin E - *The Handbook of Heart Drugs*
BL - v88 - Ag '92 - p1985 [51-250]
r LJ - v117 - Jl '92 - p76 [51-250]
Goldman, Martin S - *Nat Turner and the Southhampton Revolt of 1831*
y B Rpt - v11 - S '92 - p58 [51-250]
y KR - v60 - Ap 1 '92 - p465 [51-250]
y SLJ - v38 - Je '92 - p145 [51-250]
y VOYA - v15 - Je '92 - p123+ [501+]
Goldman, Nahum - *Online Information Hunting*
r BWatch - v13 - My '92 - p3+ [1-50]
Goldman, Nathan C - *Space Policy*
SciTech - v16 - Ag '92 - p35 [1-50]
Goldman, Ralph M - *From Warfare to Party Politics*
Pers PS - v21 - Spr '92 - p124 [501+]
The National Party Chairmen and Committees
APSR - v86 - Mr '92 - p237+ [501+]
Goldman, Robert - *Mapping Hegemony*
Choice - v29 - Jl '92 - p1671 [51-250]
Goldman, Robert M - *A Free Ballot and a Fair Count*
JSH - v58 - Ag '92 - p552+ [251-500]
Goldman, Roger - *Thurgood Marshall: Justice for All*
LATBR - Ag 9 '92 - p1+ [501+]
LJ - v117 - Jl '92 - p104 [51-250]
PW - v239 - Je 1 '92 - p47+ [51-250]
Goldman, Steve - *Vibration Spectrum Analysis*
New TB - v76 - N '91 - p1571 [51-250]
Goldman, Steven L - *Science, Technology, and Social Progress*
Isis - v83 - Mr '92 - p168+ [501+]
Goldman, William - *Hype and Glory*
Books - v5 - N '91 - p21+ [51-250]
Obs - O 20 '91 - p61
Goldmann, Nahum - *Online Information Hunting*
SciTech - v16 - Je '92 - p4 [1-50]
Goldoni, Luca - *Maria Luiga Donna in Carriera*
BL - v88 - My 15 '92 - p1667 [1-50]
Goldratt, Eliyahu M - *The Goal: A Process of Ongoing Improvement*
Mgt R - v81 - Ja '92 - p63 [51-250]
Goldreich, Gloria - *Years of Dreams*
BL - v88 - Ap 15 '92 - p1502 [51-250]
KR - v60 - F 1 '92 - p131
PW - v239 - F 3 '92 - p62
Goldring, Roland - *Fossils in the Field*
r New Sci - v134 - My 9 '92 - p40+ [501+]
SciTech - v15 - S '91 - p19 [1-50]
Goldsborough, Robert - *The Crain Adventure*
R&R Bk N - v7 - O '92 - p37 [1-50]
Fade to Black
Arm Det - v25 - Spr '92 - p251 [51-250]
y Kliatt - v26 - Ap '92 - p6 [51-250]
Fade to Black. Audio Version
Arm Det - v24 - Fall '91 - p500
y Kliatt - v26 - Ap '92 - p58 [51-250]
Silver Spire
KR - v60 - Ag 15 '92 - p1019 [51-250]
PW - v239 - Ag 31 '92 - p67 [51-250]
CS - v21 - Jl '92 - p444+ [501+]
CS - v21 - Jl '92 - p445+ [501+]
JMF - v54 - My '92 - p464+ [501+]
Wom R Bks - v9 - D '91 - p16
Goldschmidt, Arthur, Jr. - *A Concise History of the Middle East. 4th ed., Rev. and Updated*
MEJ - v46 - Win '92 - p122
R&R Bk N - v6 - D '91 - p5 [1-50]
Goldschmidt, Bertrand - *Atomic Rivals*
T&C - v33 - Ja '92 - p177+ [501+]
Goldschmidt, Georges-Arthur - *Die Absonderung*
TLS - Mr 6 '92 - p22 [251-500]
WLT - v66 - Spr '92 - p331 [251-500]
Goldschmidt, Walter - *The Human Career*
A Anth - v93 - D '91 - p977
Goldsmith, Alix - *Celebritest: Intimate Profiles of Seventy Celebrities*
FIR - v43 - Mr '92 - p130+ [51-250]
Goldsmith, Andrea - *Modern Interiors*
Aust Bk R - S '91 - p15
Goldsmith, Arnold L - *The Modern American Urban Novel*
MFS - v37 - Win '91 - p760 [251-500]
Goldsmith, Arthur A - *Building Agricultural Institutions*
Pac A - v65 - Spr '92 - p116+ [501+]
Goldsmith, Barrie - *Monitoring for Conservation and Ecology*
Choice - v29 - N '91 - p468
ECOL - v73 - Je '92 - p1134+ [501+]
New TB - v76 - S '91 - p1290+ [51-250]
QRB - v67 - Je '92 - p228 [251-500]
Goldsmith, Colin - *Extensions of Calculus*
TES - O 11 '91 - p44
Goldsmith, Deward - *The Earth Report*
HMR - S '90 - p9
Goldsmith, Donald - *The Astronomers*
y B Rpt - v10 - N '91 - p51
y WLB - v65 - Je '91 - p162
Goldsmith, Edward - *The Way: An Ecological World View*
TLS - S 11 '92 - p5 [501+]
Goldsmith, Elizabeth C - *Writing the Female Voice*
Can Lit - Aut '91 - p156+ [501+]
Goldsmith, Emanuel S - *The American Judaism of Mordecai M. Kaplan*
Choice - v29 - D '91 - p652
Goldsmith, John A - *Autosegmental and Metrical Phonology*
MLJ - v76 - Sum '92 - p259 [501+]
Goldsmith, Lynn - *Circus Dreams*
Ant & CH - v96 - N '91 - p45
Goldsmith, Olivia - *The First Wives Club*
BL - v88 - Mr 15 '92 - p1335+ [51-250]
BW - v22 - Mr 1 '92 - p12 [1-50]
KR - v59 - D 15 '91 - p1549
LJ - v117 - Ja '92 - p174
NYTBR - v97 - My 10 '92 - p17 [251-500]
PW - v239 - Ja 6 '92 - p48
Trib Bks - Mr 22 '92 - p6 [51-250]
The First Wives Club. Audio Version
LJ - v117 - My 1 '92 - p132 [51-250]
PW - v239 - My 4 '92 - p26 [51-250]
Goldsmith, Timothy H - *The Biological Roots of Human Nature*
Choice - v29 - Je '92 - p1568 [51-250]
Goldstaub, Sylvia - *Unconditional Love*
Advocate - Je 16 '92 - p117 [51-250]
Lam Bk Rpt - v3 - My '92 - p46 [1-50]
Goldsteen, Raymond L - *Demanding Democracy after Three Mile Island*
AJS - v98 - Jl '92 - p197+ [501+]
Choice - v29 - Ap '92 - p1290 [51-250]
CS - v21 - Jl '92 - p487 [251-500]
Goldstein, Allan L - *Combination Therapies*
SciTech - v16 - Je '92 - p17 [51-250]
Goldstein, Avery - *From Bandwagon to Balance-of-Power Politics*
Choice - v29 - N '91 - p515
Goldstein, Bobbye S - *What's on the Menu? (Illus. by Chris L Demerest)*
c BL - v88 - Ap 15 '92 - p1534 [51-250]
c SLJ - v38 - Jl '92 - p68 [51-250]
Goldstein, Darra - *A Taste of Russia*

***Figure 11.6** Entries from* Book Review Index. *Reprinted by permission of Gale Research, Inc.*

UNDERSTANDING/ *Title Index*

Understanding the Fourth Gospel - Ashton,
   John
Understanding the Gender Gap - Golding,
   Claudia

Figure 11.7 Title Index, Book Review Index, *1992, p. 1470.* *

A similar work, *Book Review Digest,* includes reviewers' comments in addition to the citations for book reviews. Figure 11.8 illustrates how to use *Book Review Digest.*

Figure 11.9 is a page from the subject/title index of *Book Review Digest.* Note the entry under "women—employment." It cites a review to a book by D. Tomaskovic-Devey, entitled *Gender & Racial Inequality at Work.*

The summaries of reviewers' comments of this work can be found in the main body of *Book Review Digest,* as shown in Figure 11.10. The full entry includes a description of the work being reviewed, a summary from the publisher about the book, and a listing of reviews with citations to the actual review. The number of words are included, as is the reviewer's name.

Once the full title of the book review source is identified, the journal can be retrieved by title using the library catalog. Use a title search for the source. Check the holdings screen for the specific issues you need.

Example:

t= booklist

t= choice

Indexes to Literary Criticism

Works of literary criticism contain articles or essays which evaluate or judge, describe, analyze, and compare an author's novel, poem, play, short story, or other literary work. Commentaries, criticisms, interpretations, and explanatory information about literature of all kinds—novels, plays, poetry, and short stories can be found through the online catalog, using the author of the original work and selected subheadings of the work. The following two screens from an OPAC illustrate how critical interpretations of Shakespeare's works can be found.

---

* Reprinted by permission of Gale Research, Inc.

Sample Entry

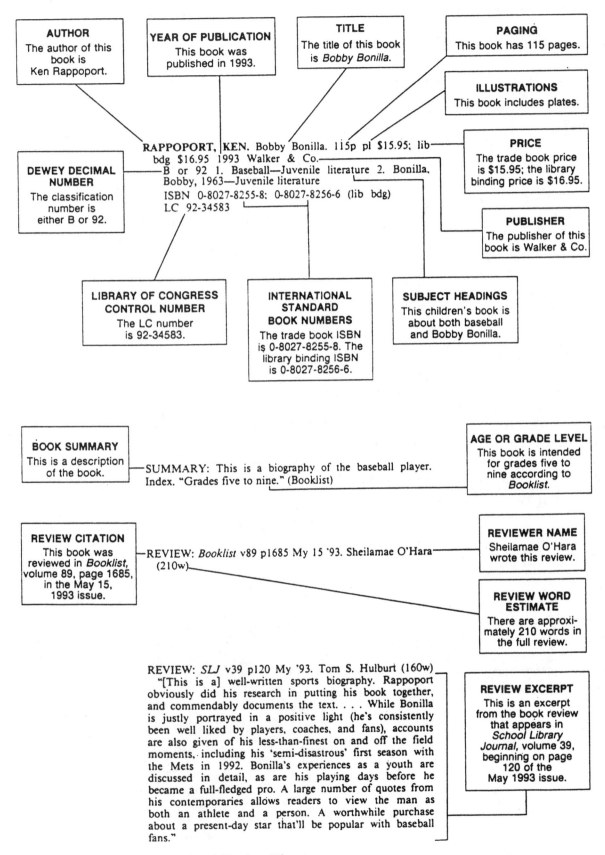

AUTHOR
The author of this book is Ken Rappoport.

YEAR OF PUBLICATION
This book was published in 1993.

TITLE
The title of this book is *Bobby Bonilla*.

PAGING
This book has 115 pages.

ILLUSTRATIONS
This book includes plates.

PRICE
The trade book price is $15.95; the library binding price is $16.95.

DEWEY DECIMAL NUMBER
The classification number is either B or 92.

PUBLISHER
The publisher of this book is Walker & Co.

RAPPOPORT, KEN. Bobby Bonilla. 115p pl $15.95; lib bdg $16.95 1993 Walker & Co.
B or 92 1. Baseball—Juvenile literature 2. Bonilla, Bobby, 1963—Juvenile literature
ISBN 0-8027-8255-8; 0-8027-8256-6 (lib bdg)
LC 92-34583

LIBRARY OF CONGRESS CONTROL NUMBER
The LC number is 92-34583.

INTERNATIONAL STANDARD BOOK NUMBERS
The trade book ISBN is 0-8027-8255-8. The library binding ISBN is 0-8027-8256-6.

SUBJECT HEADINGS
This children's book is about both baseball and Bobby Bonilla.

BOOK SUMMARY
This is a description of the book.

AGE OR GRADE LEVEL
This book is intended for grades five to nine according to *Booklist*.

SUMMARY: This is a biography of the baseball player. Index. "Grades five to nine." (Booklist)

REVIEW CITATION
This book was reviewed in *Booklist*, volume 89, page 1685, in the May 15, 1993 issue.

REVIEWER NAME
Sheilamae O'Hara wrote this review.

REVIEW WORD ESTIMATE
There are approximately 210 words in the full review.

REVIEW: *Booklist* v89 p1685 My 15 '93. Sheilamae O'Hara (210w)

REVIEW: *SLJ* v39 p120 My '93. Tom S. Hulburt (160w)
"[This is a] well-written sports biography. Rappoport obviously did his research in putting his book together, and commendably documents the text. . . . While Bonilla is justly portrayed in a positive light (he's consistently been well liked by players, coaches, and fans), accounts are also given of his less-than-finest on and off the field moments, including his 'semi-disastrous' first season with the Mets in 1992. Bonilla's experiences as a youth are discussed in detail, as are his playing days before he became a full-fledged pro. A large number of quotes from his contemporaries allows readers to view the man as both an athlete and a person. A worthwhile purchase about a present-day star that'll be popular with baseball fans."

REVIEW EXCERPT
This is an excerpt from the book review that appears in *School Library Journal*, volume 39, beginning on page 120 of the May 1993 issue.

Figure 11.8 *Sample entry from* Book Review Digest.

SUBJECT AND TITLE INDEX

The wine-dark sea. O'Brian, P.
Winged victory. Perret, G.
Wingfield, George, 1876-1959
Raymond, C. E. George Wingfield
The wings of a falcon. Voigt, C.
Wings of hope and daring. Stenberg, E.
Winik, Marion
Winik, M. Telling
Winn-Dixie Stores, Inc.
Staten, V. Can you trust a tomato in January?
The winner within. Riley, P.
Winnicott, D. W. (Donald Woods), 1896-1971
Phillips, A. On kissing, tickling, and being bored
Winnicott, Donald Woods *See* Winnicott, D. W. (Donald
Woods), 1896-1971
Winning the grand award. Iritz, M. H.
Winning ugly. Gilbert, B.
Winslow, Marcella Comès
Winslow, M. C. Brushes with the literary
Winter
> **Juvenile literature**
Honda, T. Wild horse winter
Maass, R. When winter comes
Winter camp. Hill, K.
Winter fox. Brutschy, J.
The Winter Prince. Wein, E. E.
Winter sports
> *See also*
> Sleds and sledding
Winter's orphans. Farentinos, R. C.
Wipe your feet!. Lehan, D.
Wiretapping
> *See also*
> Eavesdropping
Wisconsin
> **History**
Apps, J. W. Breweries of Wisconsin
> **Politics and government**
Woliver, L. R. From outrage to action
> **Rural conditions**
Pederson, J. M. Between memory and reality
Wise, Isaac Mayer, 1819-1900
Temkin, S. D. Isaac Mayer Wise, shaping American Judaism
The wish for kings. Lapham, L. H.
Wishbones. Wilson, B. K.
Wit and humor
> *See also* ·
> American wit and humor
> Comedy
> Jokes
> Tall tales
Grizzard, L. I took a lickin' and kept on tickin'
James, S. The adventures of Stout Mama
White, B. Mama makes up her mind
> **Juvenile literature**
Talbott, H. Your pet dinosaur, an owner's manual
Witchcraft
Gragg, L. D. The Salem witch crisis
Hester, M. Lewd women and wicked witches
The witches and the singing mice. Nimmo, J.
The witch's face. Kimmel, E. A.
Witch's fire. Butler, B.
With a Black platoon in combat. Rishell, L.
With liberty and justice for some. Kairys, D.
With teeth in the earth. Tussman, M. H.
With women's eyes
Within reach
Without consent or contract
Without remorse. Clancy, T.
Without sin. Klaw, S. ·
Witness against the beast. Thompson, E. P.
Witness for freedom
Witness to disintegration. Hixson, W. L.
A witness to genocide. Gutman, R.
Wives
> *See also*
> Abused women
> Widows
The wives of Bath. Swan, S. E.
The wizard next door. Glassman, P.
A Wizard's dozen
Woiwode, Larry
Woiwode, L. Acts
Wojnarowicz, David, 1954-1992
Wojnarowicz, D. Memories that smell like gasoline
Wole Soyinka revisted. Wright, D.
Wolf, Hugo, 1860-1903
Youens, S. Hugo Wolf

Wolf, Lucien, 1857-1930
Levene, M. War, Jews, and the new Europe
The wolf. Bradshaw, J.
The wolf & the raven. Paxson, D. L.
Wolf at the door. Corcoran, B.
Wolf children *See* Wild children
Wolf whistle. Nordan, L.
Wolfe, Michael, 1945-
Wolfe, M. The hadj
Wolfpack (Basketball team) *See* North Carolina State Wolfpack (Basketball team)
Wollstonecraft, Mary, 1759-1797
> **Fiction**
Sherwood, F. Vindication
Wolves
> **Juvenile literature**
Bradshaw, J. The wolf
Brandenburg, J. To the top of the world
Greene, C. Reading about the gray wolf
Patent, D. H. Dogs
Simon, S. Wolves
Wolves. Simon, S.
Woman at the edge of two worlds. Andrews, L. V.
A woman at war. Moore, M.
Woman changing woman. Rutter, V. B.
A woman doctor's guide to menopause. Jovanovic-Peterson, L.
The woman reader, 1837-1914. Flint, K.
A woman unafraid. Colman, P.
A woman's book of choices. Chalker, R.
The woman's heart book. Pashkow, F. J.
A woman's view. Basinger, J.
A woman's worth. Williamson, M.
Women
> *See also*
> Abused women
> Black women
> Jewish women
> Social work with women
> White women
Heidensohn, F. Women in control?
> **Bibliography**
Bindocci, C. G. Women and technology
> **Biography**
Boyer, R. M. Apache mothers and daughters
Notable Hispanic American women
Shepherd, N. A price below rubies
> *Dictionaries*
Mahoney, M. H. Women in espionage
The Norton book of women's lives
> **Books and reading**
Flint, K. The woman reader, 1837-1914
Turner, C. Living by the pen
> **Civil rights**
> *See also*
> Pro-choice movement
> Pro-life movement
Alonso, H. H. Peace as a women's issue
Costain, A. N. Inviting women's rebellion
Daniels, C. R. At women's expense
Ferraro, G. A. Changing history
> *Dictionaries*
Franck, I. M. The women's desk reference
> **Diaries**
Clarke, P. Life lines
> **Diseases**
> *See also*
> Women—Health and hygiene
Confronting cancer, constructing change
Helfant, R. H. Women, take heart
Lockie, A. The women's guide to homeopathy
McGinn, K. A. Women's cancers
Pashkow, F. J. The woman's heart book
> **Education**
Powers, J. B. The "girl question" in education
Unsettling relations
> **Employment**
Agonito, R. No more "nice girl"
Amott, T. L. Caught in the crisis
Cook, A. H. The most difficult revolution
Driscoll, D.-M. Members of the club
Glazer, N. Y. Women's paid and unpaid labor
Murphy, T. A. Ten hours' labor
Sokoloff, N. J. Black women and white women in the professions
Strom, S. H. Beyond the typewriter
Tomaskovic-Devey, D. Gender & racial inequality at work
Turbin, C. Working women of collar city

Figure 11.9 Subject and Title Index from Book Review Digest, *1994, p. 2545.*

TOLKIN, MICHAEL—*Continued*

mall. In addition, Tolkin has no sense of humour at all. . . . [The novel] is consistently, stultifyingly dull, despite its graphic descriptions of trolleys of unmatched limbs, barrels of hùman viscera in the air-crash morgue. [It] might make a good film. As a novel, however, it is still-born."

TOLLEFSON, JAMES W. The strength not to fight; an oral history of conscientious objectors of the Vietnam War. 248p $22.95 1993 Little, Brown
959.704   1. Vietnam   War,   1961-1975—Conscientious objectors
ISBN 0-316-85112-4   LC 92-36335

SUMMARY: The author examines the "experiences of conscientious objectors (CO) during the Vietnam War. The personal histories resulting from the author's interviews . . . discuss why people resisted the war, how they were able to gain CO status, and what were the consequences of their actions." (Libr J) Bibliography.

REVIEW: *Choice* v31 p664 D '93. R.E. Marcello (180w)
"Tollefson, himself a conscientious objector during the Vietnam War, has written this book based on in-depth interviews with 40 anonymous men who shared his convictions about that conflict. He does not pretend to have used a scientific sampling in selecting his subjects. Tollefson uses a clever format. Instead of writing a series of separate, individual stories, he organized the book around the major experiences of the conscientious objectors. His purpose, through these highly personal and sometimes emotional accounts, is to understand and convey accurately the experiences of his interviewees. . . . He makes no judgments, neither praising nor apologizing for nor condemning his interviewees. Good bibliography of secondary sources on conscientious objection."

REVIEW: *Libr J* v118 p154 Je 1 '93. Robert Favini (110w)
"[Tollefson] lets the collective power of many varied stories provide a chronicle of the men who sought CO status as well as the society in which they lived. This book will serve as a fine complement to Christian Appy's oral history, Working-Class War: American Combat Soldiers and Vietnam [BRD 1993]. The extensive bibliography renders the book even more valuable. Recommended for all libraries."

TOLLISON, ROBERT D. The National Collegiate Athletic Association. See Fleisher, A. A.

TOM, LINDA C., il. Random House American Sign Language dictionary. See Costello, E.

TOMASKO, ROBERT M. Rethinking the corporation; the architecture of change. 213p il $22.95 1993 AMACOM
658.4   1. Corporations 2. Management 3. Organizational change
ISBN 0-8144-5022-9   LC 93-9246

SUMMARY: This book argues against "the unstructured reduction of managerial staff. . . . Downsizing for the purpose of saving funds without significant planning and consideration of human needs and aspirations, Tomasko asserts, can lead to long-term problems. Jobs within the enterprise need to be meaningful to the workers—especially to one of the corporation's most valuable resources, the middle manager. Tomasko stresses the necessity for teamwork in planning, a diminution of hierarchy, and the use of professional as well as managerial career paths." (Libr J) Index.

REVIEW: *Bus Horiz* v37 p87 My/Je '94. Henry H. Beam (1200w)

REVIEW: *Choice* v31 p644 D '93. G. Klinefelter (170w)
"Tomasko focuses on two groups of readers; those in the organization who have the power and responsibility to bring about change and those who are on the receiving end of change. A renowned consultant in organizational structure and architectural structure, he approaches the subject of organizational planning from the perspective of an archi-

tect, covering such topics as construction of stable structures, dealing with constraints, and effectively combining several components into a unified entity. . . . An interesting and creative approach to an important topic for managers as they guide their organizations into the 21st century."

REVIEW: *Libr J* v118 p148 Je 1 '93. Littleton M. Maxwell (150w)
"Tomasko (Downsizing: Reshaping the Corporation, 1990) . . . recommends a corporate structure that is strong and economical, but, above all, not too rigid. This thought-provoking book is recommended for public, academic, and corporate collections."

TOMASKOVIC-DEVEY, DONALD. Gender & racial inequality at work; the sources & consequences of job segregation. (Cornell studies in industrial and labor relations, no27) 212p $38; pa $16.95 1993 ILR Press
331.13   1. Discrimination in employment 2. Sex discrimination 3. Race discrimination 4. Women—Employment 5. Blacks—Employment
ISBN 0-87546-304-5; 0-87546-305-3 (pa)
LC 93-16551

SUMMARY: This study is based on data from the 1989 North Carolina Employment and Health Survey. The author examines black-white and male-female inequalities in employment and job-level segregation by race and sex. "Within economic and sociological frameworks, he theorizes about such organizational and public policy issues as comparable worth and affirmative action." (Booklist) Bibliography. Index.

REVIEW: *Booklist* v89 p2019 Ag '93. David Rouse (150w)
"Librarians need no reminder that one sex or the other is usually predominant in many jobs or professions. But if they are looking for empirical, scholarly evidence of both some of the sources and many of the consequences of so-called job segregation, Tomaskovic-Devey provides it. A North Carolina State University sociology professor, he uses a 1989 North Carolina employment and health survey, unique because it included a random sample of all occupations from the general population, to develop and support his conclusions. . . . Recommended for research-oriented collections."

REVIEW: *Choice* v31 p877 Ja '94. E. Hu-DeHart (180w)
"Tomaskovic-Devey's study is a valuable contribution to what can be termed 'glass ceiling research'—that is, an inquiry into job segregation and subsequent barriers to upward mobility for groups of workers (as opposed to individuals) in the workplace. . . . [His] conclusions about race, however, are based on research concerning black workers only. Further, Tomaskovic-Devey does not thoroughly explore the intersection of gender and race. . . . Despite the obviously relevant and timely nature of this topic for the majority of American workers (women and minorities), those uninitiated in the technical discourse of social science research will not find this book very accessible."

TOMASSI, NOREEN, ed. Money for international exchange in the arts. See Money for international exchange in the arts

TOMB, HOWARD, 1959-. MicroAliens; dazzling journeys with an electron microscope; [by] Howard Tomb and Dennis Kunkel; with drawings by Tracy Dockray. 79p il $16 1993 Farrar, Straus & Giroux
578   1. Microorganisms—Juvenile literature 2. Electron microscope and microscopy—Juvenile literature
ISBN 0-374-34960-6   LC 93-1403

SUMMARY: In this book, text and photographs taken with an electron microscope examine such items as bird feathers, fleas, skin, mold, and blood. "Grades four to eight." (SLJ)

Figure 11.10 *Main entry section,* Book Review Digest, *1994, p. 2074.*

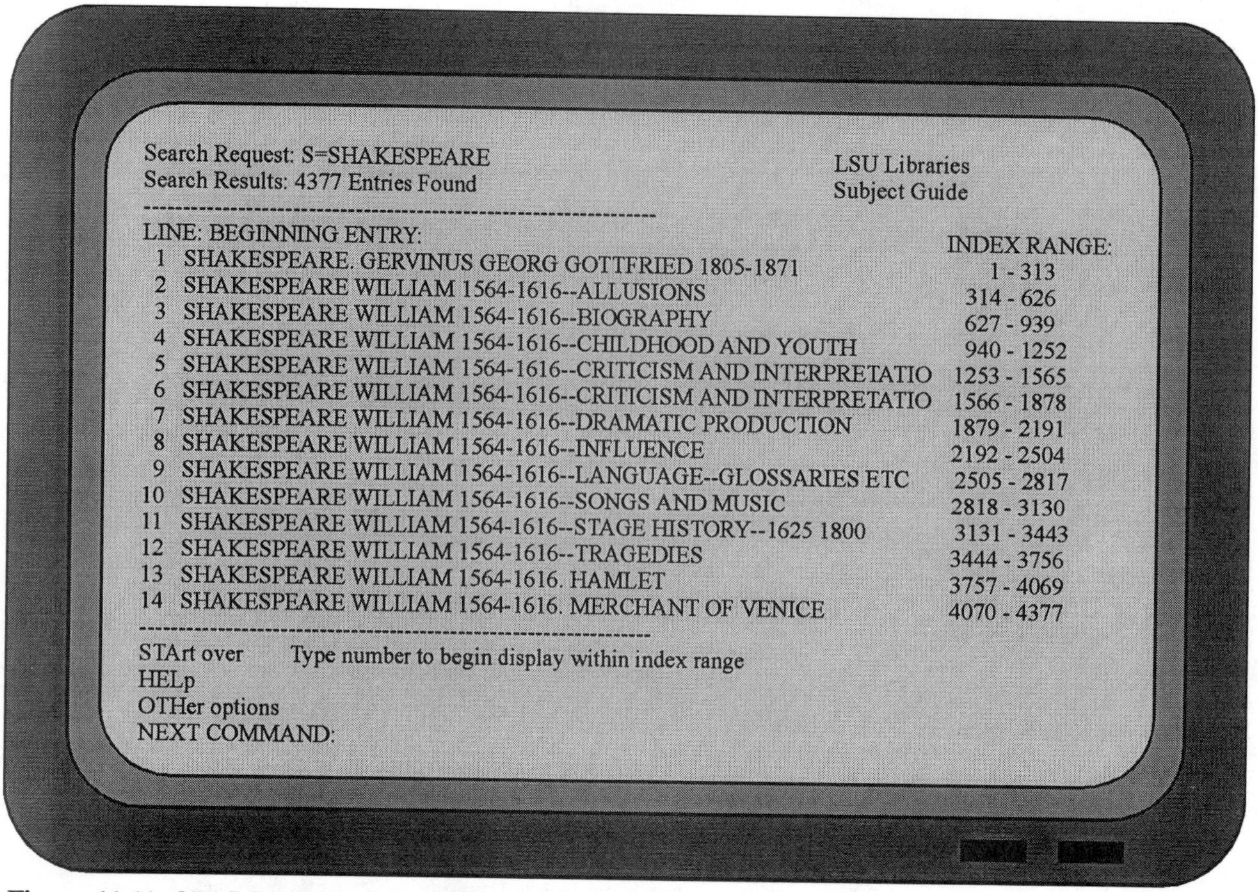

```
Search Request: S=SHAKESPEARE                          LSU Libraries
Search Results: 4377 Entries Found                     Subject Guide
--------------------------------------------------------------
LINE: BEGINNING ENTRY:                                 INDEX RANGE:
  1  SHAKESPEARE. GERVINUS GEORG GOTTFRIED 1805-1871         1 - 313
  2  SHAKESPEARE WILLIAM 1564-1616--ALLUSIONS              314 - 626
  3  SHAKESPEARE WILLIAM 1564-1616--BIOGRAPHY              627 - 939
  4  SHAKESPEARE WILLIAM 1564-1616--CHILDHOOD AND YOUTH    940 - 1252
  5  SHAKESPEARE WILLIAM 1564-1616--CRITICISM AND INTERPRETATIO  1253 - 1565
  6  SHAKESPEARE WILLIAM 1564-1616--CRITICISM AND INTERPRETATIO  1566 - 1878
  7  SHAKESPEARE WILLIAM 1564-1616--DRAMATIC PRODUCTION    1879 - 2191
  8  SHAKESPEARE WILLIAM 1564-1616--INFLUENCE              2192 - 2504
  9  SHAKESPEARE WILLIAM 1564-1616--LANGUAGE--GLOSSARIES ETC  2505 - 2817
 10  SHAKESPEARE WILLIAM 1564-1616--SONGS AND MUSIC        2818 - 3130
 11  SHAKESPEARE WILLIAM 1564-1616--STAGE HISTORY--1625 1800  3131 - 3443
 12  SHAKESPEARE WILLIAM 1564-1616--TRAGEDIES              3444 - 3756
 13  SHAKESPEARE WILLIAM 1564-1616. HAMLET                 3757 - 4069
 14  SHAKESPEARE WILLIAM 1564-1616. MERCHANT OF VENICE     4070 - 4377
--------------------------------------------------------------
STArt over     Type number to begin display within index range
HELp
OTHer options
NEXT COMMAND:
```

Figure 11.11 OPAC Subject search, Subject Guide Screen.

From the Subject Guide screen, select the subheading "criticism and interpretation." To display entries dealing with criticism and interpretations of Shakespeare's works in general, select line 6. The Subject Index screen displays individual titles of critical works.

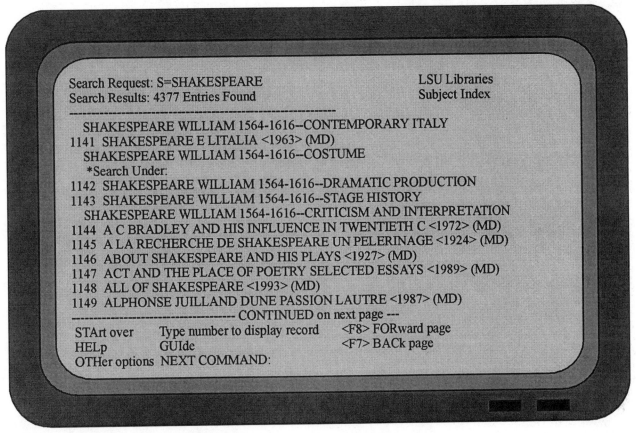

Search Request: S=SHAKESPEARE   LSU Libraries
Search Results: 4377 Entries Found   Subject Index

     SHAKESPEARE WILLIAM 1564-1616--CONTEMPORARY ITALY
1141 SHAKESPEARE E LITALIA <1963> (MD)
     SHAKESPEARE WILLIAM 1564-1616--COSTUME
   *Search Under:
1142 SHAKESPEARE WILLIAM 1564-1616--DRAMATIC PRODUCTION
1143 SHAKESPEARE WILLIAM 1564-1616--STAGE HISTORY
     SHAKESPEARE WILLIAM 1564-1616--CRITICISM AND INTERPRETATION
1144 A C BRADLEY AND HIS INFLUENCE IN TWENTIETH C <1972> (MD)
1145 A LA RECHERCHE DE SHAKESPEARE UN PELERINAGE <1924> (MD)
1146 ABOUT SHAKESPEARE AND HIS PLAYS <1927> (MD)
1147 ACT AND THE PLACE OF POETRY SELECTED ESSAYS <1989> (MD)
1148 ALL OF SHAKESPEARE <1993> (MD)
1149 ALPHONSE JUILLAND DUNE PASSION LAUTRE <1987> (MD)
-------------------------- CONTINUED on next page ---
STArt over   Type number to display record   <F8> FORward page
HELp   GUIde   <F7> BACk page
OTHer options NEXT COMMAND:

Figure 11.12 OPAC Subject Index screen.

Selected List of Literary Anthologies, Book Reviews and Literary Criticism Sources

Anthologies

Essays

Essay and General Literature Index. New York: H. W. Wilson, 1900/1933-.
  An alphabetical author, subject, and sometimes title index to thousands of essays and chapters found in books. Particularly strong in the fields of the humanities and the social sciences but covers other disciplines as well. It is an excellent source for a criticism of an author's work. Available on CD-ROM.

Plays

Keller, Dean H. *Index to Plays in Periodicals.* Rev. and expanded ed. Metuchen, N.J.: Scarecrow, 1979.
  Indexes about 10,000 plays located in 267 periodicals in one volume.

Ottemiller's Index to Plays in Collections, an Author and Title Index Appearing in Collections Published between 1900 and Early 1985. Rev. and enlarged by John M. Connor and Billie M. Connor. 7th ed. Metuchen, N. J.: Scarecrow, 1988.
  Index to full-length plays appearing in books published in England and the United States. It is divided into three sections: (1) author index with titles and dates of performance, (2) list of collections analyzed with key to symbols, and (3) title index.

Play Index. New York: H. W. Wilson, 1949-.

 The key index to 26,000 plays published from 1949 to 1986 in six volumes. The volume for 1983-1987 is an index to 3,964 plays. It is divided into two parts: Part I lists plays under authors' names and anthologies in which found. Part II includes the cast analysis by number of male and female characters needed. Part III lists anthologies with full bibliographic information. Part IV includes a Directory of Publishers and Distributors.

Poetry

American Poetry Index: An Author and Title Index to Poetry by Americans in Single Author Collections. Vol. 1, 1981-1982. Vol. 2, 1983. Vol. 3, 1984. New York: Grander Book Co., 1983.

 An alphabetical index to authors and titles of over 10,000 poems published in 190 collections which are located by number after author's name in main index.

Caskey, Jefferson D. Comp. *Index to Poetry in Popular Periodicals, 1955-1959*. Westport, CT: Greenwood, 1984.

 Indexes 7,400 poems by title appearing in American periodicals from 1955-1959. Also includes a first-line index, author index, and subject index.

_____. *Index to Poetry in Popular Periodicals, 1960-1964*. Westport, CT: Greenwood, 1988.

The Columbia Granger's Index to Poetry. 9th ed. New York: Columbia University Press, 1990.

 Continues *Granger's Index to Poetry*, 1970-1981. Indexes over 100,000 poems appearing in over 400 anthologies.

Granger, Edith. *Granger's Index to Poetry, 1970-1981*. Ed. William James Smith. 7th ed., completely rev. and enl., indexing anthologies published through December 31, 1981. New York: Columbia University Press, 1982.

 First published in 1904, this is considered the standard index to poetry. Each edition enlarges on the previous one, omitting some anthologies, adding new ones. Later editions arranged by sections as follows: (1) title and first-line index, (2) author index, and (3) subject index.

Short Stories

Short Story Index, an Index to 60,000 Stories in 4,320 Collections, 1900-1949. New York: H. W. Wilson, 1953-.

 Author, title, subject index to short stories appearing in collections. The 1984-1988 volume indexes 21,400 stories published in 1,250 collections. Kept updated by supplements.

Speeches

Mitchell, Charity. *Speech Index: An Index to Collections of World Famous Orations and Speeches for Various Occasions. Supplement, 1966-1980*. Metuchen, NJ: Scarecrow, 1982.

 Alphabetical arrangement of speeches by author, subject, and type of speech.

Sutton, Roberta Briggs. *Speech Index; an Index to 259 Collections of World Famous Orations and Speeches for Various Occasions*. 4th ed. Rev. and enl. New York: Scarecrow, 1966.

Book Reviews

Book Review Digest. New York: H. W. Wilson, 1905-.

 An alphabetical listing by authors of books. Each entry includes the title of the book, bibliographical information, and publisher's note. The publisher's note is followed by references to the reviews which appear in periodicals. Some of the references include excerpts from the book reviews. Also includes a subject and title index. A list of periodicals indexed is located in the front. Issued monthly with annual cumulation. Available on CD-ROM.

Book Review Index, a Master Cumulation. Detroit: Gale, 1955-.
 Provides citations for book reviews and includes both author and title indexes. Includes list of abbreviated journal titles.

Combined Retrospective Index to Book Reviews in Humanities Journals, 1802-1974. 10 volumes. Ed. Evan Ira Farber. Woodbridge, CT: Research Publications, 1983-1984.
 An author and title access to about 500,000 reviews from 150 humanities journals. Names of reviewers are also given. Volume 10 has a title index.

Additional sources for book reviews include *The New York Times Index*, LEXIS/NEXIS, *Readers' Guide to Periodical Literature,* and *MLA* on CD-ROM.

Indexes to Literary Criticism

Some of the following guides are limited to literature of a specific nationality, while others are international in their coverage. Both the titles and the annotations indicate in some measure the scope of the guide.

General

Contemporary Literary Criticism. Detroit: Gale, 1973-.
 Covers living writers and those who died after 1960, includes excerpts and citations from mystery and science fiction authors. "Presents significant passages from published criticism from authors" for the period covered. Provides extensive annotated bibliographies.

Essay and General Literature Index. New York: H. W. Wilson, 1900/1933-.
 As noted earlier, this is an excellent source for criticism of all types of literature. Available on CD-ROM.

Magill, Frank Northern. *Magill's Bibliography of Literary Criticism; Selected Sources for the Study of More than 2,500 Outstanding Works of Western Literature.* 4 vols. Englewood Cliffs, NJ: Salem, 1979.
 Criticisms in books, parts of books, and periodicals of poetry, drama, and fiction.

Modern Language Association International Bibliography. 1921-. CD-ROM version called
 MLA (database). Began with 1981 and is updated quarterly.

Nineteenth Century Literary Criticism. Detroit: Gale, 1981-.
 Similar to *CLC* and *TCLC*, except is limited to writers who lived between 1800 and 1900.

Twentieth-Century Literary Criticism. Detroit: Gale, 1978-.
 Similar to *CLC* and *NCLC* above, except covers authors who died between 1900 and 1960.

Novels

Abernethy, Peter L., Christian J. W. Kloesel, and Jeffry R. Smitten. *English Novel Explication. Supplement I.* Hamden, CT: Shoe String, 1976. *Supplement II,* 1981. *Supplement III,* 1987.
 Supplement IV, covers 1986 through part half of 1989. A fifth supplement is scheduled.This work supplements and updates the Palmer and Dyson guide. Extends *English Novel Explication series to 1985.*

Gerstenberger, Donna, and George Hendrick. *The American Novel, a Checklist of Twentieth Century Criticism on Novels Written Since 1789.* 2 vols. Denver: Allan Swallow, 1961-1970. Vol. 1, *The American Novel 1789-1959.* Vol. 2, *Criticisms Written 1960-1968.*
 Criticisms are listed under major authors by titles of works. Includes citations from books and periodicals.

Kearney, E. I., and L. S. Fitzgerald. *The Continental Novel, a Checklist of Criticism in English 1967-1980.* Metuchen, NJ: Scarecrow, 1988.
 Critical entries are organized under the following categories: the French novel, the Spanish and Portuguese novel, the Italian novel, the German novel, the Scandinavian novel, and the Russian and East European novel.

Palmer, Helen H., and Anne Jane Dyson. *English Novel Explication: Criticisms to 1972.* Hamden, CT: Shoe String, 1973.
Cites criticisms found in books and periodicals in English and foreign languages from 1958 to 1972.

Plays (Drama)

Breed, Paul F., and Florence M. Snideman. *Dramatic Criticism Index: a Bibliography of Commentaries on Playwrights from Ibsen to the Avante-Garde.* Detroit: Gale, 1972.
Includes critical articles from over 200 periodicals and 630 books. Main entries under authors. Includes a title and a critic index.

Eddleman, Floyd Eugene. *American Drama Criticism: Interpretations 1890-1977.* 2nd ed. Hamden, CT: Shoe String, 1979. *Supplement I,* 1984.

Palmer, Helen H., and Anne Jane Dyson. *American Drama Criticism Interpretations, 1890-1965, Inclusive of American Drama, since the First Play Produced in America.* Hamden, CT: Shoe String, 1967. *Supplement I,* 1970. *Supplement II,* 1976. *Supplement III,* 1990. Comp. by Floyd Eugene Eddleman.
Lists critical articles of American plays located in periodicals, books, and monographs. Arrangement is alphabetical by playwright.

Palmer, Helen H. *European Drama Criticism 1900-1975.* 2nd ed. Hamden, CT: Shoe String, 1977.
A source book to critical writings of representative European plays in selected books and periodicals. Information is organized in three parts: (1) alphabetical list of playwrights with critical articles which appear in periodicals and books, (2) a list of books used as sources and a list of periodicals searched, and (3) an author-title index.

Poetry

Alexander, Harriet Semmes, comp. *American and British Poetry: A Guide to the Criticism Published Between 1925-1978.* Athens, OH: Swallow Press/Ohio University Press, 1984.
Indexes criticisms located in 170 journals and 500 books published between 1925-1978.

Cline, Gloria Stark, and Jeffrey A. Baker. *An Index to Criticisms of British and American Poetry.* Metuchen, NJ: Scarecrow, 1973.
Cites critical articles on poetry published in periodicals and books between 1960 and 1970. List of abbreviations of periodicals used in entries and a bibliography of books cited are found in the back of this work.

Shields, Ellen F. *Contemporary English Poetry: An Annotated Bibliography of Criticism to 1980.* New York: Garland, 1984.

Short Stories

Short Story Criticism. Detroit: Gale. 1988-.
Criticisms are listed in chronological order. Cumulated author and title indexes are included.

Walker, Warren S. *Twentieth-Century Short Story Explication: Interpretations 1900-1975 of Short Fiction since 1800.* 3rd ed. Hamden, CT: Shoe String, 1977. *Supplement I,* 1980. *Supplement II,* 1984. *Supplement III,* 1987. Analyses of short stories appearing in books, periodicals, and monographs.

Instructor: _____   Name: _____

Course/Section: _____   Date: _____

Review Questions for Chapter Eleven

1. List the three types of sources discussed in this chapter.

    a)

    b)

    c)

2. Name an index you would use to find chapters or essays in books.

3. What is the importance of using a book review for an author's work?

4. What is the difference between a book review and a literary criticism?

5. Name two book review sources that would be useful.

6. Can book reviews be located through periodical indexes? Justify your answer.

7. How does one locate book reviews or articles on literary criticism in the library after the information has been found in an index?

8. Name two sources you could use for finding literary criticism of a particular writer.

Instructor: _____ **Name:** _____

Course/Section: _____ **Date:** _____

Essay and General Literature Index Exercise

The Essay and General Literature Index is an index to materials in anthologies. Consult the index for information on your topic or another subject you may select. After you have found your reference, answer the following questions:

1. What is the call number of the *Essay and General Literature Index?*

2. Give the date of the volume used.

3. Give the complete subject heading under which you located your topic.

4. Analyze the reference you located by giving the following information:

    a. Author of the article

    b. Title of the article

    c. Name of the book in which the article appears.

    d. Did the book have an author or an editor? Circle one or the other and record the name.

    e. Pages in the book in which the article appears.

    f. Place, publisher, and copyright or publication date of the book

5. Does the library own the book? If so, what is the call number?

6. Write a bibliographic reference to the article you have found. Use the bibliographic citation examples in Chapter 14 for citing an essay in a collection or an anthology.

7. Would this book be a good reference for your topic? Justify your answer.

Instructor: _____   **Name:** _____

Course/Section: _____   **Date:** _____

Book Review Exercise

Locate a review of a book on a topic on which you are doing research or a book you have read recently. Book reviews may be obtained from *Book Review Index, Book Review Digest* or any other book review source. Choose one of the reviews listed and answer the following questions:

1. Name and date of the book review source used:

2. Call number of the book review source:

3. Analyze one reference you found by giving the following information:

    a. Author of book selected:

    b. Title of the book:

    c. Author of review (If unsigned, mark NA.):

    d. Source in which the review appears:

        1. Complete title of the magazine or journal:

        2. Volume:

        3. Pages:

        4. Date:

        5. Number of words in review:

4. Call number of the magazine or journal in which the review appears:

5. How many other references to reviews were given?

6. Retrieve one of the reviews listed above.

7. Use the bibliographic citation examples given in Chapter 14 to write a bibliographic reference to the review.

8. Read the complete review. Is this a book which you would find useful when doing research on your topic? Justify your answer.

Instructor: _____   **Name:** _____

Course/Section: _____   **Date:** _____

Literary Criticism Exercise

Using an index to literary criticism, locate a reference to a criticism of a novel, poem, play, or short story that you have read. Locate the criticism, read it, and complete the answer sheet below:

1. Title of the index used:

2. Procedures used to locate the index:

3. Author of the literary work you selected:

4. Title of the literary work you selected:

5. Author and title of the source in which the criticism appears:

6. Place, publisher, and date of the source if a book; if a periodical, give the date and volume of the periodical and the pages on which it appears:

7. Call number of the book or periodical in which the criticism appears:

8. Use the bibliographic citation examples given in Chapter 14 to write a bibliographical citation for the criticism you found:

9. Do you agree or disagree with the critic's assessment of the work? Justify your answer.

GOVERNMENT INFORMATION

A PREVIEW

Information produced by governing bodies encompasses a broad range of topics—not only on the government itself and how it is run, but also on many subjects of interest to citizens. It is possible to find information on almost any topic in a government source. This chapter is designed to serve as a guide for locating government information. The emphasis is on U.S. Government publications, which are more numerous than those of the other entities; there are brief introductions to local, state, and United Nations documents.

KEY TERMS AND CONCEPTS

Government Information in the Research Process
U.S. Government Publications
State Government Publications
Local Government Publications
United Nations Publications

INTRODUCTION

In the United States it is an elementary—but all important— principle that the operations of government are to be open to scrutiny and criticism by citizens. This kind of uninhibited criticism makes it possible for citizens to participate in government and to contribute to the advancement of society. Indeed, the American political system, and to a large extent, the education system, rests on the widespread acceptance of ready and fair access to information about government and information produced by government. It is this principle which has led local, state, national, and even international governing bodies to produce large quantities of all sorts of information.

Government Information in the Research Process

Information from government agencies at all levels is used in research especially in the social sciences and the sciences. Although one might expect to find some government information covering topics in the humanities, that is not the norm. Aside from the intrinsic value of contributing to an informed citizenry, government publications have a number of distinctive characteristics which add to their value as reference sources.

1. *Cover a broad spectrum of subjects.* Since the government is necessarily responsive to public needs, the subjects covered in government publications range from those that are useful only to scholars and specialists in a field to those which are of interest to consumers.

2. *Ready availability.* Government publications are inexpensive or, in many cases, free of charge. One can write or call government agencies to acquire many of the publications. However, this is usually not necessary since most government publications can be found in libraries or on the Internet. It is common practice for governmental bodies to place their publications in libraries in order to make government information available to all citizens. Information from all levels of government—state, local, national, and international—is available on the Internet.

3. *Primary sources of information.* Much of the information disseminated by the government is considered to be a primary source. Statistics which are gathered first-hand fit into this category. The decennial census published by the U.S. Bureau of the Census is the result of an actual door-to-door count of U.S. citizens.

4. *Free of bias.* The individuals who work for government agencies are not supposed to represent a particular viewpoint, a particular political party, or a special interest group; as a result, government information is generally considered to be objective.

5. *Up-to-date information.* Since the government is the primary source for much of the information which appears in non-government publications, information from a government source is often more current than that in a non-government publication. This is especially true today with information that is available through the Internet.

6. *Only source of information on many topics.* Much of the information available from governmental agencies is not available from any other source. For example, the Federal government is the sole provider of information on the amounts of toxic air releases by various industries; the state government is the unique source for expenditures on state services.

In the research process one should examine the information needed to see if a government publication might not be an appropriate resource.

- Are statistics needed?
- Is there a social issue involved, such as world hunger, over population, abortion, or unemployment?
- Is it an issue that was discussed in Congress, such as use of seat belts or sexual harassment?
- Does it concern historical events, such as the war in Vietnam?
- Is it a local issue, such as the funding of public education?
- Is it scientific research that has been sponsored by the government?

Government information may show up as the various library tools are searched. For example, if government documents are included in the library's online catalog along with other materials, they will show up in the results of many subject and keyword searches. Some periodical indexes include government periodicals and reports among the sources they index. For example, *PAIS International* includes both U.S. and international government publications. The finding aids for government information that might not appear in the online catalog or other indexing sources in a routine search of the literature will be discussed below with each of the types government information sources.

United States Government Publications

Scope

The Federal government is the single largest producer of information in the world. The information sources from the United States Government are as varied as they are numerous. They come in all sizes and shapes—from one-page leaflets to works of several thousand pages and many volumes. They vary in scope from highly technical scientific research reports to popular pamphlets on such topics as diets for weight loss and caring for pets. Included in government publications are all the official documents such as laws, regulations, court decisions, presidential documents, treaties, congressional proceedings, military records, and census reports. The government issues a large number of reference books including indexes, abstracts, bibliographies, directories, atlases, handbooks, yearbooks, and almanacs. Approximately 1200 government periodicals are published on a regular basis.

Format

The format of government information is almost as varied as its scope. Until recently, government publications were published in traditional formats: paper, microfiche, film, video and cassette tapes, photographs, maps, charts, and posters. The Federal government has always been a leader in utilizing new technologies to produce, store, and retrieve information, and was the first publisher to make widespread use of CD-ROM as a publication medium. There are thousands of government titles in CD-ROM format. These include statistical sources, maps, government regulations, and reference sources such as the *Statistical Abstract of the U.S.*

Today the Government Printing Office (GPO), which is the chief publisher of U. S. Government information, is in a state of transition from a paper publisher to an electronic publisher. In 1996 Congress issued a mandate that the GPO formulate a plan to cease publishing and distributing government information in paper and microfiche format and move to electronic format. It is anticipated that before the end of the century all government information, with the exception of a few titles, will be available only in electronic format—primarily through the Internet.

Depository Libraries

The Government Printing Office (GPO) was established in 1861 for the purpose of publishing the official publications of the Federal government. Prior to that time the official documents of the U.S. Government were printed by private firms. Consequently, we have historical documents published by authority of the Federal government dating back to the Continental Congress. The GPO publishes all the official documents of the legislative, executive, and judicial branches of the Federal government—the congressional debates, laws, executive orders, annual reports, court decisions, regulations, reports, and special studies.

In 1895, Congress enacted legislation which provided for the free distribution of documents to designated libraries and institutions. The libraries receiving documents free of charge from the GPO are called *depository libraries*. Today there are approximately 1400 depository libraries in the United States. Of these, about 50 are *regional depository libraries* which receive all the publications distributed by GPO. Other libraries are *selective depository libraries*, so designated because they can choose the items which they wish to receive. The depository library provides the facilities for housing documents and the staff needed to administer the collections. The only other obligations of the depository library are to assure that the materials are cared for according to guidelines established by the GPO and to make the documents available to all citizens. Library users should inquire whether there is a depository library at their institution or in the area in order to take advantage of the full spectrum of U.S. Government publications.

Because government information is in a state of transition as of this writing (1996), the status of depository libraries is also being questioned. The role of the depository library in an electronic environment will no doubt change with the advent of an all electronic library. With government information being available primarily through the Internet, the need to house and preserve government information will cease to exist. Depository libraries will probably maintain their retrospective collections, but will assume different roles with regard to current information.

Finding Government Information

Most depository libraries house documents in a separate area arranged by Superintendent of Documents (SuDocs) number. The SuDocs system is an alpha-numeric system based on the agency which issues the document. Even though documents are shelved in a separate area, it is not unusual to find them listed in the online catalog with other library materials. However, most online catalogs contain only records of items cataloged since 1976 when GPO began creating machine readable catalog (MARC) records. Figure 12.1 illustrates how to locate documents which are shelved by SuDocs number.

Figure 12.1 Instructions for locating a U.S. Government Publication

How to find a U.S. Government Publication

As a Federal Depository Library, we receive many publications issued by agencies of the U.S. Government. These publications, which may include books, maps, posters, pamphlets, and periodicals, contain information on careers, business opportunities, space exploration, health and nutrition, energy, and many other subjects.

Federal Government publications in this collection are arranged by the Superintendent of Documents classification number. Publications are grouped together by issuing agency.' To ensure that you find all of the materials available on a particular subject, be sure to check the indexes recommended by the librarian.

The example below shows how the Superintendent of Documents classification number C 61.34:987 is constructed for the publication *U.S. Industrial Outlook:*

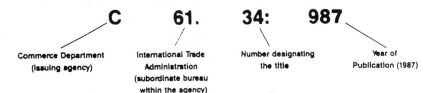

C	61.	34:	987
Commerce Department (issuing agency)	International Trade Administration (subordinate bureau within the agency)	Number designating the title	Year of Publication (1987)

Here are the prefixes from the Superintendent of Documents classification numbers for some other agencies that you may be interested in:

A	Agriculture Department
C 3.	Census Bureau (Commerce Department)
D	Defense Department
E	Energy Department
ED	Education Department
GA	General Accounting Office
GS	General Services Administration
HE	Health and Human Services Department
I	Interior Department
I 19.	U.S. Geological Survey (Interior Department)
J	Justice Department
Ju	Judiciary
L	Labor Department
LC	Library of Congress
NAS	National Aeronautics and Space Administration
S	State Department
SI	Smithsonian Institution
T 22.	Internal Revenue Service (Treasury Department)
X, Y	Congress
Y 4.	Congressional Committees .

Finding Aids

General

Monthly Catalog of United States Government Publications. Washington: GPO, 1895-.

The comprehensive index to government publications, it is used to locate government publications which are shelved by the SuDocs call number and are *not* listed in the library catalog. The main entries are arranged alphabetically by issuing agency in the main body of the catalog. Each issue contains separate indexes for subjects, titles, title keywords, authors, series reports, contract numbers, stock numbers, and SuDocs numbers. (See Figures 12.2 and 12.3).

Since 1976, GPO has been creating the *Monthly Catalog* from MARC records. Prior to this, the bibliographic entries in the *Monthly Catalog* contained less detail. Figures 12.4 and 12.5 are examples of an index entry and a bibliographic record from a pre-1976 *Monthly Catalog.*

The *Monthly Catalog* from 1976 to date, is available online through DIALOG and BRS. CD-ROM versions of the *Monthly Catalog* from 1976 to the present are available from several vendors: Autographics, Inc.; Information Access Co., Marcive, Inc.; and SilverPlatter. Figures 12.6-12.7 show a keyword search in the Marcive database, GOP/CatPac.

The *Monthly Catalog* is also available for online searching as part of the GPO Access, Federal Locator services. Once a publication is identified, a link is available to locate depository libraries that receive that publication. The database contains cataloging records published in MOCAT since January 1994 and is updated daily with preliminary cataloging records that will be edited and published in future issues of *Monthly Catalog.* Online. Available HTTP:// http://www.access.gpo.gov/cgi-bin/make430.cgi.

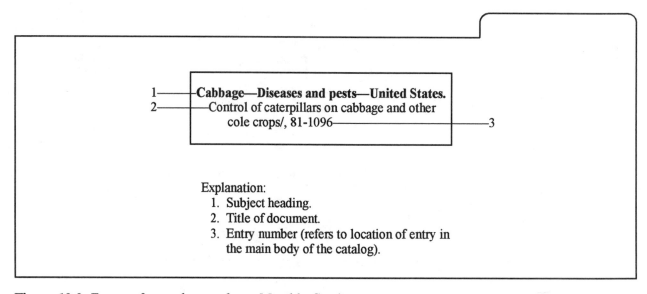

Figure 12.2 Excerpt from subject index in Monthly Catalog.

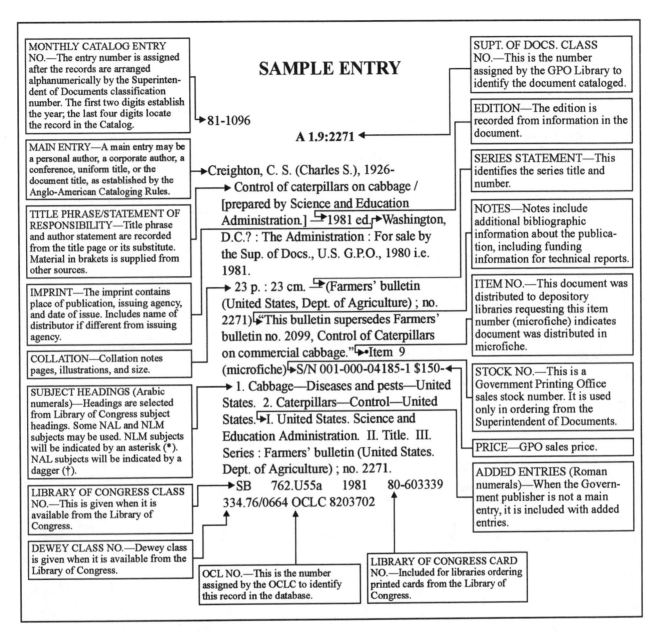

SAMPLE ENTRY

MONTHLY CATALOG ENTRY NO.—The entry number is assigned after the records are arranged alphanumerically by the Superintendent of Documents classification number. The first two digits establish the year; the last four digits locate the record in the Catalog.

MAIN ENTRY—A main entry may be a personal author, a corporate author, a conference, uniform title, or the document title, as established by the Anglo-American Cataloging Rules.

TITLE PHRASE/STATEMENT OF RESPONSIBILITY—Title phrase and author statement are recorded from the title page or its substitute. Material in brackets is supplied from other sources.

IMPRINT—The imprint contains place of publication, issuing agency, and date of issue. Includes name of distributor if different from issuing agency.

COLLATION—Collation notes pages, illustrations, and size.

SUBJECT HEADINGS (Arabic numerals)—Headings are selected from Library of Congress subject headings. Some NAL and NLM subjects may be used. NLM subjects will be indicated by an asterisk (*). NAL subjects will be indicated by a dagger (†).

LIBRARY OF CONGRESS CLASS NO.—This is given when it is available from the Library of Congress.

DEWEY CLASS NO.—Dewey class is given when it is available from the Library of Congress.

SUPT. OF DOCS. CLASS NO.—This is the number assigned by the GPO Library to identify the document cataloged.

EDITION—The edition is recorded from information in the document.

SERIES STATEMENT—This identifies the series title and number.

NOTES—Notes include additional bibliographic information about the publication, including funding information for technical reports.

ITEM NO.—This document was distributed to depository libraries requesting this item number (microfiche) indicates document was distributed in microfiche.

STOCK NO.—This is a Government Printing Office sales stock number. It is used only in ordering from the Superintendent of Documents.

PRICE—GPO sales price.

ADDED ENTRIES (Roman numerals)—When the Government publisher is not a main entry, it is included with added entries.

OCL NO.—This is the number assigned by the OCLC to identify this record in the database.

LIBRARY OF CONGRESS CARD NO.—Included for libraries ordering printed cards from the Library of Congress.

81-1096

A 1.9:2271

Creighton, C. S. (Charles S.), 1926-
Control of caterpillars on cabbage / [prepared by Science and Education Administration.] 1981 ed. Washington, D.C.? : The Administration : For sale by the Sup. of Docs., U.S. G.P.O., 1980 i.e. 1981.
23 p. : 23 cm. (Farmers' bulletin (United States, Dept. of Agriculture) ; no. 2271) "This bulletin supersedes Farmers' bulletin no. 2099, Control of Caterpillars on commercial cabbage." Item 9 (microfiche) S/N 001-000-04185-1 $150-
1. Cabbage—Diseases and pests—United States. 2. Caterpillars—Control—United States. I. United States. Science and Education Administration. II. Title. III. Series : Farmers' bulletin (United States. Dept. of Agriculture) ; no. 2271.
SB   762.U55a   1981   80-603339
334.76/0664 OCLC 8203702

Figure 12.3 Monthly Catalog of United States Government Publications.

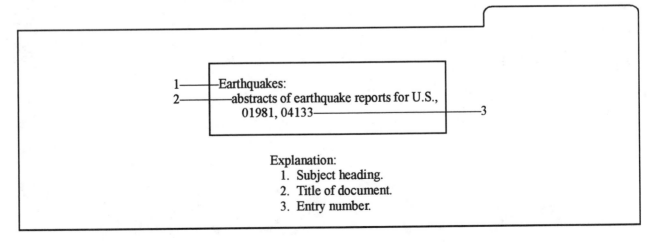

1——Earthquakes:
2——abstracts of earthquake reports for U.S., 01981, 04133——3

Explanation:
1. Subject heading.
2. Title of document.
3. Entry number.

Figure 12.4 Subject index.

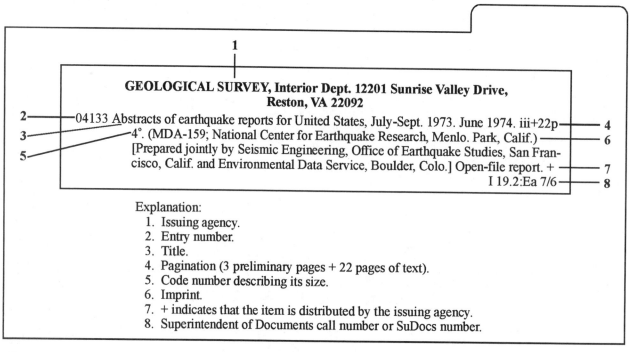

GEOLOGICAL SURVEY, Interior Dept. 12201 Sunrise Valley Drive, Reston, VA 22092

1

2 —— 04133 Abstracts of earthquake reports for United States, July-Sept. 1973. June 1974. iii+22p —— 4

3 —— 4°. (MDA-159; National Center for Earthquake Research, Menlo. Park, Calif.) —— 6

5 —— [Prepared jointly by Seismic Engineering, Office of Earthquake Studies, San Francisco, Calif. and Environmental Data Service, Boulder, Colo.] Open-file report. + —— 7

I 19.2:Ea 7/6 —— 8

Explanation:
1. Issuing agency.
2. Entry number.
3. Title.
4. Pagination (3 preliminary pages + 22 pages of text).
5. Code number describing its size.
6. Imprint.
7. + indicates that the item is distributed by the issuing agency.
8. Superintendent of Documents call number or SuDocs number.

Figure 12.5 Main entry section of the catalog.

COMBINED SEARCH: ANY- (ARTIFICIAL INTELLIGENCE) AND (CHILD*)
--- TITLE LIST ---

SEARCHING FOR:	WORD	PREVIOUS	RESULT
ARTIFICIAL	525		
INTELLIGENCE	1609	525	45
CHILD	1496		
CHILD	0	1496	1496
CHILDBEARING	0	6	6
CHILDBIRTH	6	39	43
CHILDCARE	43	1	44
CHILDCRAFT	44	1	45
CHILDERN	45	1	46
CHILDERS	46	16	62
CHILDERSBURG	62	2	64
CHILDHOOD	1496	164	1620
CHILDLESSNESS	64	2	66
CHILDREARING	66	1	67
CHILDREN			

-Move highlight [ENTER]-Select PgUp, PgDn-Page Home-Beginning End-End
F1-Help F2-Jump F5-Browse F6-Save F7-Print F9-Back F10-Main menu
PROCESSING REQUEST

Figure 12.6 GPO/CAT/PAC

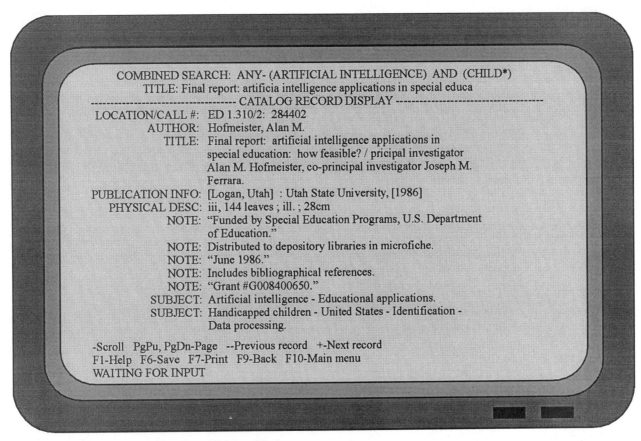

Figure 12.7 Record display from Figure 12.6

Statistical Information

Government agencies are the most prolific gatherers of statistics. The sources for statistics are discussed in Chapter 13.

Congressional Information

Congressional Information Services Index to Publications of the United States Congress. (CIS/Index). Washington: Congressional Information Service, 1970-. (Available online through DIALOG.)
A basic guide to Congressional actions. Part I provides brief abstracts of committee hearings, committee prints, House and Senate documents and reported bills, public laws, and miscellaneous publications of the U.S. Congress. Part II is a subject, name, and title index.

Congressional Masterfile. Congressional Information Service, 1789- quarterly updates. CD-ROM.
Indexes U.S. Congressional publications—including hearings, prints, documents and reports. Search by witness, witness affiliation, committee, subcommittee, bill number. Abstracts provided for documents published after 1970.

Scientific and Technical Information

Government Reports Announcements and Index. Washington: National Technical Information Service, 1970-. Bimonthly. (Available online through DIALOG. CD-ROM version also available.)
A guide to government research available through the National Technical Information Service (NTIS), a clearinghouse for government funded research as well as for many other non-depository publications by Federal agencies. Publications include all the research by private contractors which is funded by Federal

grants. The coverage is primarily in the pure sciences, but there are some reports that cover the behavioral and social sciences.

Government Information on the Internet

http://www.access.gpo.gov/su_docs/gils/gils.html
>   Government Information Locator Service (GILS) is the Federal government initiative to make government information accessible using computer and networking technology. As part of the Federal role in the National Information Infrastructure, GILS will identify and describe information resources throughout the Federal government. When it is all put together, GILS will provide forms for searching across multiple government databases.

http://www.lib.lsu.edu/gov/fedgov.html
>   Links to Federal agencies on the Internet.

http://access.gpo.gov
>   GPO's Home Page. (See Figure 12.8)

http://indigo.lib.lsu.edu/gpo/
>   Access to Congressional bills, *The Congressional Record*, *Federal Register*, Public laws, and much more.

http://ssdc.ucsd.edu/gov/
>   Many pointers to government information.

State Government Information

The individual state governments have a similar mission as the Federal government to keep their citizens informed. Although state governments publish information on a more limited scope than the national government, they, too, are prolific publishers of information. Each state provides descriptions of its governmental activities, reports of special developments in industry and economics, maps, laws, and statistics on education, crime, health, employment, business, etc. The information found in state documents is especially useful because of its timeliness. Statistics on employment, housing construction, crime, and health, for example, are gathered by the states and published in state documents before they appear in Federal documents.

Most states do not have funds to provide widespread distribution of their publications. Rather, certain libraries are designated as depository libraries for state documents and automatically receive the State's publications. The way that depository collections are organized varies among libraries. Some libraries keep their documents in a separate state collection with other special materials on the state; others house them as a separate collection within the government documents department. Still other libraries integrate state documents with their general collection. The access to state documents varies among libraries. Many states publish checklists and bibliographies listing currently available publications. A few libraries catalog state documents along with other library materials. Even so, it is difficult to identify and use state publications. For that reason, in most libraries with state documents collections, a librarian with special training and experience in state documents is usually available to assist patrons in locating information on the state level.

State Government Information on the Internet

http://www.lib.umich.edu/libhome/Documents.center/state.html
>   An excellent place to get started

http://www.state.lc.us/
>   Louisiana government information

Welcome to the U.S. Government Printing Office Home Page

About the Government Printing Office

Access to Federal Government Publications
    Superintendent of Documents
        GPO Access: On-line, On-Demand & Locator Services
        Information Available for Free Public use in Federal Depository Libraries
        Information for Sale
    Advisory Commission on Intergovernmental Relations
    Commission on the Roles and Capabilities of the United States Intelligence Community
    Congress of the United States
    Department of Interior Office of Inspector General
    Executive Office of the President
        Council of Economic Advisers
        Office of Management and Budget
    General Accounting Office
    Merit Systems Protection Board
    National Archives and Records Administration's Office of the Federal Register
    Office of Technology Assessment
    State Department

Services Available to Federal Agencies
    Customer Service
    Electronic Prepress and Document Creation
    Institute for Federal Printing and Publishing

Business and Contracting Opportunities
    Printing Procurement
    Materials Management Service

Figure 12.8 *GPO Home Page.*

Local Government Information

In the United States there are many local units of government—towns, cities, counties, and special districts. Although information about local governmental units appears in publications of the Federal government as well as in commercial publications, most of the key information is produced by local governmental units. Publications from local governments include records of their activities such as charters, laws, regulations, financial reports, city plans, maps, statistics, budgets, decisions, etc. Local publications are an important primary source of information. These documents usually are not widely distributed, making them difficult to locate and access. One way to get information from local governments is to request it directly from the local agency. Another way is through the library. Libraries, especially college and university libraries, often serve as depositories for local documents. The way local documents are handled varies among libraries. Some catalog local documents along with the other materials in the library; others keep them in separate collections which may or may not be cataloged. Since there are no quick and easy guides to local government publications, one should ask the librarian for assistance when seeking local documents or information about a local governmental unit. The librarian can direct users to the appropriate source.

Local Government on the Internet

http://www.city.net/countries/united_states/
   A searchable guide to information about cities of the world

http://lcweb.loc.gov/global/state/stategov.html
   Library of Congress' links to information on local governments

United Nations Information

The United Nations issues a large quantity of documents in mimeographed, offset, printed and electronic format. The primary purpose of United Nations documents is to serve the immediate needs of the delegates to the United Nations. However, the publications of the United Nations and its allied agencies, such as the World Health Organization (WHO) and the United Nations Education, Scientific, and Cultural Organization (UNESCO), are of great value because they deal with all the important issues in international affairs. They provide statistics and other types of information gathered from all over the globe on all facets of human endeavors. They document world problems such as hunger, illiteracy, and human rights.

The publications of the United Nations and its allied agencies may or may not be listed in the main catalog along with the other resources of a library. In either case they may be shelved in a separate collection. Libraries which serve as depository libraries for United Nations documents usually keep the publications in a separate collection shelved by the series symbol which is assigned by the United Nations. The series symbol numbers are composed of capital letters in combination with numerical notations. The elements in the numbers are separated by slash marks. The example below is the call number for the 1985 *Report on the World Social Situation.*

> ST/ESA/165
> ST   = United Nations Secretariat
> ESA = Department of International and Social Affairs
> 165 = series number designation

United Nations documents which are not listed in a library's catalog must be accessed by finding aids which are produced by the United Nations. The following indexes serve as guides to United Nations publications for the periods indicated:

Checklist of United Nations Documents. New York: United Nations, 1946-1949.

United Nations Documents Index. (*UNDI*). New York: United Nations, 1950-1973.

United Nations Documents Index. (*UNDEX*). New York: United Nations, 1970-1978.

UNDOC: Current Index. New York: United Nations, 1979-.

Index to United Nations Documents and Publications. Newsbank/Readex, 1985-. CD-ROM.
    CD-ROM version of the *UNDOC: Current Index.* Searchable by author, title, keyword, agency, and series symbol.

International and Foreign Information on the Internet

http://www.lsu.edu/guests/poli/public_html/foreign.html
    Links to many sources of information on international organizations and foreign governments

http://www.un.org
    The Home Page for the United Nations

Instructor: _____   Name: _____

Course/Section: _____   Date: _____

Review Questions for Chapter Twelve

1. What is the importance of government information to citizens?

2. Name four characteristics of government information which add to its value as a reference source.

3. Discuss the ways in which U.S. Government publications vary (a) in scope and (b) in format.

4. What are Federal depository libraries?

   Why were they established?

5. Which classification system is used to classify U.S. Government publications in many academic libraries?

6. What is the purpose of the *Monthly Catalog*?

7. What kind of information is one likely to find among the publications of state governments?

8. What is meant by "local government"' publications? What is the value of these publications?

9. Why are publications of the United Nations and its allied agencies important sources of information?

10. Is there a depository for U.S. documents at your school?

   If so, what type depository is it?

Instructor: _____   Name: _____

Course/Section: _____   Date: _____

U.S. Government Publications Exercise

Use one of the finding aids listed below to locate information on a topic which interests you or a topic which your instructor assigns.

Finding Aids:
Monthly Catalog (either the GPO printed edition or one of the CD-ROM versions)
Congressional Information Service Index

Complete the following information:
TOPIC:

1. Name of finding aid used and date:

2. Subject heading used in index and entry number of abstract, if applicable:

3. Analyze the reference you find by giving the following information:

    Author:

    Title:

    No. of pages in the document:

    Publication date:

    Agency which issued document:

    SuDocs call number:

4. Locate the document and write a brief annotation for the publication, in which you summarize its content and comment on its usefulness to the topic.

5. Make a bibliographic citation to the document. Study carefully the citations found in the textbook in Chapter 14 and then use the appropriate citation for a model.

Instructor: _____

Name: _____

Course/Section: _____

Date: _____

Online Catalog Exercise

To determine whether or not your library has any government documents, try a subject or keyword command, as shown in the following examples:

s=drugs—law and legislation
k=drugs and hearing

---

1. Find a government document on a subject of your choice. Give the exact command you typed.

2. Write the call number for two of the entries you find.

3. What classification system is used for these sources?

4. Where would these items be located in your library?

5. Locate one of the items you found.

6. Write the correct bibliographic citation for this work, as shown in the bibliographic citation examples in Chapter 14.

STATISTICAL SOURCES

A PREVIEW

There are many who agree with the notion that "there are three kinds of lies: lies, damned lies and statistics."[1] On the other hand, we know of people who take the position that "statistics don't lie." It is safe to say that neither of these two positions is altogether true. The fact is that statistics are used to prove and support research. It is also true that the researcher must evaluate statistical sources (just as they would any other information) as to reliability and usefulness. This chapter is designed to offer some suggestions for evaluating statistical information and to present a guide to locating statistical data.

KEY TERMS AND CONCEPTS

Statistics (definition)
Time Series
Secondary Source
Primary Source
Index to Statistics
Statistics on the Internet
Statistical Sources

INTRODUCTION

There are generally two definitions of statistics: (1) the science that deals with the collection, classification, analyses, and interpretation of numerical facts and data; and (2) the actual numerical facts or data. The statistical sources listed in this chapter represent both types of statistics—some of the sources present "raw" data, such as population, test scores, etc.; others have data that has been "massaged," that is, interpreted by others and then presented to prove or verify a hypothesis. The United States Government is the chief source for statistics gathered in the United States, but it is not the only one. Statistics are gathered by every level of government: international, national, state, and local. They are also collected by organizations and businesses.

---

[1] Mark Twain in his *Autobiography* attributes this remark to Benjamin Disraeli (qtd. In *Columbia Dictionary of Quotations* 870).

Why Use Statistics

Statistics are a vital element in effective research. Scientists use statistical data to support or refute a hypothesis; businesses use statistics to survey market potential; economists analyze present conditions and forecast economic trends through the use of statistics; social scientists use statistical data to understand and predict many types of human behavior. In the day to day conduct of our human activities we all use statistics in one form or another. We may want to know, for example, what is the best-selling software program for word processing; where are the top paying jobs in the country; what are the highest ranked graduate programs in business in the United States; what is the best city to live in the United States; which airline has the safest record? All rankings are based on statistics—the reliability of the statistics determines whether one can rely on the rankings.

Evaluating Statistical Sources

It is easy to fall into a trap with statistics—researchers tend to look for data which will support a hypothesis or a position, regardless of its reliability. It is always important to evaluate any information used in research; with statistics this is even more critical.

Before accepting statistical sources at face value we should ask ourselves a few questions:

- Who collected the data? Is it a business which has a "vested" interest in its publication, such as the manufacturer of a particular product who might have gathered data to support an advertising claim?

- Do the statistics reflect a bias? Political polls, for example, might be biased to reflect certain strengths or weakness of the candidates, depending on the bias of the pollsters. In this case, it is necessary to find out something about the agency conducting the poll.

- Is the data timely? Check the dates of coverage, etc.

- Is the coverage complete? In polls, for example, was the sample large enough?

- Has the data been repackaged several times so as to distort its reliability? Government data is frequently repackaged by a commercial entity, and might not include all of the original data.

- Is this a "time" series? Data gathered over a long span of time is referred to as a *time series*. It is usually considered to be a reliable source. In many cases, the research project calls for data that has a timeline.

- Is the data from a *primary* or a *secondary* source? If it is from a secondary source (for example, a periodical article), is the source documented?

Finding Statistics

Statistical data covering a wide range of topics appear in a great number of sources. There are many publications which are dedicated exclusively to statistical data. Other publications might include statistics along with other information. This is especially true of data in magazine articles.

There are several ways to access statistical information.

- Use the library's catalog

- Use a periodical index

- Use an index to statistical sources

- Use the Internet

- Use a guide that lists recommended sources

Use the Library catalog

1. For a subject search in the library catalog, use the topic with the subdivision--statistics. (Remember that statistical information in books listed in the online catalog might not be current.)

2. Check the *Library of Congress Subject Headings* (*LCSH*) or do a search in the online catalog to find the authorized subject heading. Figure 13.1 shows the authorized subject headings for "statistics." Note the "search also under" references.

3. Execute a search in the online catalog using one of the headings you located in no. 2 above. Figure 13.2 shows a search in the online catalog using a broad subject:

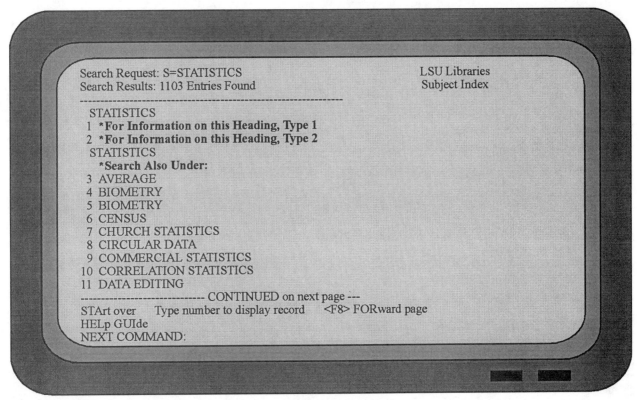

```
Search Request: S=STATISTICS                          LSU Libraries
Search Results: 1103 Entries Found                    Subject Index
------------------------------------------------------------
    STATISTICS
  1 *For Information on this Heading, Type 1
  2 *For Information on this Heading, Type 2
    STATISTICS
     *Search Also Under:
  3 AVERAGE
  4 BIOMETRY
  5 BIOMETRY
  6 CENSUS
  7 CHURCH STATISTICS
  8 CIRCULAR DATA
  9 COMMERCIAL STATISTICS
 10 CORRELATION STATISTICS
 11 DATA EDITING
------------------------- CONTINUED on next page ---
STArt over    Type number to display record    <F8> FORward page
HELp GUIde
NEXT COMMAND:
```

Figure 13.1 A broad search to determine the authorized headings.

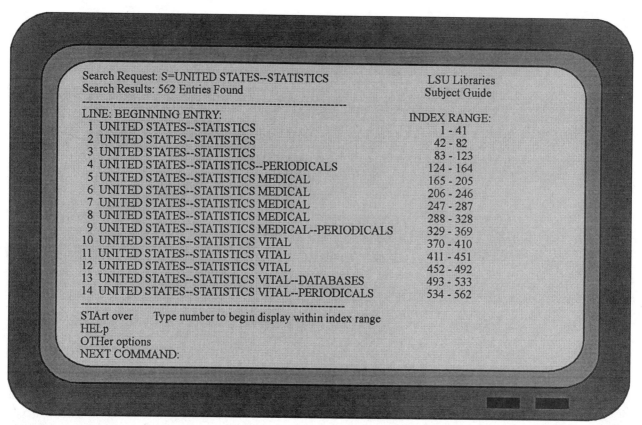

Figure 13.2 *Search using statistics as a sub-division for a geographical heading.*

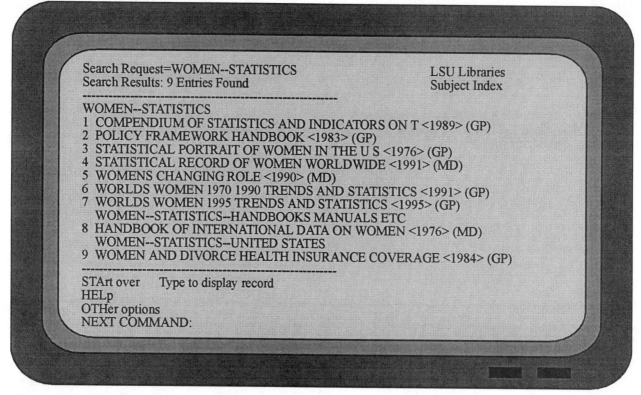

Figure 13.3 *Search for statistics on a specific topic.*

Use a Periodical Index

Although one could probably find statistics in a print index, it is much more effective to search for statistical sources in electronic format.

1. Locate an appropriate periodical index
   For example:

   > for business, use *ABI/ INFORM* or *Business Periodicals Index*.

2. Execute a keyword search:
   For example:

   > in *ABI/INFORM* search: women and salar? and statistics

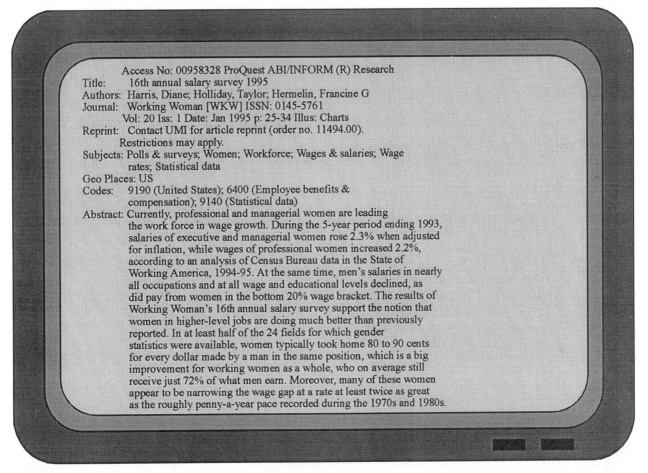

Access No: 00958328 ProQuest ABI/INFORM (R) Research
Title: 16th annual salary survey 1995
Authors: Harris, Diane; Holliday, Taylor; Hermelin, Francine G
Journal: Working Woman [WKW] ISSN: 0145-5761
          Vol: 20 Iss: 1 Date: Jan 1995 p: 25-34 Illus: Charts
Reprint: Contact UMI for article reprint (order no. 11494.00).
           Restrictions may apply.
Subjects: Polls & surveys; Women; Workforce; Wages & salaries; Wage
          rates; Statistical data
Geo Places: US
Codes: 9190 (United States); 6400 (Employee benefits &
          compensation); 9140 (Statistical data)
Abstract: Currently, professional and managerial women are leading
          the work force in wage growth. During the 5-year period ending 1993,
          salaries of executive and managerial women rose 2.3% when adjusted
          for inflation, while wages of professional women increased 2.2%,
          according to an analysis of Census Bureau data in the State of
          Working America, 1994-95. At the same time, men's salaries in nearly
          all occupations and at all wage and educational levels declined, as
          did pay from women in the bottom 20% wage bracket. The results of
          Working Woman's 16th annual salary survey support the notion that
          women in higher-level jobs are doing much better than previously
          reported. In at least half of the 24 fields for which gender
          statistics were available, women typically took home 80 to 90 cents
          for every dollar made by a man in the same position, which is a big
          improvement for working women as a whole, who on average still
          receive just 72% of what men earn. Moreover, many of these women
          appear to be narrowing the wage gap at a rate at least twice as great
          as the roughly penny-a-year pace recorded during the 1970s and 1980s.

Figure 13.4 Search in a periodical index (ABI/INFORM).*

Use an Index to Statistical Sources

There are a number of indexes to statistics. For example, to locate some of these in the online catalog, search under:

> s=united states--statistics--abstracts.
>
> **OR**
>
> s=statistics--indexes
>
> **OR**
>
> use one of the indexes listed below:

---

* Copyright © 1996 by UMI Company. All Rights Reserved. Further distribution or reproduction is prohibited without prior written permission from UMI.

American Statistics Index (ASI). Congressional Information Service, 1973-.
> A two part (index and abstracts) guide to statistical information published by the U. S. Government. Citations include the Superintendent of Documents call number as well as a microfiche reference number to the microfiche collection published by Congressional Information Service to accompany the Index. See Figures 13.5-13.8 for instructions on using *ASI*.

Index to International Statistics (IIS). Congressional Information Service, 1983-.
> A similar index to *ASI*, covering statistical sources of the United Nations and its allied agencies, foreign governments, and International Government Organizations.

Statistical Reference Index (SRI). Congressional Information Service, 1980-.
> Covers statistical publications of state and local governments, professional and trade organizations, and some commercial publishers.

CIS Statistical Masterfile. Congressional Information Service, 1973-. CD-ROM.
> A combined version in CD-ROM format of the three CIS indexes listed above.

Use the Internet

The Internet is a great source for statistics from local, state, national, and international agencies, as well as from business and professional organizations. The U. S. Government has instituted a policy requiring that Federal agencies produce and distribute information in electronic format. The result is a wealth of government-produced statistical data on the Internet.

There are several approaches to finding statistical data on the Internet:

1. Go to a well maintained Web page with links to statistical sources.

2. Go directly to a site using the URL (Uniform Resource Locator).

3. Search the Internet using one of the search engines.

Web Page Links

> http://www.lib.lsu.edu/bus/economic.html
>> An excellent collection of links to statistical sources in business and economics

> http://stats.gla.ac.uk/cti/links_stats.html
> Links to many statistical sources in the United Kingdom and the U.S.

URL Sites

http://www.lib.umich.edu/libhome/Documents.center/stats.html
> Statistical Resources on the Web through U. of Michigan

http://lapop.lsu.edu/pop.html
> Sources of demographic/census data

http://www.stat-usa.gov
> STAT-USA, a U.S. Government service providing economic, business, social, and environmental program data produced by more than 50 Federal sources. Available free through Depository libraries.

gopher://una.hh.lib.umich.edu/11/ebb
> Data from the Economic Bulletin Board - EBB, maintained at the University of Michigan

http://stats.bls.gov
> Bureau of Labor Statistics page, providing information on labor/employment in the United States

http://www.census.gov
> U. S. Bureau of the Census

Sample ASI Search

"How much did the chemicals industry invest in pollution control equipment in New Jersey?"

Step 1

Check the ASI Index Volume

Start with a "subject" approach where extensive cross-references will lead to the proper index reference from almost any likely point of entry.

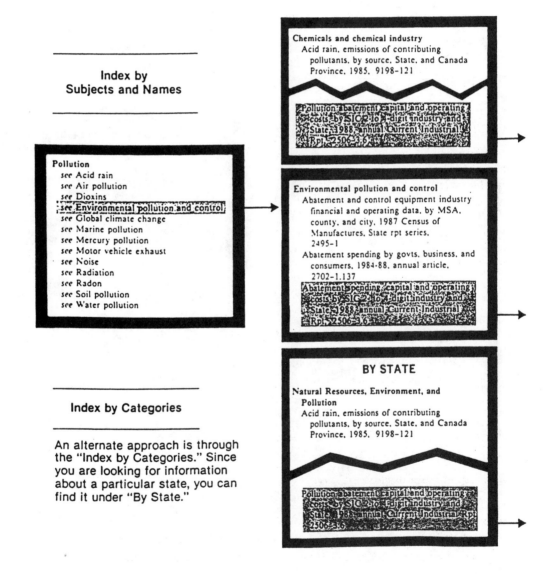

Index by Subjects and Names

Pollution
see Acid rain
see Air pollution
see Dioxins
see Environmental pollution and control
see Global climate change
see Marine pollution
see Mercury pollution
see Motor vehicle exhaust
see Noise
see Radiation
see Radon
see Soil pollution
see Water pollution

Index by Categories

An alternate approach is through the "Index by Categories." Since you are looking for information about a particular state, you can find it under "By State."

Chemicals and chemical industry
Acid rain, emissions of contributing pollutants, by source, State, and Canada Province, 1985, 9198–121

Pollution abatement capital and operating costs, by SIC 2- to 4-digit industry and State, 1988, annual, Current Industrial Rpt, 2506–3.6

Environmental pollution and control
Abatement and control equipment industry financial and operating data, by MSA, county, and city, 1987 Census of Manufactures, State rpt series, 2495–1
Abatement spending by govts, business, and consumers, 1984-88, annual article, 2702–1.137
Abatement spending, capital and operating costs, by SIC 2- to 4-digit industry and State, 1988, annual, Current Industrial Rpt, 2506–3.6

BY STATE

Natural Resources, Environment, and Pollution
Acid rain, emissions of contributing pollutants, by source, State, and Canada Province, 1985, 9198–121

Pollution abatement capital and operating costs, by SIC 2- to 4-digit industry and State, 1988, annual, Current Industrial Rpt, 2506–3.6

Figure 13.5 *From* AMERICAN STATISTICS INDEX 1995. *Reprinted by permission of Congressional Information Service, Inc.*

Step 2

Go from the index to the data description in the appropriate Abstracts volume

The ASI accession number in the index will lead to a publication entry that fully describes the document and pinpoints the tables containing the statistics you need.

2506
BUREAU OF CENSUS: MANUFACTURING
Publications in series

2506-3.6: Manufacturers' Pollution Abatement Capital Expenditures and Operating Costs, Final Report for 1988
[Annual. Sept. 1990. 55 p. MA200(88)-1. *C3.158:MA200(88)-1/990. LC 77-646295. Price not given. ASI/MF/3]

Annual report for 1988 on pollution abatement control capital expenditures and operating costs, for U.S. by SIC 4-digit industry, and for States by 2-digit industry. Data are from a sample survey of approximately 20,000 establishments with 20 or more employees, in industries with abatement capital expenditures or annual operating costs of at least $1 million.

Contents: introduction (p. 1); and 6 tables, listed below (p. 2-55).

Advance annual report for 1988 was received in Apr. 1990 and is also available on ASI microfiche under this number [Apr. 1990. 2 p. MA200(88)-1. C3.158:MA200(88)-1. Price not given. ASI/MF/3]. No advance or final reports were issued for 1987. Final report for 1986, titled *Pollution Abatement Costs and Expenditures*, is described in ASI 1989 Annual under this number.

TABLES:

[Data are for 1988. Tables show data for U.S. by SIC 2- to 4-digit industry ("a" tables) and for States by SIC 2-digit major industry groups ("b" tables). Tables 1-2 show hazardous and nonhazardous solid waste pollutants.]

1a-1b. Pollution abatement capital expenditures [for air and solid waste pollution, by pollutant type; and for air and water pollution, by abatement technique (end-of-line, production process change)]. (p. 2-21)

2a-2b. Pollution abatement operating costs by form of abatement [payments for public sewage services and solid waste collection and disposal; and for pollutants abated from air, water, and solid waste]. (p. 22-38)

3a-3b. Pollution abatement operating costs by kind of cost [depreciation; labor; materials and supplies; and services, equipment leasing, and other costs] and cost recovered by form of pollutants [air, water, solid waste]. (p. 39-55)

Step 3

Retrieve the publication

The ASI abstract contains the bibliographic information you need to locate the publication in a library's hardcopy collection or to obtain it from the issuing source, if copies are available.

Alternatively, if you have access to an ASI Microfiche Library collection, the ASI accession number will lead you directly to the correct microfiche. Or, individual publications abstracted in any ASI Monthly or Annual Supplement are available for purchase on microfiche directly from Congressional Information Service through our CIS & ASI Documents on Demand Service.

Order kits supplied to all ASI subscribers provide the necessary information about costs and how to place microfiche orders. Details are also available by writing CIS Documents on Demand.

Figure 13.6

Sample Abstract—Publications in Series

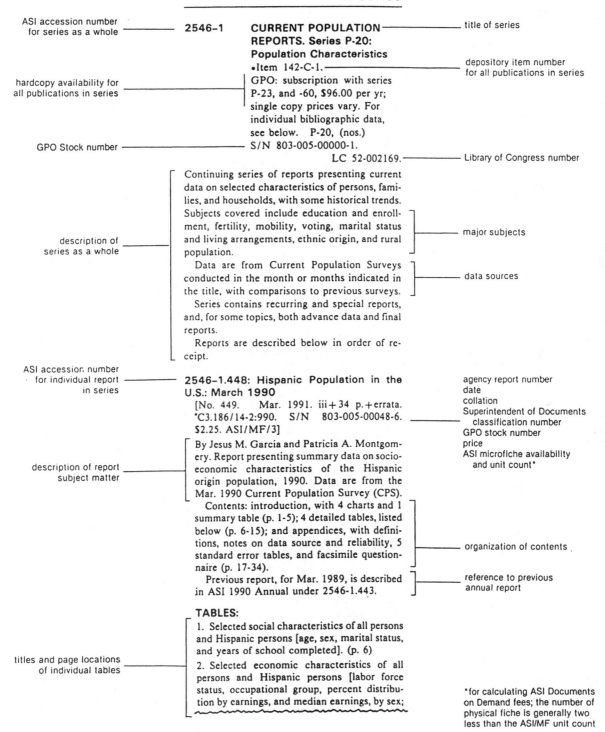

2546
BUREAU OF CENSUS:
POPULATION

Publications
in Series

ASI accession number
for series as a whole ———— **2546-1**   **CURRENT POPULATION** ———— title of series
REPORTS. Series P-20:
Population Characteristics
•Item 142-C-1. ———————— depository item number
for all publications in series

hardcopy availability for
all publications in series ———— GPO: subscription with series
P-23, and -60, $96.00 per yr;
single copy prices vary. For
individual bibliographic data,
see below.   P-20, (nos.)
GPO Stock number ———— S/N 803-005-00000-1.
LC 52-002169. ———————— Library of Congress number

description of
series as a whole ———— Continuing series of reports presenting current
data on selected characteristics of persons, fami-
lies, and households, with some historical trends.
Subjects covered include education and enrollment, fertility, mobility, voting, marital status
and living arrangements, ethnic origin, and rural — major subjects
population.

Data are from Current Population Surveys
conducted in the month or months indicated in — data sources
the title, with comparisons to previous surveys.

Series contains recurring and special reports,
and, for some topics, both advance data and final
reports.

Reports are described below in order of receipt.

ASI accession number
for individual report ———— **2546-1.448: Hispanic Population in the**   agency report number
in series **U.S.: March 1990**   date
[No. 449.   Mar. 1991. iii+34 p.+errata.   collation
*C3.186/14-2:990.   S/N   803-005-00048-6.   Superintendent of Documents
$2.25. ASI/MF/3]   classification number
GPO stock number
price
ASI microfiche availability
and unit count*

description of report
subject matter ———— By Jesus M. Garcia and Patricia A. Montgom-
ery. Report presenting summary data on socio-
economic characteristics of the Hispanic
origin population, 1990. Data are from the
Mar. 1990 Current Population Survey (CPS).

Contents: introduction, with 4 charts and 1
summary table (p. 1-5); 4 detailed tables, listed
below (p. 6-15); and appendices, with defini-
tions, notes on data source and reliability, 5 — organization of contents
standard error tables, and facsimile question-
naire (p. 17-34).

Previous report, for Mar. 1989, is described — reference to previous
in ASI 1990 Annual under 2546-1.443. annual report

TABLES:

titles and page locations
of individual tables ———— 1. Selected social characteristics of all persons
and Hispanic persons [age, sex, marital status,
and years of school completed]. (p. 6)

2. Selected economic characteristics of all
persons and Hispanic persons [labor force
status, occupational group, percent distribution by earnings, and median earnings, by sex;

*for calculating ASI Documents
on Demand fees; the number of
physical fiche is generally two
less than the ASI/MF unit count

Figure 13.7

Sample Abstract—Periodical Publication

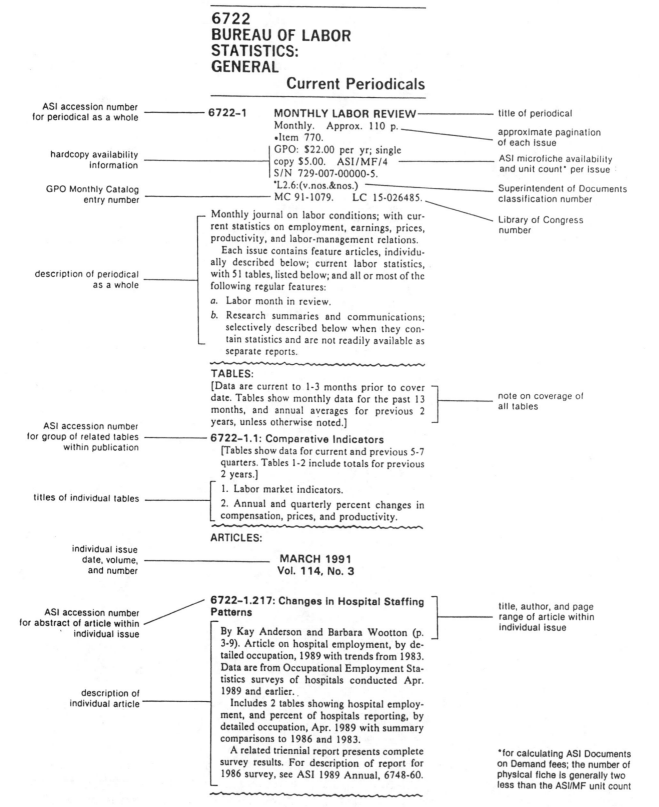

6722
BUREAU OF LABOR
STATISTICS:
GENERAL
Current Periodicals

ASI accession number for periodical as a whole ——— **6722–1**   **MONTHLY LABOR REVIEW**——— title of periodical

Monthly.   Approx. 110 p.——— approximate pagination of each issue
•Item 770.

hardcopy availability information ——— GPO: $22.00 per yr; single copy $5.00.   ASI/MF/4 ——— ASI microfiche availability and unit count* per issue
S/N 729-007-00000-5.

GPO Monthly Catalog entry number ——— *L2.6:(v.nos.&nos.) ——— Superintendent of Documents classification number
MC 91-1079.   LC 15-026485. ——— Library of Congress number

description of periodical as a whole ——— Monthly journal on labor conditions; with current statistics on employment, earnings, prices, productivity, and labor-management relations.

Each issue contains feature articles, individually described below; current labor statistics, with 51 tables, listed below; and all or most of the following regular features:

a. Labor month in review.

b. Research summaries and communications; selectively described below when they contain statistics and are not readily available as separate reports.

TABLES:

[Data are current to 1-3 months prior to cover date. Tables show monthly data for the past 13 months, and annual averages for previous 2 years, unless otherwise noted.] ——— note on coverage of all tables

ASI accession number for group of related tables within publication ——— **6722–1.1: Comparative Indicators**

[Tables show data for current and previous 5-7 quarters. Tables 1-2 include totals for previous 2 years.]

titles of individual tables ——— 1. Labor market indicators.

2. Annual and quarterly percent changes in compensation, prices, and productivity.

ARTICLES:

individual issue date, volume, and number ——— **MARCH 1991**
Vol. 114, No. 3

ASI accession number for abstract of article within individual issue ——— **6722–1.217: Changes in Hospital Staffing Patterns** ——— title, author, and page range of article within individual issue

By Kay Anderson and Barbara Wootton (p. 3-9). Article on hospital employment, by detailed occupation, 1989 with trends from 1983. Data are from Occupational Employment Statistics surveys of hospitals conducted Apr. 1989 and earlier.

description of individual article ——— Includes 2 tables showing hospital employment, and percent of hospitals reporting, by detailed occupation, Apr. 1989 with summary comparisons to 1986 and 1983.

A related triennial report presents complete survey results. For description of report for 1986 survey, see ASI 1989 Annual, 6748-60.

*for calculating ASI Documents on Demand fees; the number of physical fiche is generally two less than the ASI/MF unit count

Figure 13.8   *From* AMERICAN STATISTICS INDEX 1995. *Reprinted by permission of Congressional Information Service, Inc.*

http://leap.nlu.edu
Louisiana Electronic Assistance Program, provides statistical data for Louisiana

http://umbc7.umbc.edu/~curnoles/marystat.html
Maryland statistics sources

http://govinfo.kerr.orst/reis-statis.html
Regional Economic Information System (REIS). Provides for states, counties, and metropolitan area for the period 1969-1992.

http://www.cec.lu/en/comm/eurostat/eurostat.html
Eurostat: The Statistical Office of the European Communities

http://www.undp.org/unso_www.html
United Nations Development Program

Search Engines

http://www.yahoo.com
Yahoo: Supports boolean operators (and, or) and string searching. Displays the links along with descriptive text and the subject hierarchy under which it can be found.

http://altavista.digital.com
AltaVista: Searches World Wide Web pages and Usenet News.

http://guide.infoseek.com
Infoseek: Searches Web pages, News Groups, and Internet Frequently Asked Questions (FAQs.)

http://www.lycos.com
Lycos: Index to millions of Uniform Resource Locators (URLs).Indexes abstracts, titles, headings, subheadings.

Use A Guide to Statistical Sources

Statistics Sources. Gale, 1st ed, 1962-.
A listing of sources for statistics on a wide range of topic. Covers both U.S. and international sources. Published irregularly since 1962.

Selected Statistical Sources

General Surveys

County and City Data Book. GPO, 1949-.
Supplement to the *Statistical Abstract of the United States*, gives a wide variety of demographic, social, and economic statistics for regions, divisions, states, counties, and SMSAs.

Historical Statistics of the United States: Colonial Times to 1970. GPO, 1975.
Two volume source that contains a wide range of historical statistics for the U.S. Includes economic, political, social, and demographic data. Some tables start with the colonial period.

Statistical Abstract of the United States. GPO, 1878-.
An annual summary of data collected by the government; this publication provides statistics on a vast array of topics. The documentation following each table serves as a guide to more extensive data on the topic. Available on CD-ROM and on the Internet at: http://www.census.gov/stat_abstract/. Figure 13.9 illustrates an index entry and the corresponding table from *Statistical Abstract*.

World Almanac and Book of Facts. Funk & Wagnalls, 1893-.
Contains a wide variety of statistical information.

Annual Topical Surveys

Agricultural Statistics. GPO, 1936-.
A concise collection of data such as crop yields, market value, price, number of farms, and export/import.

Crime in the United States: FBI Uniform Crime Reports. GPO, 1930-.
Statistics on numbers of arrests, types of crimes, etc.

Digest of Education Statistics. GPO, 1975-.
Detailed coverage of public, private, vocational, and higher education statistics.

Annual Energy Review. GPO, 1982-.
Detailed data on energy production, consumption, prices, imports, exports.

Sourcebook of Criminal Justice Statistics. GPO, 1973-.
Tables give figures on prisons, prisoners, types of crimes, arrests, money spent on law enforcement and much more.

Demographics

Census of Population and Housing. GPO, 1990.
The U.S. Bureau of the Census "counts" the citizens of the United States every ten years. The data gathered includes social and economic characteristics of the population as well as head counts. The first decennial census was taken in 1790 and has continued ever since. In between the ten year periods, the Bureau of the Census conducts surveys to obtain ongoing estimates of the population.

Business and Economic—U.S.

Economic Report of the President. GPO, 1979-.
An annual report containing detailed tables showing national income, manufacturing and commercial activity, government finance, and international trade.

Monthly Labor Review. GPO, 1918-.
In addition to employment related articles, the publication features regular compilations of data related to labor/employment. It is included in a number of indexing services.

The Dow Jones Averages. 1885-1985. Business One Irwing, 1990.
Compilation of averages for 100 years.

Sourcebook of Demographics and Buying Power for every County in the USA. CACI, 1986-.
A summary of buying power based on socio-economic characteristics. Data is by country (U.S.), state, and county.

Standard and Poor's Statistical Service. Standard and Poor, 1941-.
Monthly publication with annual cumulations that contains statistics covering bank and finance, production and labor, price indexes, income and trade, building, electric powers and fuels, metals, transportation, textiles, paper products, and agricultural products. Cites data source.

Survey of Current Business. GPO, 1921-.
A monthly publication of the U. S. Bureau of Economic Analysis. Provides current and historical data on business, industry, agriculture, and manufacturing.

International Statistics

World Factbook. CIA, 1981-.

Information on countries of the world gathered from a variety of sources: the Bureau of the Census, Central Intelligence Agency, Department of State, and others. Available on the Internet at: http://www.odci.gov/cia/publications/95fa/index.html

International Financial Statistics Yearbook. IMF, 1979-.

Annual summary of many leading indicators for the nations of the world. Data includes exchange rates, interest rates, production figures, and national accounts.

National Trade Databank (NTDB). GPO, CD-ROM.

A text and statistical database source for information on international trade, with emphasis on exporting. Includes the Foreign Trader's Index (FTI) which contains a listing of overseas firms and basic information about the firm such as address and product lines.

United Nations Statistical Yearbook. United Nations, 1948-.

Statistics on a wide range of topics for countries of the world.

World Tables. International Bank for Reconstruction and Development, 1976-.

A detailed time series of data compiled from the files of the World Bank. Country statistics include balance of trade, balance of payments, manufacturing output, and significant economic indicators.

NOTE: Index citations refer to table numbers, not page numbers.

414 Labor Force, Employment, and Earnings

No. 656. Number of Workers With Earnings and Median Earnings, by Occupation of Longest Job Held and Sex: 1990

[Covers civilians 15 years old and over as of **March 1991.** Based on Current Population Survey; see text, section 1, and Appendix III. For definition of median, see Guide to Tabular Presentation]

MAJOR OCCUPATION OF LONGEST JOB HELD	ALL WORKERS				YEAR ROUND FULL-TIME				Ratio: Women to men	
	Women		Men		Women		Men			
	Number (1,000)	Median earn-ings	Number (1,000)	Median earn-ings	Number (1,000)	Median earn-ings	Number (1,000)	Median earn-ings	Number	Median earnings
Total [1]	61,732	$12,250	72,348	$21,522	31,682	$19,822	49,171	$27,678	0.64	0.72
Executive, administrators, and managerial..............	6,577	22,551	9,244	37,010	4,857	25,858	7,873	40,541	0.62	0.64
Professional specialty	8,814	23,113	8,035	36,942	4,982	29,181	6,192	41,100	0.80	0.71
Technical and related support ..	2,044	20,312	2,053	28,042	1,284	23,992	1,595	30,897	0.81	0.78
Sales....................	8,393	7,307	7,871	22,955	3,223	16,986	5,594	29,652	0.58	0.57
Admin. support, incl. clerical....	16,728	14,292	4,141	20,287	9,760	18,475	2,835	26,192	3.44	0.71
Precision production, craft and repair	1,395	13,377	13,448	22,149	795	18,739	9,412	26,506	0.08	0.71
Machine operators, assemblers, and inspectors	3,773	10,983	5,389	19,389	2,103	14,652	3,736	22,345	0.56	0.66
Transportation and material moving	511	10,805	5,056	20,053	174	16,003	3,241	24,559	0.05	0.65
Handlers, equipment cleaners, helpers, and laborers.......	995	8,270	4,885	9,912	412	13,650	2,065	18,426	0.20	0.74
Service workers............	11,722	5,746	7,801	10,514	3,769	12,139	4,106	18,550	0.92	0.65
Private household	1,007	2,166	43	(B)	183	7,309	9	(B)	20.33	(X)
Service, except private household...........	10,716	6,173	7,758	10,549	3,586	12,288	4,097	18,574	0.88	0.66
Farming, forestry, and fishing ...	680	3,810	3,548	7,881	241	10,007	1,736	14,452	0.14	0.69

B Base less than 75,000.   X Not applicable.   [1] Includes persons whose longest job was in the Armed Forces.
Source: U.S. Bureau of the Census, *Current Population Reports,* series P-60, No. 174.

Figure 13.9 Statistical Abstract of the United States

Instructor: _____   **Name:** _____

Course/Section: _____   **Date:** _____

<hr>

Review Questions for Chapter Thirteen

1. What are the two definitions of statistics?

2. Why are statistics useful in research?

3. Give three criteria you would use to evaluate statistical sources.

4. Name four ways to locate statistical information.

5. Give the commands you would use in the online catalog to find:

    a. indexes to statistics

    b. statistics about women

6. Why would you use the *ASI* in research?

7. Why would you expect to find many Federal government statistics on the Internet?

8. Name three methods you might use to locate statistical information on the Internet.

Instructor: _____   **Name:** _____

Course/Section: _____   **Date:** _____

═══

Statistics Exercise

1. Use a volume of *ASI (American Statistics Index)*, *SRI, (Statistical Reference Index)*, or another statistical index to locate a study on your topic by the U.S. Government.

   a. Title of statistical index used:

   b. Year of index you used:

   c. Subject heading you used:

   d. Abstract number/accession number/table you found:

      If you used an index volume, find the matching abstract and look for the abstract number or accession number for the publication you found.

   e. Write the title of the publication you found in the abstract or table:

   f. Give the date of the publication:

2. Use a current edition of *Statistical Abstract of the United States*. Use the index in the back of the book to find a table of statistics on a topic of your choice.

   a. What subject did you select?

   b. How many tables did you find on this topic?

   c. Write the name of one table here.

3. Use the sample bibliographic format included in Chapter 14 of this text and write the correct bibliographic citation for this table.

THE RESEARCH PAPER

A PREVIEW

One of the ways that a student learns to locate, evaluate, and use information resources is through the research paper assignment. The goal of this chapter is to provide the student not only with clear and precise technical counsel as to planning, researching and documenting a research paper, but also to provide a concrete illustration of and model for this process. It is hoped that the advice given in this chapter will sharpen the student's ability to make critical judgments in selecting and using information sources.

KEY TERMS AND CONCEPTS

Research Paper
Topic
Thesis
Outline
Search Strategy
Evaluating Sources
Taking Notes
Writing the Paper
Documenting the Research
Plagiarism

INTRODUCTION

Research fills a variety of information needs from finding out telephone numbers to engaging in complicated investigations of the origin of the universe. For the college student, library research is an integral part of the learning process. Undergraduate students are expected to prepare themselves for living by learning how to locate and use information. Graduate students are expected to prepare themselves to become participants in the creation of new knowledge. Teachers seeking to develop their students' skills will usually rely on some type of formal research project. The most common type of research project is the research paper, usually a formal essay requiring library research. The research paper offers the student an opportunity to examine issues, locate material relevant to an issue, digest, analyze, evaluate, and present the information with conclusions and interpretations.

Earlier chapters of this book were intended to provide an introduction to the academic library and to appropriate resources to use in research. This chapter will focus on the techniques and the mechanics of preparing a research paper.

Steps in Preparing a Research Paper

It is helpful to approach the research paper assignment as a series of stages or steps. Some rather obvious steps are:

1. Selecting a topic

2. Formulating a thesis

3. Preparing the outline

4. Preparing the search strategy and gathering information

5. Taking notes

6. Writing the text of the paper

7. Documenting the sources

Selecting a Topic

Sometimes the initial step in the preparation of a research paper is the most challenging one. The selection of a topic is also the most crucial one in determining the success of the research paper. If the instructor assigns a topic, the student need only determine how to proceed with the research. In most cases, however, students must choose their own topics.

Several overriding principles which should be considered in selecting a research topic are provided in Figure 14.1.

SELECTING A TOPIC

Initial considerations:
- interest of researcher
- prior understanding of topic
- terminology
- content
- manageability of topic
- length of assignment/project
- type of assignment/project
- due date of assignment/project
- availability of research materials

Carefully consider topics that may be too:
- recent
- regional
- emotional
- complex
- broad
- narrow

Conduct a preliminary library search:
1. use the *Library of Congress Subject Headings (LCSH)*--for appropriate subject headings
2. use general encyclopedias--for overview of topic
3. use the library catalog--for books and other background material
4. use periodicals--magazines, newspaper and journal articles for ideas on a topic

---

Figure 14.1 Selecting a topic.

Formulating a Thesis

After the student has become somewhat familiar with the topic selected, the second step is to determine the *thesis* of the paper. What is the purpose of the paper? What will be the focus? What is to be proven or shown in the paper? The thesis statement is a concise statement of the paper's purpose and the approach to be used.

The *search strategy*, or process to be used in locating information, is determined by the thesis since the information located must support the thesis. Some preliminary reading from one or two sources such as an encyclopedia article or a periodical article is probably sufficient to help formulate the thesis statement.

FORMULATING A THESIS

Developing a Thesis:

- Begin with a question--not an opinion. Don't just give the purpose of the paper.
- Conduct research to look for points that will shape or form an opinion.
- Final statement indicates that the thesis is supported by evidence. (Thesis statement should be brief--no more than three sentences.)

Sample Topic:	Discrimination of Women
Initial Thesis:	Does discrimination against women exist in the United States?
After Further Research:	What evidence is there of discrimination against women? Is there segregation by sex? Inequality in pay? Inequality in education and professional opportunities?
FINAL Thesis Statement:	Working women are discriminated against in many ways. One of the most obvious is the inequality in pay which exists in traditional "male" occupations such as managers, business executives, and entertainers.

Figure 14.2 Formulating a thesis.

Preparing the Outline

The third step is to prepare a working outline that includes all facets of the topic to be investigated. The same preliminary sources used as a guide to narrow the topic and formulate the thesis statement are also helpful in compiling the outline. To be useful the outline should divide the thesis into a number of major points; each of the points should be further divided and subdivided until the writer can visualize the outline as a guide for research and as a skeleton for the final report. The process of subdividing should follow a logical sequence with related points grouped together. The major points should be parallel, just as the subdivisions under each heading should be parallel. The main points in the outline should support the thesis statement. These should be assigned Roman numerals. The first subdivisions are given capital letters; the second, Arabic numbers; the third, lower-case letters. If it is necessary to subdivide any further than this, Arabic numbers in parentheses are used.

Since each heading or subheading in the outline denotes a division, there must be more than one part if it is to be logical. Thus, if there is a I, there must be a II; if there is an A, there must be a B, etc. The working outline is important to the search strategy since the search should be directed to the relevant points in the outline.

In the process of locating information, it is probable that other aspects of the topic not included in the working outline will be discovered and that the final outline will be changed and improved. As information is gathered the outline can be revised and new headings or subheadings added.

Example:
Thesis statement:
```
I.        First major point
     A.        First subdivision
          1.        Second subdivision
               a.        Third subdivision
               b.
                         (1) Fourth subdivision
                         (2)
          2.

     B.
II.       Second major point
```

Figure 14.3   Outline form.

Example of a Preliminary Topic Outline
```
I. History and definition of discrimination
     A. Types of discrimination
          1. Age
          2. Race
          3. Sex
II. Sex discrimination against women
     A. Employment
          1. History of women in the labor movement
          2. Sex segregation in the workplace
               a. Maternity leave
               b. Sexual politics
          3. Wages
               a. Equal pay for equal work
               b. Affirmative action
     B. Education
          1. Opportunities
          2. Laws
          3. Statistics
III. Wage discrimination
     A. Career women
     B. Trends and issues
     C. Job satisfaction
```

Figure 14.4   Example of preliminary topic outline.

As the search strategy is developed and further research is conducted, a more complete outline can be formulated based on information found.

Developing a Search Strategy

Using the thesis statement and the outline as a basis, the researcher should develop a *search strategy* or plan of research. This strategy involves analyzing the information needed and determining which sources are appropriate to consult in order to get that information. It is helpful to begin by analyzing the information according to specific factors that are involved in answering the research questions.

SELECTION CRITERIA	
Factors to Consider	**Criteria to Consider:**
FOCUS	1. approach (discipline or aspect): Humanities, Social Sciences, or Science? 2. scope of information covered: complete coverage or narrow aspects? 3. pro or con?
TIME FACTOR	1. historical, current, or a combination? 2. timeline of published information: daily / weekly/ monthly/ quarterly/ yearly
TREATMENT	1. *popular:* Intended for widespread readership; often written by journalists or staff writers; contains illustrations, advertisements, anecdotal accounts; deals with current events and issues. 2. *scholarly:* Written by experts and scholars (based on research) usually lengthy; documented; describes results of experiments and studies
FORMAT	newspaper, magazine or journal, book, CD-ROM, cassette, microformat, Internet, etc.
TYPE OF SOURCE	1. general information: background material 2. specific facts 3. geographical factors 4. biographical 5. statistical 6. *primary*—original source of information; eyewitness account (diary, interview, experiment); statistics. *secondary*—second hand; usually a commentary based on primary (books, articles about an event; encyclopedia article; reported after the fact; removed from the event).

Figure 14.5 Selection criteria.

The informational needs must be identified and matched with the appropriate information source as part of the search strategy. Students should be familiar with the library's services and should know how its materials are organized. But more than this, they should know the characteristics of the more basic information tools so that they can know which of these to use for specific information.

Figure 14.6 analyzes the major sources to consult in the library search. Once some knowledge of these sources has been acquired, it is possible to determine the most appropriate tools to be consulted in order to answer a specific question.

SELECTING APPROPRIATE SOURCES		
INFORMATION	**SOURCES TO CONSULT**	**FINDING AIDS**
Preliminary Ideas	LCSH, general encyclopedias, current periodicals	guides to reference sources
Overview of Topic	general encyclopedias, books, current periodicals	ask reference staff, library catalogs, indexes
Definitions	dictionaries	library catalog
Primary Sources	newspapers, research reports, manuscripts, archives, government publications.	library catalog, newspaper, LEXIS/NEXIS, Internet
Secondary Sources	books, magazine and journal articles, subject encyclopedias	library catalogs, indexes and abstracts, online databases, Internet, LEXIS/NEXIS, browsing reference stacks
Facts	almanacs, yearbooks, government publications, statistics	library catalog, statistical indexes
Current Information	periodicals (newspapers, magazines, journals)	periodical indexes, online databases, Internet, LEXIS/NEXIS
Historical Information	books, encyclopedias, reference sources	library catalog, browsing reference stacks
Evaluative Sources	book reviews, author information, publisher information	book review indexes, directories

Figure 14.6 *Selecting appropriate sources.*

Asking for Help

Reference librarians can provide valuable assistance with research questions if they know what information is being sought. For the researcher, the key to getting assistance is knowing which questions to ask. Following are guidelines to observe in order to get maximum help from the librarian:

1. Explain the purpose of the research.

2. Give the assignment specifications. For example, length of paper, number of sources needed, and due date.

3. Explain the level of difficulty—scholarly, technical, easy-to-understand, etc.

4. Give the time framework—current, historical.

5. Describe the kinds of sources needed—primary or secondary.

6. Ask for assistance with specific questions that may be difficult to locate—statistics, dates, little known facts.

Evaluating Sources

As information is gathered, it is important to be critical about the sources. The information should, of course, be relevant to the outline and to the thesis. The same questions raised in planning the search strategy should be kept in mind as the search is executed. Is the information sufficiently up-to-date? Is the latest edition of a work available? Is the source reliable? Does the work reflect a particular prejudice? There are several ways to determine the reliability of a source. Some of these are listed in Figure 14.7.

EVALUATION CRITERIA	
Factors to Consider	**Criteria to Consider**
Author	information on educational background, professional experience, reputation
Publisher	reputation: not "vanity presses," major university or publishing house
Content	scope of information covered: in-depth or selected aspects of topic? objectivity? bias?
User Aids	illustrations, index, charts, graphs, finding tools, etc.

Figure 14.7 Evaluation criteria.

Taking Notes

A convenient way to record information is to keep notes to identify the author's last name or short title of the source being used, and all important facts and opinions that are relevant to the topic. It is best to *paraphrase* the words of the author, although sometimes *direct quotations* are needed for emphasis or for authoritativeness. In either case it is important to retain the original meaning. Since material used out of context can be manipulated to distort the author's intended meaning, it is important to use the material to convey the author's intent. If statements are quoted directly, they should be copied exactly as they appear in the original and placed within quotation marks. The page or pages should be correctly noted.

It is important to keep a complete bibliographic record of the information along with the call number and location of each item. It is also helpful to know which bibliographical form the instructor requires before undertaking the actual research so that the necessary details need be copied only once.

Writing the Paper

Once the researcher is satisfied that sufficient information has been gathered to support all the topics in the original outline, it is time to begin on the first draft of the paper. The notes should be sorted so that they are grouped under headings to fit the topics in the outline.

The research paper, by definition, is based primarily on evidence gathered from authorities and scholars. It demands a great deal of creativity to assimilate evidence and present it so that it gives the reader a new perspective. Sufficient time should be allowed for the actual writing. It may take several drafts to achieve the well-written research paper. In writing the paper, all the elements of good writing should be employed—effective phrasing of ideas, good paragraph development, and attention to logical flow of the paragraphs into a unified paper.

Documenting the Research

It is expected that a research paper will be documented since by definition it includes ideas and facts gathered from other sources. To document a research paper means to state the sources used or consulted. There are several acceptable methods of acknowledging the material used in writing a research paper. Three of these will be discussed below:

1. parenthetical references in the text keyed to a list of works cited;

2. full bibliographic references within the text of the paper; and

3. notes.

There are a number of style manuals which serve as guides for documenting research. Some scholarly disciplines recommend a style which is peculiar to that field. The style manual that is used in this text is the *MLA Handbook for Writers of Research Papers*, by Joseph Gibaldi (4th ed. New York: The Modern Language Association of America, 1995), hereafter referred to as the *MLA Handbook*. It is widely used in the humanities and social sciences.

Plagiarism

The appropriation of ideas or the copying of the language of another writer without formal acknowledgment is *plagiarism*. Plagiarism is a serious violation of legal and ethical canons; yet many students who would not dare copy another's examination paper think nothing of "borrowing" ideas and even exact language from another writer without giving credit. This is not to say that writers must document every single thing they write. Those ideas which evolved in the writer's own mind, even though they are a result of the research, do not require documentation. Nor is it necessary to document facts considered common knowledge. Ordinarily the writer should not have difficulty determining what is common knowledge. Some facts will appear over and over in the readings. Well-known facts, such as the date of America's entry into World War I, require no documentation. Little known facts, or facts about which the writer has no prior knowledge, such as details of President Wilson's peace proposals, would require documentation. If there is doubt in the writer's mind as to whether or not a fact is common knowledge, the source should be acknowledged.

Parenthetical References

The *MLA Handbook* (sec.4.2) recommends the use of parenthetical references in which citations in the text are keyed to a list of "Works Cited" as the preferred method. The "Works Cited" is a list with full bibliographic descriptions of all the sources that were used and acknowledged in the text. The source in the text is identified by a brief reference in parenthesis to the corresponding reference in the list of "Works Cited." Usually the author's last name and the page(s) cited in the text are sufficient for identification:

> "...although women have jobs with lower pay and less authority than men they are equally satisfied with their jobs and employers." (Phelan, 95)

If the author is mentioned in the text, it is not necessary to repeat the author's name in the citation:

> Jo Phelan believes that there are five possible explanations of the paradox of the contented female worker. (95)

The entry would appear in the list of "Works Cited" as:

Phelan, Jo. "The Paradox of the Contented Female Worker: An Assessment of Alternative Explanations." *Social Psychology Quarterly* 57.2 (1994): 95-105.

If the parenthetical reference is to a work that is listed by title in the "Works Cited," the title, or a shortened form of the title, may be used. The reference "Gender Discrimination" is sufficient to identify the title and page reference for the article cited below:

"Gender Discrimination in the Workplace: a Literature Review." *Communications of the ACM* 38.1 (1995): 58-59.

Full Bibliographic References in Text

The use of a full bibliographic reference in the text to cite a source is acceptable only when one or two references are cited. The reference above to the *MLA Handbook* is an example of this form of documentation.

Notes

When notes are used for documentation, the documented material in the text of the paper is indicated by a "superscript" (a raised Arabic number) placed after the punctuation mark of material that is cited. The numbers are keyed to numbers in the notes. The first reference to the work contains full bibliographic information. Subsequent references to the same work are cited in brief. The note numbers should be consecutive throughout the paper. Notes used to document works cited in the text may appear at the bottom of the page (footnotes) or at the end of the paper (endnotes). When endnotes are used for documentation, it is not necessary to include a separate bibliography in the paper.

Example:

Book

[1] Barbara F. Reskin and Irene Padavic, *Women and Men at Work* (Thousand Oaks, CA: Pine Forge Press, 1994) 135.
[2] Reskin 186.

Periodical Article

[3] Maury Gittleman and Mary Joyce, "Earnings Mobility in the U.S., 1967-91," *Monthly Labor Review* 118.9 (1995): 10.
[4] Gittleman 16.

The terms *ibid.* (meaning "in the same place"), *op. cit.* ("in the work cited") and *loc. cit.* ("in the place cited") are no longer used in many style manuals. Rather, the work being cited is identified with the relevant page numbers. In most cases the author's last name is sufficient to identify the work. If two or more different titles by the same author are being cited, the citation should include a shortened form of the title after the author's last name. References to John Grisham's *The Client* and his *The Firm* would be cited in subsequent references as follows:

[5] Grisham, *The Client* 48.
[6] Grisham, *The Firm* 150.

Bibliography or Works Cited

A bibliography is a descriptive list of sources of information—books, articles from periodicals, government documents, theses and dissertations, articles from reference books, and other sources of information. A bibliography may list works by one author (an *author* bibliography), or it may list references on a subject (a *subject* bibliography). A *selective* bibliography includes only some of the possible references, while a *complete* bibliography lists all the references available. Bibliographies with descriptive notes about each entry are called *annotated* bibliographies.

The preferred term for a bibliography in a research paper is "*Works Cited*." It includes all the sources of information used in writing the paper and is placed at the end of the paper (*MLA Handbook* 4.3). The term "*Works Consulted*" should be used if the list includes additional works which were not cited in the text of the paper.

The items in a bibliography may be grouped according to their form of publication. For example, books may be listed in one group and periodicals in a second group. Within each group, the items are arranged in alphabetical order. In the Bibliographic Citations provided at the end of this chapter, the MLA style is used and works are separated by type of source.

Items in the bibliography are arranged alphabetically according to the last name of the author. If a work has more than one author, only the first name listed is inverted. If an item is listed by title rather than author, it is placed alphabetically by words in the title, excluding the initial articles "a," "an," or "the." For example, *The Encyclopaedia Britannica* would be alphabetized by "Encyclopaedia." If two or more entries have the same author, the author's name is not repeated. A three space line is used to indicate the omission of the name. The first line of each entry is placed in hanging *indention*. That is, it begins about four spaces to the left of the following lines in the entry.

An example of "Works Cited" for a research paper on women and wages is provided at the end of this chapter.

General Rules - Notes and Bibliography

Regardless of the method used to document research, one needs to know certain elementary forms of documentation. While there is no one "correct" form for documentation, convention dictates that the writer of scholarly papers follow a prescribed style—one that is consistent throughout and which communicates clearly and accurately the sources which are being documented. The writer should consult a style manual in other disciplines if the MLA style is not appropriate.

Style Manuals

Chicago Manual of Style. 14th ed. Chicago: University of Chicago Press, 1993.

Garner, Diane L. and Diane H. Smith. *The Complete Guide to Citing Government Information Resources: A Manual for Writers & Librarians*. Rev. ed. Chicago: American Library Association, 1993.

Gibaldi, Joseph. *MLA Handbook for Writers of Research Papers*. 4th ed. New York: Modern Language Association of America, 1995.

Li, Xia and Nancy C. Crane. *Electronic Style: A Guide to Citing Electronic Information*. Westport, CT: Mecklermedia, 1993.

_____. "Electronic Sources: MLA Style of Citation." Online. Available HTTP: http://www.uvm.edu/~xli/reference/mla.html.

Publication Manual of the American Psychological Association. 4th ed. Washington: APA, 1994.

BIBLIOGRAPHIC CITATIONS (MLA STYLE)

I. Books

Items to include in documenting a book:

1. Author's full name. If there are more than one, but less than four authors, all of the authors' names are included. When there are four authors, it is permissible to cite all the names or to give the first one listed on the title page followed by "et al." or by "and others." If there are more than four authors, only the first one listed is cited followed by "et al." or by "and others."

2. Title of part of book if only citing one part.

3. The title of the book, as it appears on the title page.

4. Editor, translator, compiler (if any).

5. The edition if other than the first.

6. Volume if part of a multivolume set.

7. The series (if any).

8. The imprint

   a. The city of publication. If more than one place is listed on the title page, only the first one listed is used. The name of the state is included if the city is not well known.

   b. The publisher. The shortened name of the publisher is used unless there is confusion in identification. The shortened forms of publishers' names are found in the *MLA Handbook* (6.3).

   c. The date of publication. Publication date is found on the title page. If there is no publication date given, the latest copyright date is used. If neither a publication date nor a copyright date is given, the abbreviation, n.d., is used.

9. Page citation for a note entry or inclusive pages when citing a part of a book.

Examples

The examples below include first reference note form and bibliographic form for each entry.

A. Book by one author

Notes:

[1] Ethel Hausman, *The Illustrated Encyclopedia of American Wildflowers* (Garden City: Garden City Pub., 1947) 28.

Bibliography:

Hausman, Ethel. *The Illustrated Encyclopedia of American Wildflowers*. Garden City: Garden City Pub., 1947.

Explanation: Cite author, title, and imprint (place of publication, publisher, date). The publisher's full name is given only when there is confusion with the name of the city.

B. Book by two or more authors

Notes:

    [2] Wallace K. Ferguson and Geoffrey Bruum, *A Survey of European Civilization*, 2nd ed. (Boston: Houghton, 1952) 73.

Bibliography:

Ferguson, Wallace K., and Geoffrey Bruum. *A Survey of European Civilization*. 2nd ed. Boston: Houghton, 1952.

Explanation: The name of the first author is inverted in the bibliographical entry. Names of other authors are given in regular order. These are given in the order in which they appear on the title page. Remainder of entry cites edition, place of publication, publisher, and edition.

B.2 Book by two or more authors with the same last name

Notes:

    [3] Will Durant and Ariel Durant, *A Dual Autobiography* (New York: Simon, 1977) 10.

Bibliography:

Durant, Will, and Ariel Durant. *A Dual Autobiography.* New York: Simon, 1977.

Explanation: Author, title, imprint. Last name of second author is given.

B.3 Book by more than three persons

Notes:

    [4] James Davis, et al., *Society and the Law: New Meanings for an Old Profession* (New York: Free, 1962) 102.

Bibliography:

Davis, James, et al. *Society and the Law: New Meanings for an Old Profession.* New York: Free, 1962.

Explanation: Author, title, imprint. May also use Davis, James, and others, or give all names in full.

C. Book by a corporate author

Notes:

    [5] Center for the Study of Democratic Institutions, *Natural Law and Modern Society*, contrib. John Cogley, et al. (Cleveland: World, 1973) 157.

Bibliography:

Center for the Study of Democratic Institutions. *Natural Law and Modern Society.* Contrib. John Cogley, et al. Cleveland: World, 1973.

Explanation: Corporate author, title, contributors, imprint.

D. Book that is an edited work

Notes:

    [6] Phillip green and Michael Walzer, eds. *The Political Imagination in Literature: A Reader* (New York: Free, 1969) 28.

Bibliography:

Green, Phillip, and Michael Walzer, eds. *The Political Imagination in Literature: A Reader.* New York: Free, 1969.

Explanation: Editors, title, imprint.

E. A book that is part of a series

Notes:
[7] Lacy H. Hunt, *Dynamics of Forecasting Financial Cycles: Theory, Technique, and Implementation*, Contemporary Studies in Economic and Financial Analysis (Greenwich: JAI, 1976) 18.

Bibliography:
Hunt, Lacy H. *Dynamics of Forecasting Financial Cycles: Theory, Technique, and Implementation.* Contemporary Studies in Economic and Financial Analysis. Greenwich: JAI, 1976.

Explanation: Author, title of book, title of series, imprint.

F. Book that is one volume of a multivolume work, one author, each volume a different title

Notes:
[8] Dumas Malone, *Jefferson and the Ordeal of Liberty, Vol. III of Jefferson and His Time* 6 vols. (Boston: Little, 1962) 243.

Bibliography:
Malone, Dumas, *Jefferson and the Ordeal of Liberty.* Vol III of *Jefferson and His Time.* 6 vols. Boston: Little, 1962.

Explanation: Author, title of Vol. III, title of set, number of volumes in set, imprint.

G. Book that is one volume of a multivolume work with one general title

Notes:
[9] Charles Warren, *The Supreme Court in United States History,* rev. ed. 2 vols. (Boston: Little, 1926) I: 231.

Bibliography:
Warren, Charles. *The Supreme Court in United States History.* Rev. ed. 2 Vols. Boston: Little, 1926.

Explanation: Author of book, title, edition, number of volumes, imprint.

H. Book that is a translation of an author's work

Notes:
[10] Friedrich Nietzsche, *The Birth of Tragedy and the Genealogy of Morals*, trans. Francis Golffing (Garden City: Doubleday, 1956) 42.

Bibliography:
Nietzsche, Frederick. *The Birth of Tragedy and the Genealogy of Morals.* Trans. Francis Golffing. Garden City: Doubleday, 1952.

Explanation: Author, title, translator, imprint.

I. Short story in a collected work (anthology)

Notes:
[11] William Faulkner, "Dry September," *Ten Modern Masters: An Anthology of the Short Story*, ed. Robert G. Davis (New York: Harcourt, 1953) 340.

Bibliography:
Faulkner, William. "Dry September." *Ten Modern Masters: An Anthology of the Short Story.* Ed. Robert G. Davis. New York: Harcourt, 1953. 339-350.

Explanation: Author of short story, title, of short story, title of book in which story appears, editor of book, imprint, pages on which story appears.

J. Essay or article in a collected work (anthology)

Notes:

[12] James D. Barker, "Man, Mood, and the Presidency," *The Presidency Reappraised*, ed. Rexfor G. Tugwell and Ghomas E. Cronin (New York: Praeger, 1974) 208.

Bibliography:

Barker, James D. "Man, Mood, and the Presidency." *The Presidency Reappraised.* Ed. Rexford G. Tugwell and Thomas E. Cronin. New York: Prager, 1974. 205-214.

Explanation: Author of article, title of article, title of book in which article appears, editors of book, imprint, pages on which article appears in book.

II. Reference Books

In citing articles form encyclopedias, yearbooks, biographical dictionaries, and other well known reference books, the following items are included:
1.   The atuhor of the article, if known.
2.   The title of the article as it appears in the book.
3.   The title of the book in which the article appears.
4.   The edition, if other than the first, and the date of publication.
5.   The volume number if one of a multivolume set, unless entire set is alphabetically arranged.
6.   The inclusive paging for a bibliographical entry; specific page for a note entry. If the articles are arranged in alphabetical order in the work, page numbers should be omitted.

Examples

A. Article from a multivolume general reference book

Notes:

[13] Leroy D. Vandam, "Anesthetic," *Encyclopaedia Britannica: Macropaedia*, 1974.

Bibliography:

Vandam, Leroy D. "Anesthetic." *Encyclopaedia Britannica: Macropaedia.* 1974.

Explanation: Author of the article, title of the article, title of the book, publication date.

B. Article from a single volume general reference book

Notes:

[14] Romulo Betancourt, "Latin America, Its Problems and Possibilities," *Britannica Book of the Year, 1966* (1966) 26.

Bibliography:

Betancourt, Romulo. "Latin America, Its Problems and Possiblities." *Britannica Book of the Year, 1966.* 1966. 19-40.

Explanation: Author of the article, title of the article, title of the book, publication date, inclusive pages.

C. Article from a multivolume subject reference book

Notes:

[15] Eleanor Flexner, "Woman's Rights Movement," *Dictionary of American History,* ed. Joseph G.E. Hopkins and Wayne Andrews, 6 vols. (New York: Scribner's 1961) VI. Supp. 1: 301.

Bibliography:

Flexner, Eleanor. "Woman's Rights Movement." *Dictionary of American History*. Ed. Joseph G.E. Hopkins and Wayne Andrews. 6 vols. New York: Scribner's, 1961. VI, Supp. 1: 301-03.

Explanation: Author of the article, title of the article, title of the reference book, editors, total volumes, imprint, volume number and inclusive pages of the article. Note: If the reference book is not a familiar one or if there are other books with the same title, it is necessary to give full publication information.

D. Article from a biographical dictionary (unsigned)

Notes:

[16] "Sellers, Peter (Richard Henry)," *Who's Who 1976-1977,* 1976.

Bibliography:

"Sellers, Peter (Richard Henry)." *Who's Who 1976-1977*. 1976.

Explanation: Full name of biographee or subject of article which is used as title of article, title of biographical dictionary, and date.

E. Article from a biographical dictionary (signed)

Notes:

[17] Arthur C. Cole, "Webster, Daniel," *Dictionary of American Biography*, 1936.

Bibliography:

Cole, Arthur C. "Webster, Daniel." *Dictionary of American Biography,* 1936.

Explanation: Author of article, name of biographee, title of biographical dictionary, copyright date.

F. Book of quotations

Notes:

[18] Samuel Johnson, "He who praises everybody praises nobody...," *The Oxford Dictionary of Quotations*, 2nd ed. 237.

Bibliography:

Johnson, Samuel. "He who praises everybody praises nobody...." *The Oxford Dictionary of Quotations*. 2nd ed. 237.

Explanation: Author, first line of quotation, title of book, edition, page.

III. Periodical and Newspaper Articles

In citing articles from periodicals the following items are included:

1. The author of the article if it is a signed article.
2. The title of the article.
3. The title of the periodical.
4. The volume number and/or issue number if it is a journal.
5. The date.
6. The inclusive pages in a bibliographical entry; the specific page reference in a note entry. If an article is not printed on consecutive pages, that is, if it begins on one page and continues on later pages, cite the beginning page followed by a "+."

Examples

A. Article from a monthly magazine (signed)

Notes:

[19] Roger Starr, "A Kind Word about Money," *Harper's* April 1976: 90.

Bibliography:

Starr, Roger. "A Kind Word about Money." *Harper's* April 1976: 79-92.

Explanation: Author of article, title of article, title of magazine, date, page(s). With a monthly magazine only the date and pages, not the volume are cited.

B. Article from a monthly magazine (unsigned)

Notes:

[20] "First National Data on Reading Speed," *Intellect* Oct. 1972: 9.

Bibliography:

"First National Data on Reading Speed." *Intellect* Oct. 1972: 9.

Explanation: Title of article, title of magazine, date, page.

C. Article from a weekly magazine (signed)

Notes:

[21] James D. Meindl, "Microelectronics and Computers in Medicine," *Science* 12 Feb. 1982: 793.

Bibliography:

Meindl, James D. "Microelectronics and Computers in Medicine." *Science* 12 Feb. 1982: 792-797.

Explanation: Author of article, title of article, title of magazine, date, page(s).

D. Article from a weekly magazine (unsigned)

Notes:

[22] "Behind the Threat of More Inflation," *Business Week* 18 Nov. 1972: 77.

Bibliography:

"Behind the Threat of More Inflation." *Business Week* 18 Nov. 1972: 76-78.

Explanation: Title of article, title of magazine, date, page(s).

E. Article from a journal with continuously numbered pages throughout the volume

Notes:

[23] Gerald Runkle, "Is Violence Always Wrong?" *Journal of Politics* 38 (1976): 250.

Bibliography:

Runkle, Gerald. "Is Violence Always Wrong?" *Journal of Politics* 38 (1976): 247-291.

Explanation: Author of article, title of article, title of journal, volume number, year, and page(s).

F. Article from a journal with separately numbered pages in each issue

Notes:

[24] Jay Martin, "A Watertight Watergate Future: Americans in a Post-American Age," *The Antioch Review* 2 (1975): 18.

Bibliography:

Martin, Jay. "A Watertight Watergate Future: Americans in a Post-American Age." *The Antioch Review* 33.2 (1975): 7-25.

Explanation: Author of article, title of article, title of journal, volume number, issue number, year, and pages.

G. Book review (signed)

Notes:

[25] Robert Sherrill, rev. of *The Time of Illusion*, by Jonathan Schell, *New York Times Book Review* 18 Jan. 1976: 1.

Bibliography:

Sherrill, Rev. of *The Time of Illusion*, by Jonathan Schell. *New York Times Book Review* 18 Jan. 1976: 1-2.

Explanation: Author of review, title of book, author of book, periodical in which review appears, date, page(s).

H. Book review with title (signed)

Notes:

[26] Robert Hughes, "The Sorcerer's Apprentice," rev. of *Journey to Ixtlan*, by Carlos Castaneda, *Time* 6 Nov. 1972: 101.

Bibliography:

Hughes, Robert. "The Sorcerer's Apprentice." Rev. of *Journey to Ixtlan*, by Carlos castaneda. *Time* 6 Nov. 1972: 101.

Explanation: Author of review, title of review, title of book, author of book, periodical in which review appears, date, page.

I. Book review (unsigned)

Notes:

[27] Rev. of *The Efficacy of Law*, by Harry W. Jones, *Choice* 7 (1970): 941.

Bibliography:

Rev. of *The Efficacy of Law*, by Harry W. Jones. *Choice* 7 (1970): 941.

Explanation: Title of book, author of book, name of periodical in which review appears, volume number, date, page.

J. Newspaper article (signed)

Notes:

[28] Tom Goldstein, "New Federal Tax Law Could Foster Growth of Plans to Provide Prepaid Legal Services," *New York Times* 28 Sept. 1976, eastern ed.: A36.

Bibliography:

Goldstein, Tom. "New Federal Tax Law Could Foster Growth of Plans to Provide Prepaid Legal Services," *New York Times* 28 Sept. 1976, eastern ed.: A36.

Explanation: Author of newspaper article, summary title of article, name of newspaper, date, edition, section, page.

K. Newspaper article (unsigned)

Notes:

[29] "College Enrollment Decline Predicted for South in '80's," *Morning Advocate* [Baton Rouge] 28 Sept. 1976: B7.

Bibliography:

"College Enrollment Decline Predicted for South in '80's." *Morning Advocate* [Baton Rouge] 28 Sept. 1976: B7.

Explanation: Summary title of article, name of newspaper, city, date, section, page. Note: the name of the city is in brackets because it is not part of the title.

L. Editorial from a newspaper

Notes:

[30] "Takeovers Yes, Hold-ups No," Editorial, *New York Times* 28 Nov. 1986, eastern ed.: A26.

Bibliography:

"Takeovers Yes, Hold-ups No." Editorial. *New York Times* 28 Nov. 1986, eastern ed.: A26.

Explanation: Title of article, type of article, title of newspaper, date, edition, section, page.

IV. Unpublished Thesis

Notes:

[31] Carol A. Runnels, "The Self Image of the Artist...," Thesis, Louisiana State University, 1975, 10.

Bibliography:

Runnels, Carol A. "The Self Image of the Artist...." Thesis, Louisiana State University, 1975.

Explanation: Author, title, descriptive label (thesis), degree-granting institution, year, and pages in note citation.

V. Phonographic Recordings

Notes:

[32] Elise Bell, *The Bronze Bow*, based on the book by Elizabeth George Speare, Newberry Award Records, NAR 3029, 1972.

Bibliography:

Bell, Elise. *The Bronze Bow.* Based on the book by Elizabeth George Speare, Newberry Award Records, NAR 3029, 1972.

Explanation: Performer, title of recording, source, producer of record, catalog number, date.

VI. Musical Score

Notes:

[33] Kelly Bryan, *March—Washington D.C.* (London: Novello, 1971).

Bibliography:

Bryan, Kelly. *March—Washington D.C.* London: Novello, 1971.

Explanation: Composer, title of composition, imprint.

VII. Computer Software

Notes:
[34] *Dollars and Sense with Forecast*, computer software, Monogram, 1984, IBM PC, PCjr., XT.

Bibliography:
Dollars and Sense with Forecast. Computer software. Monogram, 1984. IBM PC, PCjr., XT.

Explanation: Title of program, descriptive label, distributor, year of publication, operating system for which the program is designed.

VIII. Videotapes

Notes:
[35] *Our National Parks*, videocassette, prod. Wolfgang Bayer Productions, National Geographic Book Service, 1989, 30 min.

Bibliography:
Our National Parks. Videocassette. Prod. Wolfgang Bayer Productions. National Geographic Book Service, 1989. 30 min.

Explanation: Title of tape, type of tape, producer, distributor, date, running time.

IX. Microform Format

Notes:
[36] Robert M. Spalter-Roth and Heidi I. Hartmann. *Increasing Working Mothers Earnings* (Washington: Institute for Women's Policy Research, 1991): ERIC Microfiche ED 370825.

Bibliography:
Spalter-Roth, Robert M. and Heidi I. Hartmann. *Increasing Working Mothers Earnings*. Washington.: Institute for Women's Policy Research, 1991: ERIC Microfiche ED 370825.

Explanation: Cite author, title, imprint, ERIC Microfiche number.

X. Electronic Format

A. Newspaper

Notes:
[37] John Ellement, "Equal Pay for Women Backed; Court Upholds WWII-era Law, " *The Boston Globe* 13 December 1995: Metro/Region p.33. Available NEXIS Library: NEWS File: MAJPAP.

Bibliography:
Ellement, John. "Equal Pay for Women Backed; Court Upholds WWII-era Law." *The Boston Globe* 13 December 1995: Metro/Region p.33. Online. Available NEXIS Library: NEWS File: MAJPAP.

Explanation: Cite author, title of article, and title of printed source, date, vol. (if applicable) page, medium (Online), database.name, and file identifier or number.

B. CD-ROM

Notes:

[38] "Sex by Employment Status," *1990 U.S. Census of Population and Housing, STF 3c*, CD-ROM, Washington: U.S. Bureau of the Census, 1990.

Bibliography:

"Sex by Employment Status." *1990 U.S. Census of Population and Housing, STF 3c*. CD-ROM. Washington: U.S. Bureau of the Census. 1990.

Explanation: Article title, title of print version of the work, medium, imprint, date.

C. Internet

Notes:

[39] "Widening Wage Inequality," Policy and Research Report, Online, The Urban Institute, Available HTTP: http://www.urban.org/periodcl/prr25_1b.htm.

Bibliography:

"Widening Wage Inequality." Policy and Research Report. Online. The Urban Institute. Available HTTP: http://www.urban.org/periodcl/prr25_1b.htm.

Explanation: Article title, title of print version of the work, medium, supplier, available protocol.

XI. Interview

Notes:

[40] Michael Harrris, Personal Interview 3 February 1996.

Bibliography:

Harris, Michael. Personal Interview. 3 February 1996.

XII. Television Program

Notes:

[41] *Firing Line*, host William Buckley, prod. and dir. Warren Steibel, PBS, WLAC: Baton Rouge, LA, 27 May 1990.

Bibliography:

Firing Line. Host William Buckley. Prod. and dir. Warren Steibel. PBS. WLAC: Baton Rouge, LA, 27 May 1990.

XIII. Class Lecture

Notes:

[42] John Wilson, Sociology 1001: "Women in the Labor Force," State University, University Station, LA 18 Feb. 1996.

Bibliography:

Wilson, John. Sociology 1001: "Women in the Labor Force." State University, University Station, LA 18 Feb. 1996.

XIV. Government Publications

A. *Agency publication*

Notes:

[43] William J. Reid, Jr., and F.P. Cuthbert, Jr., *Aphids on Leafy Vegetables: How to Control Them*, Agricultural Research Service, Farmers' Bulletin No. 2148 (Washington: GPO, 1976) 15.

Bibliography:

Reid, William J., Jr., and F.P. Cuthbert, Jr. *Aphids on Leafy Vegetables: How to Control Them.* Agricultural Research Service, Farmers' Bulletin No. 2148. Washington: GPO, 1976.

Explanation: Authors of publication, title, Government agency responsible for publication, series title and number, imprint, pages (notes).

B. *Congressional hearings*

Notes:

[44] U.S. Cong. Senate. Select Committee on Nutrition and Human Needs, *Federally Supported Food Program*:..., 95th Cong., 1st sess. (Washington: GPO, 1977) 16.

Bibliography:

U.S. Cong. Senate. Select Committee on Nutrition and Human Needs. *Federally Supported Food Progoram*:.... 95th Cong., 1st sess. Washington: GPO, 1977.

Explanation: Senate committee as author, title, session of Congress, imprint, page (for note).

C. *Congressional bills, reports, documents*

Notes:

[45] U.S. Cong. House. Committee on the Judiciary, *Opposing the Granting of Permanent Residence in the United States to Certain Aliens*, Report to accompany H. Res. 795, 95th Cong., 1st sess., H.R. no. 691 (Washington: GPO, 1977) 3.

Bibliography:

U.S. Cong. House. Committee on the Judiciary, *Opposing the Granting of Permanent Residence in the United States to Certain Aliens*. Report to accompany H. Res. 7u95. 95th Cong., lst sess. H.R. no. 691. Washington: GPO, 1977.

Explanation: House committee as author, title, document type (Report, etc.), session of Congress, imprint, page (for note).

D. *Laws, decrees, etc.*

1. Citation to the *Statutes at Large*

Notes:

[46] PL 96-511 (Dec. 11, 1980), Paperwork Reduction Act of 1980, 94 Stat. 2812.

Bibliography:

PL 96-511 (Dec. 11, 1980). Paperwork Reduction Act of 1980. 94 Stat. 2812.

Explanation: public law number, date approved, title of law, volume number of the *Statutes at Large*, abbreviation for *Statutes at Large*, page number.

2. Citation to the *United States Code*

Notes:

[47] 20 U.S.C. 238 (1980).

Bibliography:

20 U.S.C. 238 (1980).

Explanation: title number of code, abbreviation of *United states Code*, section number, and edition date.

E. Court case

Notes:

[48] Brewer v. Williams, 430 U.S. 389 (1977).

Bibliography:

Brewer v. Williams, 430 U.S. 389 (1977).

Explanation: Name of case, volume 430 of *U.S. Reports*, page 389, date 1977.

F. Congressional Record

Notes:

[49] *Cong. Rec.* 121 (1975): 40634.

Bibliography:

Cong. Rec. 121 (1975): 40634.

Explanation: *Congressional Record*, volume number, year, page number. Notice that it is not necessary to cite the subject or title of the article or its author.

Abbreviations

anon.—anonymous
bibliog.—bibliography
bibliog. f.—bibliographical footnote
bull.—bulletin
c—copyright
cf.—compare
col., cols.—column(s)
comp.—compiler, compiled by
Cong.—Congress
Cong. Rec.—Congressional Record
ed., eds.—editor(s), edition(s), edited by
e.g.—for example
enl.—enlarged
et al.—and others
f., ff.—and following
facsim.—facsimile
GPO—Government Printing Office
H. Doc.—House document
HR—House of Representatives
HR #—House bill (e.g., HR 190)
H. Rept.—House report
H. Res—House resolution
ibid.—in the same place
loc. cit.—in the place cited

introd.—introduction
illus.—illustrated (by), illustrator, illustration(s)
n. d.—no date
n. p.—no place of publication, no publisher
n. pag.—no pagination
op. cit.—in the work cited
p.—page
pp.—pages
por., pors.—portrait, portraits
pref.—preface
pseud.—pseudonym
q. v.—which see
rev.—revised by, revision, review, reviewed (by)
    Review should be spelled out if there is any
    confusion as to meaning.)
S—Senate
S #—Senate bill (e.g., Senate 45)
S. Doc.—Senate document
S. Rept.—Senate report
S. Res—Senate resolution
[sic]—thus, so
trans. or tr.—translator, translation, translated by
vol., vols.—volume(s)

Works Cited

Brown, Clair and Joseph A. Pechman, eds. <u>Gender in the Workplace</u>. Washington: Brookings Institution, 1987.

Taeuber, Cynthia M. <u>Statistical Handbook on Women in America</u>. Phoenix, AZ: Oryx Press, 1991.

England, Paula, et. al. "The Gendered Valuation of Occupations and Skills: Earnings in 1980 Census Occupations." <u>Social Forces</u> 73:1 (1994): 65-99.

Gittleman, Maury and Mary Joyce. "Earnings Mobility in the U.S., 1967-91." <u>Monthly Labor Review</u> September 1995: 3-13.

Harris, D. "Salary Survey 1995." <u>Working Woman</u> January 1995: 25-30+.

Hill, Elizabeth T. "Marital History, Post-School-Age Training and Wages: Women's Experiences." <u>Social Science Journal</u> 31.2 (1994): 127-138.

Reskin, Barbara F. and Irene Padavic. <u>Women and Men at Work</u>. Thousand Oaks, CA: Pine Forge Press, 1994.

Schneider, Dorothy and Carl J. Schneider. <u>The ABC-CLIO Companion to Women in the Workplace</u>. Santa Barbara, CA: ABC-CLIO, 1993.

Sochen, June. "Women's Rights." <u>Compton's Encyclopedia</u> 1991. 271-279.

Instructor: _____   Name: _____

Course/Section: _____   Date: _____

Review Questions for Chapter Fourteen

1. Name the steps involved in writing a research paper.

2. What three things should be considered in developing a thesis?

    a.

    b.

    c.

3. What are the major library sources to consult when doing library research?

4. List three evaluation criteria you would consider in selecting sources for research.

    a.

    b.

    c.

5. Define plagiarism.

6. Explain the difference between a "primary" and a "secondary" source.

7. Explain the difference between a "popular" and a "scholarly" source.

8. What is the purpose of documentation in a research paper?

9. Name and describe three methods of documenting a research paper.

   a.

   b.

   c.

10. What is the difference between a list of "Works Cited" and a list of "Works Consulted"?

11. Name the items which are usually included in a bibliographic reference to most non-reference books.

12. How do bibliographic citations for reference books differ from those of non-reference books?

13. Name the items which are included in bibliographical references to periodical articles.

Instructor: _____   **Name:** _____

Course/Section: _____   **Date:** _____

═══

Topic Exercise

The first step in writing a research paper is to select a topic. This exercise will help you focus on a topic and the aspect you want to research. Select a topic you might want to use for a 10 page research paper in one of your classes.

1. TOPIC (Subject): _____

2. Write three questions or statements you can make about this topic today, based on what you already know about it.

    a)

    b)

    c)

3. Would you approach this topic from a social sciences, humanities, or science perspective?

4. What keywords or terms might you use to find information on this topic?

5. What kind of informational sources might you use for this topic?
    (ex. books, articles, statistics, etc.)

6. Would you expect to find mostly popular or scholarly sources?

7. Would you expect to find mostly primary or secondary sources on this topic?

Instructor: _____   Name: _____

Course/Section: _____   Date: _____

Background Research

TOPIC: _____

**General Background
Information:**
**(list sources used to find
overview of topic)**

_____

(Use *LCSH*) to find:

Main approved terms

Narrow terms

Broader terms

Related terms

_____

Perspective: **What approach do you plan to take for this topic?
(Humanities, Social Science, or Science)**

_____

Suggested initial thesis statement:

Instructor: _____   **Name:** _____

Course/Section: _____   **Date:** _____

Research Project Worksheet

Record information from the titles consulted for a research project or research paper on this form. Items which do not apply should be labeled N/A.

1. Give the title of the source you selected.

   a) How did you locate this source?

   b) Give the subject heading or command you used to find the source.

2. If this is a reference work, give the subject heading used within the work.

3. If this is an index or abstract, give the name of the index or abstract, the volume, year, and subject heading used within the index.

4. Write out a correct bibliographic citation for this source.

5. Call number of source: Library location:

6. Evaluation of the material used:

7. Write any notes you wish to take from this source on the back of this sheet. Paraphrase the words of the author. Use direct quotes for emphasis or authoritativeness. Enclose quotations in quotation marks. Record page numbers of materials used.

Instructor: _____   **Name:** _____

Course/Section: _____   **Date:** _____

Search Strategy Practice

1. What is the topic for your research paper?

2. What subject headings have you used to find books in your library catalog? Did you use subject or key-word commands?

3. Which periodical indexes will you use to locate citations for popular articles? Why did you choose these indexes?

4. What subject headings will you use in these indexes?

5. Which scholarly periodical indexes or databases will you use? Why did you select these?

6. What subject headings will you use?

7. Write a formal thesis statement for your paper.

8. Write a preliminary outline for your paper, based on the research you've found thus far.

Instructor: _____   Name: _____

Course/Section: _____   Date: _____

The Research Process:
Selecting and Evaluating Sources

Instructions

The guide below is designed to provide information on a topic. It should help you identify information sources and the correct terminology to use in a literature search, and direct you to good books, the best indexes, and other pertinent literature. Any of the sources you use can be in electronic format or in paper.

Write complete bibliographic citations for each entry using the forms found in Chapter 14. Put the call numbers at the end of the citation.

1. Select a **topic** for your guide from the list provided by your instructor. Write the topic you select here.

2. Give a **brief summary** of your topic in two or three sentences. Define your subject as specifically as possible. The statements should reflect the scope of your research. That is, it should state which aspects of the topic are to be included in the search, and which questions you would like to answer. It should enable you to develop a search strategy for the topic.

3. An **introduction to the topic** appears in:
    (A general or subject encyclopedia or dictionary will often provide a suitable discussion--a simple definition is not enough. Alternate sources include handbooks or good general books on the subject.)

4. **Specific terms** dealing with the topic are listed in the *LCSH* under these subject headings:

    Most specific term(s):   More general term(s):   Related term(s):

5. Some useful **books** on this topic are:
    (Find at least three books that are relevant to your topic.)

6. Some **reference books** on this topic are:
    (Choose your sources from the library catalog, by browsing in the reference stacks, or with the help of a librarian. Your sources must actually contain information on the topic, such as that found in manuals, texts, handbooks, gazetteers, atlases, subject dictionaries, or encyclopedias. Indexes and bibliographies should not be used here.)

7a. **Two indexes** which would identify articles on the topic in popular magazines or newspapers are: (Write the names of the two best indexes for your topic. Then write the subject term(s) to use in each index to get an article on your topic. Include the call numbers and specific library locations.)

    Look under the subject heading(s):

7b. Three **periodical articles** from these indexes which have useful information on this topic are: (Put journal call numbers at the end of the citation.)

8a. Some **subject indexes** to be used in a search are:
(Find at least two subject indexes or abstracts which would provide scholarly information on this topic.)

Look under the subject headings:

8b. Three **periodical articles** from these indexes which have useful information on this topic are: (Put journal call numbers at the end of the citation.)

9. One source on the **Internet** that is relevant to the topic is: (Use one of the search engines listed in Chapter 7.)
Search engine used:

Command:

Information on this topic is available at: (Give the URL for the source you found.)

10. One index to help locate **government documents** dealing with the topic is:

Subject term(s) used in the index:

A useful government document on this topic is:

11. Use one of the books you found on this topic and find a **review** of it. Sources to consult include *Book Review Digest* and *Book Review Index*. Write the correct bibliographic citation for the review below.

12. Locate **biographical information** on the author of one of the books or articles you found during this project. Some sources to consult are *Biography and Genealogy Master Index, Biography Index, Current Biography, American Men and Women of Science, Who's Who in America*, etc. Give full bibliographic citations.

13. **Select two of the best sources you located and** give a brief evaluation of their usefulness to your topic. Use Figures 14.6 and 14.7 in the text to formulate your evaluation comments.

IF YOU ARE UNABLE TO LOCATE MATERIAL IN ANY OF THESE CATEGORIES, SEE YOUR INSTRUCTOR.

Instructor: _____   **Name:** _____

Course/Section: _____   **Date:** _____

The Research Process:
Selecting and Evaluating Sources

Instructions

The guide below is designed to provide information on a topic. It should help you identify information sources and the correct terminology to use in a literature search, and direct you to good books, the best indexes, and other pertinent literature. Any of the sources you use can be in electronic format or in paper.

Write complete bibliographic citations for each entry using the forms found in Chapter 14. Put the call numbers at the end of the citation.

1. Select a **topic** for your guide from the list provided by your instructor. Write the topic you select here.

   Discrimination against women in employment

2. Give a **brief summary** of your topic in two or three sentences. Define your subject as specifically as possible. The statements should reflect the scope of your research. That is, it should state which aspects of the topic are to be included in the search, and which questions you would like to answer. It should enable you to develop a search strategy for the topic.

   Are women still discriminated against in the workplace? One area where this is clearly evident is in salary discrepancies.

3. An **introduction to the topic** appears in:
   (A general or subject encyclopedia or dictionary will often provide a suitable discussion—a simple definition is not enough. Alternate sources include handbooks or good general books on the subject.)

   Sochen, June. "Women's Rights." Compton's Encyclopedia. 1991. 271-279.
   REF AG 5 C73 1991

4. Specific terms dealing with the topic are listed in the *LCSH* under these subject headings:

Most specific term(s):	**More general term(s):**	**Related term(s):**
sex discrimination	discrimination	equal pay for equal
wages—women	sex discrimination against	work
	women	
	women's rights	
	women—employment	

5. Some **useful books** on this topic are: (Find at least three books that are relevant to your topic.)

   Reskin, Barbara F. and Heidi L. Hartmann, ed. Women's Work, Men's Work: Sex Segregation on the Job. Washington: National Academy Press, 1986. HD 6060.5 U5 W66 1986

   1993 Handbook on Women Workers: Trends & Issues. Washington: U.S. Department of Labor, Women's Bureau, 1994. L36.108: W84/3

   Schneider, Dorothy and Carl J. Schneider. The ABC-CLIO Companion to Women in the Workplace. Santa Barbara, CA: ABC-CLIO, 1993. HD 6095 S34 1993

6. Some **reference books** on this topic are:
(Choose your sources from the library catalog, by browsing in the reference stacks, or with the help of a librarian. Your sources must actually contain information on the topic, such as that found in manuals, texts, handbooks, gazetteers, atlases, subject dictionaries, or encyclopedias. Indexes and bibliographies should not be used here.)

"Sex Discrimination." <u>Handbook of American Women's History</u>. New York: Garland, 1990. REF HQ 1410 H36 1990

Taeuber, Cynthia M. <u>Statistical Handbook of Women in America</u>. Phoenix, AZ: Oryx, 1991. REF HQ 1420 T34 1991

7a. Two **indexes** which would identify articles on the topic in popular magazines or newspapers are: (Write the names of the two best indexes for your topic. Then write the subject term(s) to use in each index to get an article on your topic. Include the call numbers and specific library locations.)

<u>Readers' Guide to Periodical Literature</u> REF AI 3 R48 Table 19, Reference Room

Dynix VISTA, Reference Room

Look under the subject heading(s): women--employment, wages, women and discrimination, women and wages

7b. **Three periodical articles** from these indexes which have useful information on this topic are: (Put journal call numbers at the end of the citation.)

Friedman, D. R. "Working Women: Findings from a Sweeping New Study." <u>U.S. News and World Report</u> 22 May 1995: 55. Microfiche 1713, Microforms Room

Ares, B. Drummond, Jr. "Efforts to End Job Preference Are Failing." <u>New York Times</u> 20 Nov 1995:A1:1. Microfilm 27, Microforms Room

"1994 Hall of Shame." <u>Working Woman</u> Dec 1994:28-31. Online. Dynix VISTA 3/18/96.

8a. Some **subject indexes** to be used in a search are:
(Find at least two subject indexes or abstracts which would provide scholarly information on this topic.)

<u>Sociological Abstracts</u>   REF HM 1 S67
<u>PsycLit</u>   LSU Libraries' LAN
<u>ABI/Inform</u>   LSU Libraries' LAN

Look under the subject headings: women, wages, women and discrimination, and women and employment

8b. **Three periodical articles** from these indexes which have useful information on this topic are: (Put journal call numbers at the end of the citation.)

McGoldrick, K. "Do Women Receive Compensating Wages for Earnings Uncertainty?" <u>Southern Economic Journal</u> 62(1) 1995: 210-222. HC 107 A13 A67

Hill, Elizabeth T. "Marital History, Post-School-Age Training and Wages: Women's Experiences." <u>Social Science Journal</u> 31(2) 1994: 127-138. H1 R6

England, Paula, Melissa A. Hebert, et. al. "The Gendered Valuation of Occupations and Skills: Earnings in 1980 Census Occupations." <u>Social Forces</u> 73(1) 1994: 65-69. HN 51 S5

9. Find one source on the **Internet** that is relevant to your topic. Use one of the search engines listed in Chapter 7.

Search engine used: Lycos   Command: women and work

Information on this topic is available at: (Give the title and URL for the source you found.)

"Women's Contract with America." Online. Women Leaders Online, 1995. Polwoman@aol.com. Available at HTTP:// http://worcester.lm.com/women/contract.html

10. One index to help locate **government documents** dealing with the topic is:

American Statistics Index   REF Z 7554 U5A46 1995

   a) Subject term(s) used in the index:

   Earnings, general

   b) A useful government document on this topic is:

   Gittleman, Maury and Mary Joyce. "Earnings Mobility in the U.S., 1967-91." Monthly Labor Review Sept 1995: 3-13. L2:6:118/9

11. Use one of the books you found on this topic and find a **review** of it. Sources to consult include Book Review Digest and Book Review Index. Write the correct bibliographic citation for the review below.

   Rouse, David. Rev. of Gender & Racial Inequality at Work: the Sources & Consequences of Job Segregation, by Donald Tomaskovic-Devey. Booklist Aug. 1993: 2019. Z 1035 A49

12. Locate **biographical information** on the author of one of the books or articles you found during this project. Some sources to consult are *Biography and Genealogy Master Index, Biography Index, Current Biography, American Men and Women of Science, Who's Who in America*, etc. Give full bibliographic citations.

   "Goldin, Claudia Dale." Who's Who in America. 50th ed. 1996. REF E663 W56

13. Select two of the best sources you located and give a brief evaluation of their usefulness to your topic. Use Figures 14.6 and 14.7 in the text to formulate your evaluation comments.

   From the index to Compton's Encyclopedia I was able to find woman as a subjectheading, then a reference to women's rights. An article entitled "Women's Rights" included a full discussion of the history of women's role in society and was helpful in formulating the thesis for this assignment. One section, "Women at Work," was particularly helpful in giving an overview of the topic of discrimination against women in the workforce. The article was easy to read, longer than in other encyclopedias consulted, and was presented in chronological order. Several bibliographical references were given for further consideration.

   The book Women and Men at Work, by Barbara Reskin and Irene Padavic, was helpful in that it defined "sex segregation," "sex inequality," and the "gender-role socialization theory" in light of the employer/employee relationship. It also provided an insight into future trends, listing particular occupations which might experience growth. The authors mention the need for upgrading and deskilling to keep up with the changing trends in the job market. Two other trends they mention include the rise of temporary workers and workforce diversity. This work could contribute substantially to information on this topic and would lend supporting evidence to the thesis statement that discrepancies in wages exist. It includes a thorough glossary/index of terms and several pages of references to related works.

Instructor: _____   Name: _____

Course/Section: _____   Date: _____

Evaluating Sources Exercise

Select two sources on a topic of your choice and retrieve them.

First source:

Title:

call number:

Method used to retrieve this source:

Would you consider this source a popular or a scholarly work? Give several reasons for your decision.

Are primary or secondary sources used in the work? Give specific examples.

Second source:

Title:

call number:

Method used to retrieve this source:

Would you consider this source a popular or a scholarly work? Give several reasons for your decision.

Are primary or secondary sources used in the source? Give specific examples.

Instructor: _____   Name: _____

Course/Section: _____   Date: _____

Group Project and Presentation

Each group of 2-5 people will research a topic, hand in the results of their research to the instructor, and make a 5-minute presentation in class. The entire group will receive the same grade for the project. Participation by each group member is required.

Each group must decide how to divide up the work so that each member can make a meaningful contribution to the project. The project will serve as a review for the final exam. Please type or write your final product very neatly.

This group research assignment requires you to use various library tools (reference books, indexes, abstracts, computer databases, the OPAC, etc., to gather information on a topic of your choice. You will construct a research plan and then use the various library tools to produce a list or bibliography of resources found at the library.

For each source or library tool you use, explain why you thought it was an appropriate source.

Document the search statement or strategy you used for each selected source.

Grading will be based on: Why you selected this source.
Why it is relevant to your research.
Whether you document it properly.

Directions

Select a broad topic such as literature, business, biology, agriculture, psychology, music, etc. and narrow it down to a manageable topic, using *LCSH*, the online catalog, or a general or subject encyclopedia.

1. Identify the subject/topic you selected.

2. Find **background information** on this topic. Tell which source you used to find the information. List the sources you find.

3. Write a focused thesis statement describing the exact angle you are using to pursue your research.

After you have decided on a thesis, continue with your research.

4. Find at least two magazine and/or newspaper articles on this topic. Write a citation for each. (Follow the examples in Chapter 14.)

5. Find at least three scholarly journal articles related to your topic. Write a citation for each.

Find any of the following that applies to your thesis statement:

6. Statistics to support your thesis. (Cite the table or article you find.)

7. Biographical information, either on an author or one of your works, or on a person well known in your subject area for the topic. Write a citation for this biography.

8. An Internet site on your topic. (Cite it using the HTTP address.)

Glossary

abstract — a type of index which gives the location of an article in a periodical or a book and a brief summary of that article.

annotated bibliography — a list of works with descriptions and a brief summary or critical statement about each.

annotation — critical or explanatory note about the contents of a book or article.

anthology — any collection of varied literary compositions; includes under one title many different titles of shorter works.

appendix — section of the book containing supplementary materials such as tables or maps.

article — a complete piece of writing that is part of a larger work.

bibliography — list of sources of information.

book catalog — list of library holdings in book form.

book number — last letter/number combination in a call number. Stands for the author of the book and sometimes the title.

Boolean operators — the terms "and," "or," "not" used in keyword searching to broaden, narrow or limit a search.

CD-ROM — (Compact disk, read only memory) A compact disk containing text and/or images that is accessed by computers.

call number — the identification number which determines where a book or other library material is located in the library.

card catalog — library holdings recorded on 3 x 5 cards, filed alphabetically.

citation — a reference to an exact source of information.

class number — top part of call number which stands for subject matter of the book.

COM catalog — (computer output microform), a listing in microform that is generated from computer tapes.

commands — symbols and/or terms used to retrieve computer stored information.

copyright — the legal right to control the production, use, and sale of copies of a literary, musical, or artistic work.

contemporary — belonging to the same time period in history.

controlled vocabulary — standardized terms used in databases or catalogs as subject headings or descriptors.

cross reference — a reference from one term or word in a book or index to another word or term.

cumulation — an index which is formed as a result of the incorporation of successive parts of elements. All the material is arranged in one alphabet.

current — existing at the present time.

database	units of information which are stored in machine readable form and retrieved by use of a computer.
depository library	specially designated libraries that receive U.S. Government publications free of charge.
direct source	information presented in such a way that is not necessary to consult another source.
discipline	a branch of knowledge (e.g., humanities, social sciences, science).
dissertation	research that is completed in partial fulfillment of the requirements for a doctoral degree.
document delivery	service provided by libraries to borrow or copy materials from other libraries or vendors.
documentation	a reference to a source used or consulted in research.
edition	all copies of a book printed from a single type setting.
endnotes	identification of sources used in a text, placed at the end of the text or, in a book, at the ends of chapters.
entry	description of individual sources of information.
field	The different elements or access points by which records are retrieved in an electronic database.
footnotes	identification of sources used in a text, placed at the bottom of the page.
free-text search	a search for words regardless of where they appear in a record.
full-text database	database which provides the complete text of material as it appeared in the original source.
glossary	a list with definitions of technical or unusual terms used in the text.
imprint	place of publication, publisher, and either publication or copyright date.
in-house database	one created within the library that can be stored on hard disks, floppy disks, or magnetic tape.
index	alphabetical list of the subjects discussed in the book with corresponding page number; also separate publication which points to information found in other sources.
indirect source	a guide to information which is located in other sources.
information	knowledge in the form of ideas, facts, or data created by the human mind.
information processing	all of the ways that humans transmit, record, store, retrieve and use information.
integrated catalog	an online system that provides bibliographic records for periodical indexes in the same database as the online catalog.
Internet	a network that connects computers to one another, allowing for the free flow of information among them. (See Chapter 7 for a detailed glossary of terms.)
introduction	describes the subject matter and gives a preliminary statement leading to the main contents of the book.
italic	kind of type in which the letters usually slope to the right and which is used for emphasis.
journal	scholarly periodical usually issued monthly or quarterly.

keyword search	"free-text searching"; electronic searching using non-standardized subject headings.
library network	libraries linked together via telecommunication facilities for the purpose of sharing resources.
MARC	machine readable cataloging records.
microform	printed materials which are reduced in size by photographic means and can only be read with special readers.
notes	identification of sources used in a text; also explanatory material.
online	databases stored on a remote computer and accessed locally.
online catalog	library catalog records in machine readable form which are accessed by use of computers.
online search	a search that is carried out by means of a computer.
OPAC	acronym for online public access catalog.
parenthetical references	citations placed in the text and keyed to the list of "Works Cited."
periodicals	magazines and journals.
plagiarism	appropriation of ideas or the copying of the language of another writer without formal acknowledgment.
positional operators	terms used to refer to the order in which words appear in a record--adj, adj#, with, same.
preface	gives the author's purpose in writing the book and acknowledges those persons who have helped in its preparation.
primary source	a firsthand or eyewitness account of an event.
prompt	a message on a computer screen that asks the user for information or a command.
record	individual entries in an electronic database.
reprint	copies of the same edition printed at a later time.
scope	the range of material covered in a book or article.
search strategy	the process to be used in locating information.
secondary source	literature which analyzes, interprets, relates, or evaluates a primary source or other secondary sources.
see also reference	a listing of additional headings to consult for information.
see reference	a reference from a term that is not used to one that is used.
serial	publications issued on a continuing basis at regularly stated intervals.
series	publication similar in content and format.
short-title	first part of a compound title.
stacks	groups of shelves on which books are placed in a library.
subject search	using a controlled vocabulary (such as *LCSH*) to search a record.
subheading	a subdivision of a major heading.
subtitle	second part of a compound title which explains the short-title.

table of contents   a list of chapters or parts of a book in numerical order with the pages on which they are located.

thesis   a research project completed in partial fulfillment of the requirements for the master's degree.

thesis statement   a statement of purpose in a research paper.

title page   page in front of the book which gives the official author, title, and often the imprint.

truncation   abbreviation of words in the commands given to search an online database.

vendor   one who markets databases to subscribers.

vertical file   files containing ephemeral materials such as pamphlets, pictures, and newspaper clippings.

volume   written or printed sheets put together to form a book. One book of a series. All the issues of a periodical bound together to make a unit.

INDEX

Note: Only reference books and indexes that are discussed in the text are listed in this index by title. For additional titles consult the lists at the ends of the chapters.